C000097473

VILLAGE VOICES

It was while I was researching a book called *The English Vicarage Garden* (Michael Joseph, London,1988) that I first came into contact with the WI. It happened in a village called Eversley in Hampshire. I had gone to interview the woman who now owns the rectory there, once the home of Canon Charles Kingsley, author of *The Water Babies* and an inspired naturalist. At the end of the interview I was told I should get in touch with local archivist Mrs Sarah Beer, who had some photographs of Kingsley and his family . . . What I found was a wonderful scrapbook that captured perfectly both the feel of Eversley in the 1850s and the personality of Kingsley himself. The scrapbook had been made by the local women's institute, one of hundreds made by institutes throughout the country.

In the days that Kingsley was rector, his parishioners epitomised the rural idyll, working in sympathy with the rhythms of nature, steeped in traditions centuries old. But, as elsewhere in the countryside, Eversley was already under threat by the Industrial Revolution, which drew more than half the country population into the towns and almost laid low our ancient rural culture. As I set about my research for *Village Voices*, I began to realise just how appropriate an introduction Eversley had been. For the Women's Institute movement arose, in 1915, in response to the Great Change, and as an attempt to rekindle a spirit in the homes of ordinary country folk, to revitalise a lost world.

Village Voices is not a straightforward history of the WI. As the title suggests, it is an oral record, a celebration of the 75 years that the WI has been engaged in its main purpose to improve the quality of life for countrywomen everywhere.

The first stage of my research was to make contact with WI members who were prepared to share with me their memories of each decade from 1915 to 1990. I wrote to every County Secretary, asking for names and addresses of possible contributors, and later I wrote a long letter for everyone to see in the organisation's magazine, *Home and Country*.

The response I had was almost overwhelming.

The second stage involved me in correspondence with literally hundreds of people who had indicated that they were prepared to help, and the third saw me travelling all over the country – as far as Embleton on the North East coast of Northumberland to Madron near Land's End in Cornwall – my tape recorder and camera keeping me company in a rather battered Cortina, bought for the purpose.

I have, of course, only been able to include material from those who responded to the call, and alas, it would have been impractical to include all that I did gather – over half a million words in interview alone. My apologies are due, therefore, to those whom I left out and to those whose contributions had, perforce, to be whittled down to a manageable size. I have tried to make these difficult editorial decisions with an ear for the true rhythms of life which have sustained the Movement's phenomenal rise from its humble beginnings in September, 1915, and which I have no doubt at all will continue to sustain its purpose in the quite different context of the 21st Century.

PIERS DUDGEON, *London, 1989*

VILLAGE VOICES

A Portrait of Change
in England's Green and Pleasant Land
1915~1990

*A 75th Anniversary Celebration
of Rural Britain by the W.I.—
Britain's Foremost Women's Movement*

Edited by Piers Dudgeon

First published in Great Britain in 1989 by
Sidgwick & Jackson Limited
1 Tavistock Chambers
Bloomsbury Way
London WC1A 2SG

Copyright © 1989 Pilot Productions Limited

All rights reserved. No part of this publication may be
reproduced, stored in a retrieval system, or
transmitted in any form or by any means, electronic,
mechanical, photocopying, recording or otherwise,
without the prior written permission of the copyright owner.

Designed by Malcolm Smythe
Studio work by Keith Shannon

Acknowledgements
Photographs, other than those taken by the editor, are
reproduced by kind permission of the Women's Institute, Nick
Wright, Birmingham Museums and Art Gallery, Topham Picture
Library, Landesbildstelle, The Museum of English Rural Life,
Greenpeace Communications Ltd, Hastings Museum and Art Gallery,
The Sutcliffe Gallery, *Farmer's Weekly*, Popperfoto, the Milk
Marketing Board, *Home and Country* Magazine, *The Independent*, and
Derry Brabbs (from *Rural England* by David Puttnam and Derrick
Mercer, published by Queen Anne Press).

Quotations from *Farmer's Glory* by A G Street (Oxford
University Press, 1983) and *Notes Towards the Definition of
Culture* by T S Eliot (Faber and Faber, 1983)

Typeset in Ehrhardt by Dorchester Typesetting, Dorset, England
Printed by Mandarin, Hong Kong
for Pilot Productions Limited
17 Munster Road
London SW6 4ER

ISBN: 0-283-99886-5

Contents

Chapter One
THE VILLAGE, PRE-1915   7

Chapter Two
WOMEN IN A MAN'S WORLD   16

Chapter Three
PROJECT PRODUCE, 1916   24

Chapter Four
POWER TO COUNTRYWOMEN   34

Chapter Five
THE ORGANISATION   38

Chapter Six
EDUCATING THE MEMBERSHIP TO POWER   48

Chapter Seven
PART OF A GLOBAL VILLAGE   72

Chapter Eight
WOMEN AT WAR   76

Chapter Nine
PLANNING FOR A NEW AGE   98

Chapter Ten
EDUCATING AND EXPANDING IN THE NEW AGE   114

Chapter Eleven
WIDENING HORIZONS   120

Chapter Twelve
POST-WAR BABIES AND SOCIAL REVOLUTION   130

Chapter Thirteen
WOMEN IN A WOMAN'S WORLD   138

Chapter Fourteen
THE AGE OF SCIENCE   148

Chapter Fifteen
MIRROR TO THE FUTURE   164

Epilogue   175

Chapter One

THE VILLAGE, PRE-1915

'For we are the people of England,
and we have not spoken yet.'
G K CHESTERTON

A Yorkshire farmer, 1920. Official concern for rural
communities now focused on the welfare of the farmer's wife.

In 1801 four-fifths of the population lived in the countryside, but by 1901 more than half had moved to live in large towns and cities. The bare statistics of rural de-population caused by the Industrial Revolution – harsh though they are – describe only the most visible aspect of an economic and cultural depression which reached deep into the heart of the rural community and precipitated the formation of the WI.

Traditionally, a farmer made a living by supplying the neighbouring town with his produce and spending his money on goods which his townsmen customers had to offer; business was a simple, normal exchange of products to the mutual advantage of both groups. But as the Industrial Revolution gathered pace and Britain built up her export trade in manufacturing goods, food became the currency with which foreign nations paid, to the detriment of the British farmer. Improved modes of

transport (in particular, the steamship and railway) made it feasible to import and distribute produce from Europe and America, and our farmers were simply not set up to offer competition. By about 1880, the imports of cheap corn and meat from overseas had ended the once Golden Age of British agriculture. Between 1871 and 1900 over two million acres of arable land went out of cultivation in Britain, and life in rural villages, once busy, happy and prosperous, became, for many, hard and bleak. Capital ceased to be spent on improvements in buildings and equipment, and landlords and tenants were forced to neglect the repairs needed to prevent the ensuing delapidation of farms and cottages.

In response, a Royal Commission was set up in 1893 and its report observed that the smallholder seemed to be surviving better than most provided that he employed little or no labour and, with his wife and family, worked his holding with minimum waste. Clearly the smallholder, his wife, and his family should be given every opportunity to do better still, and there arose a fresh sense of the importance of agricultural education – an education not only in new farming methods, but in initiative, in enterprise, and in the need to think and act together in co-operation. In 1901, the Agricultural Organisation Society (AOS) was formed in Britain with the avowed purpose 'to start local societies of farmers, smallholders, and growers so that they may co-operate together to buy what they needed, sell what they grew, and in any other way to the benefit of agriculture'. In 1912 the Board of Education published a report on an investigation into agricultural instruction in France, Germany and Belgium, and drew particular attention to the Belgian women's movement, the Cercles des Fermières, in which was found 'the most powerful lever for the economic and social elevation of farmers and their wives'. Its author drew attention to the fact that while 'other wives are concerned professionally only with the care of a house and children, the farmer's wife is a partner in a business. On her good management of the dairy, poultry yard, and piggery much of his profit depends', yet she was often also engaged in the never-ending toil of bringing up a large family on a miserably low income. It was at this point in the chain of depression that it was felt something could be done to regenerate country life. Bring fresh interest to her life, raise her consciousness in the best Liberal tradition of the day, organise women's groups to educate her in ways to improve country life, increase the comfort and prosperity of the home, and you will 'stem the tide of rural depopulation, and heal a national canker.'

This focus upon the important role of farmer's wife was quite new, a revolutionary concept in the minds of men concerned with the revival of rural England and the farming community in particular. That she had little respite from a gruelling daily round may be seen from this extract from the prize-winning scrapbook of Llangernyw WI in North Wales, in which Mrs A E Jones recalls her mother's life early this century:

'There lived at the farmhouse a maid, teamsman, cowman and teenage lad. Breakfast was around 7.00 am, milking finished, horses fed and groomed. There was a mid-morning snack to prepare at 10.00. The maid would take this out to the men wherever they'd be working. Dinner was at mid-day, an old sheep bell, hung by the front door at our home, announced "dinner ready!". Tea was at 3.00, evening meal at 6.00, and during harvest another meal was served later.

'Besides preparing meals and general housework, wife and maid were responsible for feeding calves (each having its allowance of meal and skimmed milk in a

The maid would take the mid-morning snack to the men wherever they would be working.

bucket), the sow, the hens, ducks and geese, and of course collecting eggs. Monday was always washing day, using tub and dolly. The whites were boiled in a copper boiler heated with sticks and small logs, the fire was lit early to bring the clothes to the boil by the time breakfast was over; later mother had a hand wringer which was screwed onto the edge of the sink, thus doing away with hand wringing. On wet days clothes would be hung in the loft or hay shed to dry. Most farms were fortunate in having a well near the house (or were the farmhouses built near the wells? – probably). Others had to walk to the nearest well. It was not until the mid-1950s that mains water was available in this area.

'Farming was a way of life. The poverty was dreadful but they created enormous happiness as well.' Lady Elizabeth Brunner.

'Monday was also butter-making day; in the evening the round pounds were wrapped, and the eggs counted into a bucket ready for market the next day in Llanrwst.

'Tuesday's journey to market was six miles by horse-drawn cart. It was customary in hot weather to lay rhubarb leaves at the bottom of the basket and on top of the butter, in the belief that they helped keep the butter cool. Tuesday was the day when the shopping was done; the list was not long – only what was necessary was bought: tea, sugar, cheese, yeast, and flower for bread-making in 1cwt bags. These bags were made of strong white cotton and made very nice table cloths. The *Farmer and Stockbreeder* was bought on market day – our only weekly farming paper. Mother used to enjoy a sit-down after tea on market days to read some of the Women's and Poultry sections.

'After tea on Tuesdays the ironing was done using the old flat iron. If one was not an expert at controlling the fire, the iron would be either too hot or too cold; smoke or soot would sometimes touch the iron and if not careful, would mark the clothes and flare the temper! Sheets and towels were put through the mangle, not ironed.

'Baking was often done on Wednesdays, bread, bara brith, buns and cakes. Eight or ten large loaves were baked in a large brick oven heated with timber (ours was in an outhouse not far from the back door). The bread would be in for about two hours and taken out about tea-time. I have often wondered how one could tell when the oven was hot enough to put in the dough, I believe it was according to the colour of the bricks. When the bread was taken out, a large dish full of rice

Besides preparing meals, the farmer's wife looked after the calves, the sow, the hens, the ducks and the geese.
'The home is the centre of farm business. A large part is played in the farm economy by the farmer's wife.' 1929 WI AGM.

pudding was sometimes placed in the oven for a couple of hours then sticks were put in. They would be nice and dry, ready to start next week's fire. The cakes were baked in the kitchen grate oven. There were never any failures, and that, without a thermometer, or thermostat! Mother judged the heat of the oven by putting her hand on the brass handle.

'Thursday was bedrooms day – five bedrooms, two flights of stairs, parlour and dining room also had an extra "do". Oatcakes, which were on the menu daily, had to be baked every seven or ten days. Making these was quite an art. The oatmeal was mixed with water and rolled into rounds of about twelve inches diameter, baked on a griddle above the coal fire, using sticks as well if necessary to keep the heat up, turned over once, and then left in front of the fire (on a stool) to dry a bit and curl inwards – rather hot work and time consuming.

'Friday meant windows had to be cleaned. Old oak furniture polished, brasses done – not forgetting mending and sewing – also knitting, always knitting on the go (farmers always wore hand knitted stockings).

'Saturday, the kitchen had a good turn out. The big

The table in Erland Lee's home in South Wentworth where the first WI was discussed and the constitution drawn up.

The home of Erland Lee, who organised the first WI meeting in Stoney Creek, Canada.

white table (sycamore) was well scrubbed. The cutlery had an extra sparkle using "bathbrick", the old black leaded grate seemed with its fender and stool to have an extra shine on Saturdays. An extra supply of sticks and coal was brought in to last over Sunday. Vegetables were also prepared for Sunday dinner. The grandfather clock was always wound up on Saturday evenings.

'Only essential work was done on Sundays. the chapel was well attended and we thought nothing of walking one and a half miles to the service with others joining us on the way. Most Sundays we attended the three services – 10.00 am, 2.00 pm and 6.00.'

In 1904, in a book entitled *The Organisation of Agriculture in England and Other Lands*, rural historian Edwin Pratt praised the aim of the AOS to engender a new spirit in the farming community but showed how far other countries were ahead of our own. He wrote of Canada and described the Farmers' Institutes there and their 'sequel', the Women's Institutes. He wrote too of what

English rural community was not just economic, its effect not just to extinguish a hundred old agricultural and everyday rural crafts, but to threaten a whole manner of life and values woven into the ancient fabric of the rural community. Now, those conscious of what had happened were calling upon the women in our rural communities to bring the countryside back to life. The Women's Institute Movement in Canada had been established in affiliation with the Farmers' Institute of South Wentworth, and the first WI meeting was held in the village of Stoney Creek, Ontario, in 1897. It spread fast: thirty-six institutes with 3,000 members, by 1902, over 800 ten years later.

In February 1915, Mrs Alfred Watt, a founder member of the Metchosin Institute in Canada, travelled to London and attended a conference on industrial and agricultural co-operation – England was at war; it had become vital that farming should prosper, that food should be grown at home and brought quickly to the great city markets. The conference was opened by the

The Canadian WI was inspired by the tragic death of Adelaide Hoodless's first baby, due, she felt, to her ignorance

about food hygiene. The call came during a talk she gave in King Street, Stoney Creek, in 1897. Below right: The

Homestead, where Adelaide Hoodless lived until 1881. Centre: J Nugent Harris of the AOS.

Women's Institutes might do in Britain to educate countrywomen, to bring fresh interest to village life, and to relieve 'what must too often be its unspeakable dullness. . . It was indeed a happy inspiration which led the wives and daughters of Canadian farmers to conclude that, inasmuch as women generally play so important a part in the work of a farm, they should have an organisation of their own which would enable them to do what they could to advance the welfare both of home life and of agriculture.'

The blow that industrial materialism had dealt the

Secretary of the AOS, Mr Nugent Harris. Mrs Watt sat in the front row listening and knitting as one speaker followed another. Near the end of the meeting she put her knitting aside, rose, and began to tell the story of the Women's Institute movement in her own country and its co-operative ideals. Nugent Harris was immediately possessed by the conviction that here – precisely – was the catalyst that would help fulfil the needs of Britain's agricultural community.

Not much later, Mrs Watt was appointed to the AOS staff for a period of three months with the express purpose of organising WIs in Britain. A Governor of the AOS, who was present at the meeting which ratified her appointment, one Colonel the Hon R Stapleton-Cotton, shrewdly advised that the Movement's beginnings should be made in Wales because every Welsh village supported a number of different places of worship, each with its own social organisation for women attached. The WI, he held, should present a non-denominational, non-political profile which would unite these little mutually exclusive groups in a single community effort.

Colonel Cotton duly arranged a small conference at Bangor in North Wales to which he invited influential people who might be useful in the formation of such a movement, and a few days later, on September 11th, 1915, in the Colonel's home village of Llanfairpwllgwyngyllgogerychwyrndrobwllllandysilliogogogoch, on the isle of Anglesey, the first women's institute in Britain was formed.

Colonel Richard Southwell George Stapleton-Cotton was born in 1849, the second son of the second Viscount Combermere. His connection with Anglesey stems from the fact that his sister became mother to the sixth Marquess. WI member, Miss Dorothy Sargent, daughter of the sixth Marquess's game-keeper, recalls that a disability brought Colonel Stapleton-Cotton to settle in Anglesey, in the early years of the century. He had been living in Antigua, where he had plantations, until,

during a terrific storm, he was cut down by a bolt of lightning and thereafter paralysed below the knees. 'That was why he came to live at Plas Llwynonn, the old dower house to Plas Newydd, on the estate of his nephew, the sixth Marquess of Anglesey.'

He and Mrs Cotton apparently settled down quickly and become actively involved with the economic life of the village. 'There was always some new idea waiting to be developed,' recalls Mrs Sargent. 'His first was a bulb growing enterprise – daffodils, narcisi, tulips – it looked like a miniature Holland, the farm where he grew them. The Colonel was a frequent sight driving in his donkey chaise along the peaceful and traffic free roads of Llanfairpwll. The donkey chaise was like an elaborate invalid chair, but much bigger, and it had a donkey harnessed to it. And wherever the Colonel was – meetings, services – Tinker, his dog, was also in evidence. When he went to the little church on Lord Anglesey's estate, the donkey would be stabled in the church hut while the Colonel was wheeled into his place by the font. But the dog would go in with him and sit there – his behaviour as impeccable as one of Trollope's clergy! I knew the family well and became playmates with the Colonel's only grand-daughter, Penelope, who later married John Betjeman, the Poet Laureate.

'From the start of World War I, the Colonel had all the local women working on the land, and others working for the comforts of the troops. Another of his

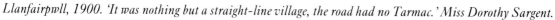

Llanfairpwll, 1900. 'It was nothing but a straight-line village, the road had no Tarmac.' Miss Dorothy Sargent.

Plas Newydd. 'The Colonel came here when the present Lord Anglesey's father inherited.' The Marchioness of Anglesey.

Plas Llwynonn, where Colonel Stapleton-Cotton lived on Lord Anglesey's Estate.

Llanfairpwll station, where Colonel Stapleton-Cotton set up his egg marketing depot.

enterprises was an egg collecting depot, set up on the railway station platform. And willows were grown in the local football field for basket making.'

Mary Blanche Roberts, a lifelong friend of Dorothy Sargent, remembers other enterprises of the Colonel: 'We used to pick blackberries and take them to him, and he would send them to England for jam making. I often wondered if that is where the WI jam-making tradition stemmed from. They had an old hut and some old fashioned scales, and we used to put the blackberries we had picked into these tall pans we used for carrying water from the wells. We would fill those; the Colonel would weigh them up, and then you got so much a pound. I think if you filled one pan you got about sixpence.

'His egg marketing enterprise was sort of similar. He had, again, a sort of hut on the railway platform where he'd test the eggs. They would hold the eggs in front of a lamp and if they were bad they would discard them. There'd be a big bowl for cracked and broken eggs, and you could have those very cheaply. My mother used to strain them and use them for omelettes or custards.

'During school holidays, we used to go egg collecting with William Owen in his van. We'd take sandwiches with us, start at 8.00 am and meander round the farms up the Hollyhead Road, branching off to Newborough and those sort of places. You see, the Colonel was offering a marketing service to the farmers in the days when distribution was very badly organised. Once collected and sorted, they would be packed away and sent off on the train. Just like all the bulbs from the Colonel's bulb fields. He was a wonderful character, and we all looked up to him. He also ran a chicory farm and owned a bacon factory, so he employed a lot of labour in the area.'

Clearly the Colonel practised the tenets of the organisation he represented, and in calling the meeting at which the first Women's Institute was actually formed he would not have felt that he was doing anything very radical. Already impressed with the war work of women in the village, here was another opportunity for co-operation – the key word of the AOS. There are sparse records of the meeting itself, but here is a unique memory of one participant – Rhiannon Morris Jones: 'It makes me feel very old to think that I attended the first WI meeting ever held in this country. Let me hasten to add that I was a schoolgirl at the time, and that my chief duty on this great occasion was to carry chairs there which my mother had lent for the meeting.

'When the suggestion of forming a WI was put to the Colonel he went scouring round the village looking for a room where they could meet. As the Movement was supposed to be non-denominational and non-political none of the church or chapel rooms would do. Then his eyes fell on a large disused shed, where garden chairs were kept, in the garden of a house called Graig on the outskirts of the village. He gained the consent of the owner [Mr W E Jones, County Surveyor and Estate Agent for the Marquess of Anglesey], and it was here that the first meeting was held. Subsequent meetings of course I did not attend as I had to go back to school.

'I wish I could tell you what went on in that first meeting, but alas I have forgotten all about it, except that it was a beautiful sunny day and the garden was full of flowers, perhaps a good omen for the future of the Women's Institutes.'

What the schoolgirl cannot now remember – perhaps not surprisingly – is that the meeting was almost exclusively about business. A committee of ten was elected including a President (Mrs Stapleton-Cotton), a Vice President and Treasurer (Mrs W E Jones, whose shed it was) and an Honorary Secretary (Mrs Wilson of Bryn). All very much in the business-like tradition of the WI Movement. But it was not until September 16th, five days later, that Mrs Watt came to formalise the proceedings and explain in detail the object of the Movement. She arranged for a number of resolutions (motions, formal proposals) to be put to the meeting, namely that a Women's Institute should be created in Llanfairpwll, that there would be regular monthly meetings on the first Tuesday in each month at 2 pm, that the membership fee should be two shillings, a reasonable proportion of the agricultural wage which in 1921 was forty-six shillings.

The object of the Movement was declared as follows:
a. Studying home economics.
b. Providing a centre for educational and social intercourse and for all local activities.
c. Encouraging home and local industries.
d. Developing co-operative enterprises.
e. Stimulating interest in the Agricultural Industry.

Mrs Watt explained that the institute should be non-sectarian and non-political, and that no controversial subject which might cause friction or lead to serious differences was to be brought forward for discussion. Further that all elections should be by ballot, and a majority of the votes cast should be necessary to a choice. All thoroughly democratic. The duties of the committee

The disused shed at Graig, where garden chairs were kept, where the first meeting of the WI in Britain took place in 1915.

'It was a beautiful sunny day, and the garden was full of flowers . . . a good omen for the future.' Mrs Morris Jones.

were clearly laid out as was the procedure at meetings:

1. Opening
2. Minutes
3. Correspondence
4. Roll Call
5. Reports
6. New business
7. Reception of new members
8. Programme and discussion
9. Adjournment

Number 8 was an important aspect of the meetings. Talks on cookery, household affairs and gardening were the most popular, and occasionally a lecturer from the nearby university college would visit. Otherwise, the Colonel would step in to 'give us a talk from his wide knowledge of the world, of persons or of things'.

It is interesting what elements of the WI rules survived these early days when the Movement was under the protective wing of the AOS. The emphasis on rigid and democratic procedure, co-operation and education has remained, but when, a few years later, the 'new women' brought the Movement its independence, the original rather parochial conception as a non-political force was immediately dropped.

The members of the first institute in Britain, outside the shed at Graig.

Chapter Two
WOMEN IN A MAN'S WORLD

*'We weren't ambitious in those days,
there weren't the opportunities.'*
MRS GLADYS MORRIS

*Mrs Adelaide Hoodless. Her WI was
not bound up with women's rights.*

It would be wrong to suggest that Mrs Watt's success in establishing the first institute in Britain had come easily. In 1899 Mrs Adelaide Hoodless, the Canadian Movement's founder, had travelled to England as a representative to the World's Congress for Women and when she returned to Ontario she claimed to have been 'deluged with enquiries, even from such important leaders of the agricultural movement as Lady Warwick.' But when, in 1913, Mrs Watt first came to England to turn words into action she was driven to despair by the apathy she found. 'I was disgusted,' she later confided to Nugent Harris, 'the way my appeals to start Women's Institutes in England were received.' And he could only agree: 'I became impressed by the "out-of-touch" of the

women folk on the farms with those questions that affect the life of every citizen.' In an effort to have the Farmers' Associations open their membership to women he had persuaded the Manchester and District branch to agree to an experiment. A number of women – wives and daughters of farmer members – were permitted to attend a meeting. 'But the women sat silent and took no part in discussions. . .they sat there like oysters!'

Afterwards Nugent Harris discovered that many of the women had not agreed with decisions taken at the meeting. 'Why did you not say so?' he asked. 'If we had spoken, you know what we'd get when we got home,' came the reply.

It is difficult to imagine the repressive atmosphere

Left: *Mrs Alfred Watt, member for Metchosin WI in Canada and Wivelsfield WI in Sussex. At the beginning, she was the only salaried organiser of institutes in Britain, and it was largely due to her personality and hard work that news of the Movement spread. The great leaders who came afterwards and took the WI to independence from its government-backed sponsors, shared her aims, but saw the education of women into positions of power as the essential means of achieving them. Edith Rigby (right), first President of Hutton and Howick WI was a suffragette, gaoled seven times, once for planting a bomb in the Liverpool Corn Exchange.*

which women – especially countrywomen – suffered in silence in those days. The very idea of an organisation in which they could play an important and individual role was revolutionary. Mrs Margaret Jones of Criccieth WI has not forgotten what it was like to grow up in the shadow of men who, in the words of Gervas Huxley (later to become Honorary Treasurer to the Movement), 'believed in the mental, moral and physical inferiority of women'. The idea of marriage as a partnership of equals was almost completely alien: 'The women didn't get money like they do today. The man kept the purse, I don't know how it was in England but that is what happened in Wales. If they wanted something extra, women had to go to the shop and ask for tic. There are books in Welsh which show the women's shopbooks for the week. I remember somebody from a farm had bought several things from the local shop – flour, rice and so on, and then there's mention of "a quarter of tea (not to tell Evan)". Evan was the husband, you see. Tea had become fashionable but it wasn't necessary, so the women had to smuggle it in, and they would meet together when the men were out working in the fields and brew this tea. But they were afraid to let their husbands know. And if a woman wanted a new ribbon for her hat, then she had to put it down as "bicarbonate of soda" or something like that, and the shop account would show something different in case the husband should find out.

'Down-trodden? . . . you have no idea! I'll say they were down-trodden, we are still fighting! Never mind we will get there. Men have always been chauvinistic. It is the fault of the women a lot of it. I think the women brought up their sons to be chauvinistic, I'm quite convinced of that from my experience of my own mother. I had to clean my brothers' boots; I loathed the job. I loathed it when I was young, why should I do it? There were three brothers, all older than me, who were quite capable of cleaning their own boots. I said then to my mother when I was rebelling, you know, "Never will I clean a man's boots," and then of course I had five sons! I cleaned their shoes when they were small, but when they became seven years of age, they cleaned their own boots and shoes and I have never done it since. Two husbands and five sons and I've never cleaned their shoes.'

Of course the repressive atmosphere clouded not only the family context. There was so little opportunity outside the family that 'ambition' was a meaningless word to countrywomen. 'We weren't ambitious in those days,' recalls Mrs Gladys Morris, 98-year-old member of Talybont WI. 'It wasn't the same as today. Even if I had been ambitious there weren't the openings. I remember domestic service was very popular.' The professions were almost exclusively a male preserve; up to the beginning of the century there were no female secretaries or typists let alone executives or civil servants.

For practically all women marriage and child-bearing were the order of the day. 'I was twenty years old in 1915 when the WI was launched,' said Mrs Chipperfield of Cleeve WI. 'I was living in Manchester as a teacher at the time, one of the few jobs a women could do in those days. But I only worked for eight years in my whole life because then I got married. You see it wasn't done to work when you were married, unless you were down-and-out or the husband was ill.'

The first step to equality of opportunity for women was deemed to be the Vote. Vociferous and certainly most militant among those fighting for women's rights were

members of the Women's Political and Social Union, led by Mrs Emily Pankhurst. They were not in fact fighting for all women to have the vote, just property owning women. One member of the Union, Mrs Edith Rigby, was later to become a founder member and first President of Hutton and Howick WI in Lancashire. Mrs P A Townson, President today, tells Edith's story, a story which shows that in its earliest days the Women's Institute Movement made a natural progression for at least one fervent feminist.

'Edith was born in 1873, the daughter of a Preston doctor. She was a suffragette and was gaoled on seven occasions, once for planting a bomb in the Liverpool Corn Exchange and again for burning down Lord Leverhulme's house on Rivington Pike. For the attack on Lord Leverhulme's property in 1913 she enlisted the help of a man whose wife was also a suffragette, as she needed someone to drive the car and help her carry the paraffin cans up the hillside to within sight of the large bungalow called Roynton Cottage. Mrs Rigby then dismissed the gentleman and after making sure no one was in residence she started several fires by breaking windows and pouring paraffin in. The house, which was wooden, went up like a tinder box. She gave herself up to the police on 10th July, 1913. From the dock she made this statement – "I want to ask Sir William Lever whether he thinks his property on Rivington Pike is more valuable as one of his superfluous houses occasionally to be opened to people, or as a beacon lighted for King and Country, to see here are some intolerable grievances for women."

'Edith had been brought up amongst the poor of Preston where her father had his practice and all her life worked for their welfare, visiting factories in the area where she thought the girls were underpaid, and approaching the management. She was a strong Socialist and entertained many famous people in her home, including Kier Hardy. She also founded a club for working girls, mainly weavers in 1899. There they would have an evening social with tea and biscuits and entertainment, but she also organised classes in English Literature and History as well as gymnastics and elementary hygiene. They were also marched off to the local park to play cricket (in their clogs) and to the newly opened swimming baths.

'In 1912 when Asquith (the Prime Minister) put a stop to the Conciliation Bill (the product of an all-party Committee on Suffrage which proposed giving the Vote to property-owning women), it again provoked an angry response from Edith who poured acid on the green of

Left: *Mrs Pankhurst arrested outside Buckingham Palace, 1914.* Inset: *Mrs Pankhurst fund raising for the cause.*

the local golf course and ordered a friend to plant a bomb in the mouth of a cannon in a Blackburn park. The lady, having time to spare before returning to Preston, set fire to the stands at Blackburn Rovers Football Ground. Like many suffragettes who were gaoled, Edith went on hunger strike and was forcibly fed.

'Edith was also very critical of the wealthy neighbours in Winckley Square, Preston, where she lived with her doctor husband, Charles. They confined their servants to attics or basements during non-working hours. Her own maids had the run of the house, eating in the dining room, having the evenings free, and did not wear uniforms which Edith considered badges of servitude.

'Edith's devoted husband, Charles, bore all this silently, as the only occasion he complained resulted in even more uncomfortable conditions. It happened after a particularly tiring day for the doctor, who came home to find only sandwiches for tea, as the cook had gone out to the theatre. He remarked that he deserved a hot meal after such an exhausting day, and told Edith that she couldn't even cook let alone earn her living at anything. As usual, when

Margaret Hitchcock: 'If only women would use their votes to insist that the morality of men conform to that of women.'

rebuked, Edith said nothing and left not just the room but the house. Quite used to her behaviour, her husband passed the first week without much concern, but by the second he had hired two detectives. Nothing was heard for a further month, then one day he received a message to say that his wife – alias Polly Sharples – was employed as under house maid by a titled family in London. Her employer had become suspicious when "Polly" volunteered to translate an important business letter written in French. Charles took the train to London and went to the house. He was shown into a small room and after some time Edith appeared in a maid's outfit. When he asked how she could do this to him, she replied: "I'm sorry, Sir, but we're not allowed followers."

'Apparently her experience at the house did show her that some of the aristocracy treated their servants well.

'When the First World War started Edith bought a cottage outside Preston with two acres and set about doing her war effort by producing vegetable, fruit and honey from her land, leaving her long-suffering husband living in Winckley Square and visiting the cottage at weekends. There she would dress in breeches, haymaking smock and trilby. She was a devotee of organic gardening; it was during this period that she helped form our institute and became President.'

Few people today, either within or outside the WI, would credit the emergence of the Movement from a background of such unrest, but as Dorothy E Williams of the Worcestershire Federation put it so succinctly, 'The institutes were in some sense the rural counterpart of the banding together of women in the urban areas, in a common fight for freedom and independence of thought and action. The husband of one enthusiast for the new Movement understandably interpreted "WI" as standing for "Women's Independence".'

Nor is it pure coincidence that the Movement's first Chairman came from a non-militant organisation dedicated to securing the Vote not just for property owners but for all women, or that the first private secretary to this Chairman – Mrs Margaret Hitchcock – was a suffragist who had worked as Secretary of the Colchester Suffrage Society and later as full-time organiser for the Liberal Women's Suffrage Union in London, or that the Movement's first Treasurer – Mrs Helena Auerbach

Ripley, the bus shelter a local WI effort. 'If anyone wanted anything doing the Estate would send their man out.' Mrs Mary Smith.

– who played a crucial role in enabling the WI to become independent of the Government, had been Honorary Treasurer of the National Union of Women's Suffrage Societies until the passing of the Act in 1917 which gave women the parliamentary vote.

The fact is that the women who took control of the WI Movement away from the AOS and the government that funded them were not only 'thinking' women who wanted equality, they were real leaders of their day, women who today might be leading businesswomen, publishers, civil servants, or politicians. And their vision of equality was perceived not only in relation to men, but also and as important, amongst themselves. This, too, was fairly revolutionary, as Miss Vera Thompson of Brenchley WI recalls: 'What I liked about the WI, we all got together and there was no class consciousness. It was the first time that people from all walks of life in the place got together on an equal basis. We were Liberals in our family, very strong Liberals. My mother and father were very old friends of Ramsay MacDonald, and the talk around the vicarage was very much not approved by some.'

Most villages were still run on pretty much a feudal basis. Even where the Lord of the Manor no longer held sway, his place as leader or patron had very often been taken by a wealthy industrialist. Today there are some villagers with long memories who argue that this form of very local government worked well, especially before improved eduacational and work opportunities provided villagers with wider horizons. 'My mother started the WI here in Ugley in 1921,' says Miss Nancy Tennant, 'My father built a war memorial and a village hall where for the first time we had somewhere where we could meet. My parents were, in a way, parents to the village. You have to understand that people were so helpless in those days. This is what is so impossible for people to realise today. People were so vulnerable, that was the awful thing. You could get turned out of your house at the end of the week, and if your husband got ill, there was nothing behind you, and therefore my parents (because we never had a proper parson) felt responsible for the welfare of the village. My father was a very ardent Liberal and the idea of being called a Squire was something that would send him into a real fury or horror, but our house became a place where you would go when you needed help, or fun!

'At my ninetieth birthday there were wonderful octogenarians who could remember coming to the school treats at my parents' home, and who still had little treasures which they had kept since then. My parents were very beloved in the village. They weren't at all autocratic.'

Surely this was patronage in the best sense – guardianship without condescension – and there's a hint that where something akin to it exists today it might even be preferable to our Welfare State. Lady Ingilby of Ripley in West Yorkshire is in the unusual position of still maintaining a 'loose' patronage in a village of between 120 and 150 people: 'Until quite recently the Estate owned all the houses in the village except the Rectory and the Glebe, and the Glebe Cottage, and the school house and the school. But now a few new houses have been built and private people own them. The freehold properties that were always part of the Estate are still so. You need a lot of staff if you run a business like this. It was designed as an Estate village and there were two working farms in the village.

'It's a loaded question as to whether I think that people have benefited from private rather than State patronage, and I'm biassed. But I can say that people always want to come and live here and I think most people want to attach themselves to something or someone, and therefore they like a village where there's a centre, where there's someone in charge. Also I think they find it useful. It does help to solve village squabbles.'

Ripley Castle.

If Ugley and Ripley are models of what was good in the old feudal system, there were plenty of examples in other squirearchies for which Mrs Watt's democratic ideal of 'one woman one vote' came as a serious shock. Nugent Harris told how one Lady of the Manor, when she had grasped what was to her the well-nigh incomprehensible notion of complete democracy upon which the WI was founded, wrote to say that she with her husband refused to sanction the formation of 'such a radical organisation'.

Again, Mrs Chipperfield of Cleeve: 'The first time that I went to the WI, I wondered what I had come into. There they all were, huddled round these four or five oil heaters. There was an old lady behind me, Mrs Leam who lived in the beautiful old Georgian house, which was the last house in Cleeve. She had been out in India I remember with her husband who was a Major in the army, and she was used to "the boys" doing everything. Well, I was sitting there and suddenly I got a tap with a stick on my back. Now, you have to remember I came from a rather posh suburb of Manchester, and I wasn't used to country life, though I loved the countryside and we spent all our spare time in the country, but I wasn't a

'I wasn't used to country life . . . I thought I'd come into the feudal system.' Mrs Chipperfield of Cleeve.

'My parents were, in a way, parents to the village . . . there was a family party feeling.' Miss Nancy Tennant.

countrywoman. So, I got this tap on my back and I turned round and this woman pointed her stick at the window. She wanted the curtain drawn. She wasn't going to do it herself, she didn't care who did it and I was the one in front of her. I just stared at her, I couldn't believe it. Surely she would ask me to draw the curtain. I was a real live wire at that time, you know, not hobbling about like I do now. A little later, after I had done nothing, the same performance happened again, this time she glowered at me, so I took no notice. I was waiting for her to ask me. I wasn't used to that.

'I learnt later that she was the Secretary and had been for twelve years and as soon as I got in harness I got that changed. Now President and Secretary move on every five years. I thought I had come into the feudal system, the only difference was we, in Cleeve, had the Imperial Tobacco Company – Baron Sinclair of Cleeve - rather than a Lord and Lady, and they didn't look after all the families like the Lords did in their day, but they ruled the roost none the less.'

Mrs Watt, a Canadian, was astonished by the hard lines of the British class system, but soon realised that she could not build her organisation in Britain without the help of the ruling class.

Miss Viola Williams, Durnford and Woodford WI: 'I can remember way back when an institute in this country was formed, almost without exception the President was the Lady of the Manor, the Secretary was a school mistress (because she was probably the most literate), and the Treasurer, very often, was the doctor's wife, and that was the hierarchy. I can remember that quite clearly. When I went out to Malaya to form institutes there, the hierarchy was the same: the President was the Chief's wife, the Secretary was the school mistress because she was the only one who could read and write, and the Treasurer was the local DO's wife. It was an absolutely identical pattern. And that wasn't anybody's influence, that was simply what was available. It was exactly the same situation in this country. What was available at the time.'

The alternative, as Gladys Morris explains, was simply impracticable: 'It was always the Lady of the Manor who was President – the others wouldn't have felt confident to have taken it on.' It was that deeply ingrained reticence for responsibility, which had its roots in the class system, to which the first leaders of the Movement immediately addressed themselves. As we shall see, the method they chose was education – the education of ordinary members in skills of leadership, the skills required to run an organisation efficiently.

Chapter Three
PROJECT PRODUCE, 1916

*'Success cannot be achieved unless
every member takes her share of responsibility.'*
LADY DENMAN

*Bron Eifion, home of Mrs Dorothy Drage, who started the
first WI market during World War I.*

In spite of Mrs Watt's difficulties, the Movement spread fast. By the autumn of 1916 there were twenty-four institutes, and the New Year of 1917 saw forty thriving – the British WI had come farther in fifteen months than the Canadian organisation in its first five years. Much of the work during this early, frenetic period of expansion fell to Mrs Watt herself, the Movement's only salaried organiser. The success bears testimony to Mrs Watt's incredible energy, stamina, and stubborn resolve. She was completely dedicated to the task in hand and, clearly, from this record of the formation of Criccieth WI, one of the very earliest, she would not take No for an answer. Mrs Dorothy Drage, whose father, John Whitehead-Graves, had come to Criccieth from the

Midlands to start a quarrying industry, was a key person in the village and the obvious target for Mrs Watt. Mrs Drage describes their meeting in 1915:

'My impression of Mrs Watt was first not too enthusiastic, but on talking to her, her absolute sincerity and devotion to the work of helping countrywomen to which she had given her life, impressed me, against my will. We already had so much to do for the Red Cross, for our servicemen and for our soldiers, it was hard to know if we could undertake anything new. But her brilliant power of speaking and force of interest in the work at last persuaded me and my friends that we would consider forming a WI.'

Mrs Drage describes Mrs Watt as 'short and sturdy –

good looking to a degree with dark, very penetrating eyes.' Miss Nancy Tennant, who knew Mrs Watt well, adds a more human touch to the portrait: 'She was a very warm character, a kind of Mrs Tiggy-Winkle, but with an indomitable determination. I remember her coming to stay at our home in Ugley when she was stomping around Essex. She suddenly arrived in my father's study in what appeared to be her dressing gown and lovely mop cap – he looked awfully surprised. It really was very funny and now seems a very long time ago.'

With the Movement's early success came serious interest from the Government. The AOS was largely funded by the Board of Agriculture which saw a use for the WI in linking together countrywomen in more organised war work. What they needed was a real leader. Mrs Watt wouldn't do, they said, what was required was a woman with title and position, someone able to handle the Ladies of the Manor and turn the expanding organisation to the advantage of a nation beleaguered by war. Mrs Stapleton-Cotton and Mrs Drage helped form a special sub-committee of the AOS dedicated to WI affairs, and began to look around for a leader. Many names were discussed, but they finally agreed to make

an approach to Lady Salisbury. In the opinion of Mrs Roland Wilkins, a Governor of the AOS and acting Chairman of the sub-committee, Lady Salisbury was not the ideal choice, and when she declined, Mrs Wilkins pressed for an invitation to be sent to one Lady Gertrude Denman.

'Trudie' Denman was the daughter of Weetman Pearson (first Viscount Cowdray), Yorkshireman, staunch Liberal, oil magnate, and newspaper baron. Their relationship was close, and Trudie's father took great pains to pass on his experience of the world to a daughter whom he clearly intended to do great things. His letters to her demonstrate that Weetman believed it his paternal duty to prepare his daughter for success in the New World, a world where for the first time women would wield real power. In January 1903 he wrote:

''Tis always well to remember that a reputation is a most dangerous possession. Those who own it have, willingly or unwillingly, the almost irresistible temptation to live up to it. The beautiful woman takes to dyeing and generally touching up (by adding to or taking from – in the latter case so far, of course, as possible) in her

'Lady Denman's contribution towards the happiness and progress of rural life is one of the greatest that has been made in our time.' HRH Queen Elizabeth, May, 1946.

The Movement spread fast, thanks particularly to the energy of Mrs Watt, who travelled all over the country promoting it. In 1917 she formed the first Nottinghamshire institute at Southwell (left: view from the Old Bishop's Palace) when she happened to be staying there with a relative.

thirties and forties; the brilliant woman must shine at whatever strain or effort to herself or perhaps misery to others at being made to appear ignorant or foolish; the rich must continue to spend when possibly they would be much happier (and truer to their own interests) by being careful; the bold rider has often to take foolish chances for fear of being considered commonplace; and so *ad infinitum*. No! The only true course to follow is to remain as near commonplace and average as your surroundings will allow you. This conduct will save many heartburnings, many disappointments and many false positions. But, at the same time, it is necessary to have large reserves, so that at any time you can push your way to the front should it be necessary or advisable to do so. This line of conduct brings respect and love and "gets you there at the finish". Hence be careful to avoid having nothing behind. If you can make a splendid show in the window, do so, so long as there will be no disappointment when the interior of the shop is examined.'

And on another occasion, he advised, 'Dame Fortune is very elusive; the only way to succeed with her is to sketch a fortune which you think you can realise and then go for it bald-headed.'

At nineteen Trudie married Thomas Denman, a young Liberal peer, the third Baron Denman. It was a suitable match in that it added title to money, but one which Trudie herself was less sure about than her mother. And in fact the marriage was not a happy one, the experience prompting Trudie to give this advice to her own daughter on the subject: 'Never get married unless you are certain that you would be absolutely miserable if you said No. That is the best way a girl can test whether she is really in love or only thinks she may be.'

Her suitability for the leadership of the WI Movement went further than title, connections and money, however. She had already demonstrated a spirit of enterprise, social concern, organisational ability and commitment to the rights of country folk.

Mrs Wilkins had originally met her over a housing improvement scheme which Lady Denman had undertaken at her 3,000-acre property in Sussex – Balcombe

Balcombe Place, the 3,000-acre property in Sussex which Trudie Denman's father bought for her when she married.

Place. The estate cottages had been provided with their own water supply and sanitation – rare luxuries in those days. It was just such practical changes to everyday life that were to concern the WI Movement under Lady Denman's leadership. Additionally, through the influence of her mother, she had in 1908 been elected to the Executive of the Women's Liberal Foundation, a non-militant organisation of more than 100,000 members campaigning for the Vote for all women, which was led by Lady Carlisle. From Lady Carlisle, Trudie Denman learned a very great deal. Her plans for the organisation and constitution of the WI would be based upon those of the Women's Liberal Foundation, and that organisation's strict pursuance of its aims through existing establishment channels (rather than by militant protest) became the *modus operandi* of the new Movement.

Towards the end of 1910 Trudie accompanied her husband to Australia, where he was appointed Governor General. Australian women already had the right to vote for both State and Federal parliaments. Trudie Denman became involved in work being undertaken by the National Council of Women to educate its members to use that vote, to improve housing, to implement improvements in opportunity in other areas, for example in the appointment of women magistrates. It might have been a forward vision of her early concerns as Chairman of the WI. It was here too that she showed where her most impressive contribution to WI work would lie – in the sphere of organisation. She championed interstate conferences designed to bring together opinion from the farthest reaches of the continent, sharpen aims, and co-ordinate action to achieve them.

Back in England, in 1914, she soon became involved in war work, started a charity called 'Smokes for Wounded Soldiers and Sailors Society', which raised the sum – incredible in those days – of £67,000 for troops abroad, and with her friend Nellie Grant began an enterprise to increase egg production. The success of this venture, launched from an office in Pimlico where she designed a model back-yard hen-house and dispensed information to the interested, led to her starting a poultry farm of her own at Balcombe Place.

Mrs Wilkins' approach came in 1916, and Lady Denman's signature appeared for the first time on the minutes of a WI executive meeting held on October 3rd of that year. From the start, Lady Denman planned for independence from her Government sponsors. Why was independence important to an organisation declaring itself to be non-political? Well, Lady Denman was about to do something about that as well, and her plans were aided by a government anxious to get the WI show on the road to feed a nation at war.

Between the beginning of 1917 and the following autumn a further 100 institutes were formed. Mrs Watt could no longer handle the burden of field work alone, and quite clearly some arrangement, other than operating on an AOS budget as a special sub-committee of that organisation, had to be made.

The Board of Agriculture, who saw its main purpose as getting the WI involved in war work, particularly in food production, proposed that its administration should henceforth come under the Women's Branch of the Board's Food Department that had been set up to form a Women's Land Army – a mobile force of workers who would work the land in place of male farm workers now fighting abroad.

By the autumn of 1917 the food situation was desperate, for it was in that year that the submarine blockade became effective. England was cut off, a beleaguered island; by September there was only three weeks' food supply left. Writing of his first day at boarding school, Evelyn Waugh conveyed the reality perfectly: 'She gave us tea that afternoon in her drawing room and said that it was a "patriotic" tea; we could eat with a good conscience because none of the cakes contained flour; some were made of potatoes, some of rice. . . As a treat, before going to school I had been taken to hear Harry Lauder, the Scotch music-hall comedian, who after his songs had addressed us on the subject. "When you cut yourself another slice of bread," he had declaimed, "look at the knife. There's blood on it. The blood of a British soldier you have stabbed in the back."'

Given the drastic situation Lady Denman could not have been in a better position to negotiate independence when she went to meet Dame Meriel Talbot, Director of the Board's new Women's Branch, but she was far from sure of success in her own mind: 'The 140 Institutes scattered through England and Wales were not then a Federation – a few of us had been discussing the need for a proper constitution, but how was I to convince a government department that if these village societies were to be controlled by a Ministry or by Local Authorities their value would be nil? I arrived at my interview prepared for battle and ready to spin a yarn that there'd be a riot in the countryside if the Women's Institutes became official organisations. Luckily my truthfulness was not put to the test, for Dame Meriel took it for granted that the institutes must unite to manage their own affairs. Their formation was thus undertaken by the Government – but after that they became the responsibility of the National Federation; in other words the institutes themselves laid down policy and made their own rules at the annual general meeting of the Federation, and by these decisions all the women's institutes were and are bound. Thus, owing to the understanding and to the lack of red tape of a government department of those days, the Women's Institutes became self-governing.'

At the institutes' first AGM, held in the Central Hall, Westminster, on October 16th, 1917, the National Federation was duly formed, and a Central Committee of Management elected.

For the institutes themselves, produce work was the order of the day, whatever ambitions or high ideals the new leader of the movement had in store for the future.

The 'programme', the part of the monthly meeting at which visiting lecturers or demonstrators would speak and demonstrate the skills which members would be required to perform in their war work, was a serious business everywhere. At the first WI meeting at Heddon-on-the-Wall, the first institute to be formed in Northumberland, 'general regret' was expressed by the President Mrs Wise that members had not taken notebooks. 'It was hoped,' read the minutes, 'that all members would bring notebooks to take down notes on lectures and discussions.'

Left: *A pruning test undertaken by members in 1918 as part of their education for the war effort.* Bottom left: *Members of Northumberland's first institute at Heddon-on-the-Wall, ticked off for not bringing notebooks to the food production demonstrations.* Right: *Fruit picking in Kent. With Britain's men away fighting the war, the nation's food supply depended upon women, and the WI was the only organisation through which it could be organised at that time.* Below right: *The production of jam by the WI in two world wars gave the Movement a media image which has served to obscure its contribution since 1915. Nevertheless the preserving skills, and the sheer good humour and fellowship that has always gone with them, are as evident today as they always have been, as these two members at the Essex Show in 1988 clearly demonstrate.*

On April 8th, 1918, a message was received at Heddon from the Board of Agriculture and Fisheries – 'Sugar must be granted to those who wish to buy fruit and make jam' – and was carried unanimously. In fact allocations of rationed sugar were made to all institutes for organised jam making in 1917, 1918 and 1919, and demands for production were met in a competitive spirit. The example set by Colonel Stapleton-Cotton in Llanfairpwll was copied throughout the institutes, an effort now organised centrally from the institutes' own National Federation office (NFWI). Local women were also bonded together either working on the land or making clothes for the comfort of the troops. And Dame Meriel Talbot left no doubt in the minds of the delegates to the first AGM, that food production was indeed the priority: 'There is only one thing, I believe, which could possibly shake the resolution of our race in carrying this war to a finish, and that one thing would be hunger . . . Every ounce of food which can be grown in this country must be grown . . . every woman who can give a hand in this vastly important work must give a hand . . . she must also become, and be encourage to take every opportunity for becoming, more skilled in land work, and therefore in the production of food.'

The exhortation to action was given a strongly nationalistic flavour by Lady Denman in her opening address. One has to remember how isolated from the wide world were so many of the tiny villages that now had institutes. Communications were less effectual; people were not just geographically isolated, they were isolated from information and government propaganda about co-operation in the war effort. In the speech Lady Denman sets out to convert members' personal interest in the welfare of their own sons and husbands fighting at the front, into a determination to work together as a movement for the benefit of the whole nation: 'I feel that just as any institute's success cannot be achieved unless every member of the institute takes her share of the responsibility, so the whole Movement will not succeed unless every institute is interested in every other institute; and that we all feel that we are not only members of our own institute, but members of the great

Epping WI Market – the 1st War gave birth to the markets. In 1988 they turned over £8,250,000.

national Women's Institute Movement as well.'

If the post-industrial depression of the rural community and the new focus on women as equal partners inspired the formation of the WI in Britain, the catalyst which assured its expansion and development as an independent movement was the 1st World War. Not only did it increase the Movement's funding and hasten its independence, it also helped bind together the institutes into a strongly unified whole.

In the immediate business of food production, lines were being laid for what was – in a somewhat different form – to become the single most successful commercial operation with which the WI has ever been involved; today it generates more than £8,250,000 a year. The first WI Market began in Criccieth, North Wales, as a wholesale, not retail, operation in response to a wartime need to encourage the producer. There would have been no point in encouraging people to work the land and produce more food if it could not be distributed.

Mrs Dorothy Drage, Criccieth WI: 'Criccieth WI, in the summer of 1916, was mainly occupied by collecting and marketing fruit and vegetables. The object was helping the food supply by encouraging the producer. The sale was held twice a week in the WI room by voluntary workers. Goods were sold wholesale to the trade til 4.00 pm after which, retail sales finished the day. At the end of three and a half months trading on these lines, it was found that £250 had been turned over to the producer members. We took turns in collecting and selling. We had anxious moments on several days wondering how much produce was going to come in, and welcomed with joy the larger amounts from the larger gardens and farms, as our sales included eggs as well as vegetables and fruit.'

However, the enterprise ran into some opposition. In their efforts to encourage producers by offering higher prices, some retailers' profits had been seriously hit. 'Adverse comment was aroused by the fact that by giving the producers a slightly better margin of profit we had reduced a little the large percentage of profit the retailers of fruit and vegetables had been accustomed to.'

Matters came to a head when the WI received 'two letters written by two friends of retailers complaining that their margin of profit was, owing to our activities, not up to the standard they would like.' As a result of these two letters, Mrs Drage recalls, 'we heard from the Executive Committee of the National Federation that I might have to be superseded and I was sent for to be interviewed in London by three officers of the Committee and asked many questions. They were very kind to me, but I was told that another lady had been nominated to take my place. I was terribly distressed as I was already very interested in the work and had hoped that

we were helping the nation's food supply. When I returned home, many other of our members and good friends were also considerably troubled. In order to get the matter straight, a meeting was held soon after my London interview under the Chairmanship of Colonel Stapleton-Cotton.'

Subsequently Criccieth market was put under the authority of a new team comprising both women and men and it was never again as successful as it had been. Once the WI market lowered its prices, a price war ensued with other wholesale suppliers, and the retailers proved to be as disloyal to the WI market as, when WI prices were higher, they had been critical.

Nevertheless, the idea of a retail version of the Criccieth market was taken up elsewhere, in Lewes in Sussex; it opened on December 14th, 1919, in the old Market Hall. Mrs Vera Cox, who became Markets Organiser for the WI in 1932, recalls: 'Its start was entirely due to the sound common sense and enthusiasm of Miss Brand, who realised that if you encourage people to grow extra food you must find a market for the surplus produce, so she started the Lewes Market for the benefit of WI members and ex-Servicemen from the Ringmer Land Settlement, and today you will still find the market working in the old grey Market Hall up the steep High Street.'

If the markets grew out of a need made urgent by war, they also exposed a need among farmers generally for more effective marketing services. Gladys Morris remembers that farming was difficult at the turn of the century precisely because of problems in selling produce: 'I can remember my Mum bringing eggs back from Brecon – she wasn't able to sell twenty for a shilling. I suppose it would have been at the plentiful time of year and of course there wasn't the money about that there is now.' More likely her mother failed even to obtain this pitifully low price because at the time egg producers were in the hands of dealers who had the markets tied up. The Colonel's egg depot at Llanfairpwll was the first enterprise anywhere to take egg distribution out of the hands of the dealers. Dealers took farmers' eggs to market and sold them at prices which they themselves fixed. The Colonel introduced the testing and grading of eggs, and paid commission upon the quantity received at the depot. In the first year, 380,222 eggs were collected and sold there; by September 1916 the number had increased to 1,478,822. An article appeared in 1917 in *The Ladies Field* which ran, 'Anglesey eggs are in great demand; in fact so much so that orders have frequently to be declined. The success achieved by the Anglesey Egg Collecting Depot should act as an incentive to others to organise their forces and thus keep in the hands of British Agriculturists a portion

ESSEX WOMENS

'The purpose of the markets was to provide anyone who could make things, cook things, grow things, preserve things, an outlet by which they could earn a little money. It depends where the market is, but they usually take about 10% commission and the rest goes back to the producer. You don't have to be a WI member to produce, you can be a man if you want to! We do more organic than inorganic, but it's not exclusively organic – I produce vegetables for three markets and I don't think I could do them without some sort of inorganic control.' Miss Viola Williams.

at least of the £9,500,000 which, in normal times, is the amount expended on eggs imported into this country.'

The notion of village communities getting together and marketing their own produce was of course entirely consistent with the main principle of co-operation that had been one of the founding purposes of the AOS and the WI Movement. In peace-time when siege conditions were relieved, the same co-operative spirit helped the women of the village in different ways – Vera Cox: 'In the early days the money from markets was often spent on grim necessities – boots for children and husbands, warm clothes, and replacements for the home. Sometimes this market money was the first money that a woman had had to call her own since she married. One old couple went for their first holiday. To the owners of larger gardens, market money meant help towards wages, repairs to greenhouses or fences – or better seeds. To others it meant help with school fees. Since the farmhouse is often the last part of the farm to be modernised, quite a lot of the money has gone towards labour-saving equipment, from mixers to fridges. A retired Naval officer has augmented his pension, a child has made rock-cakes towards buying a pony, two women market-gardners established their business, in the beginning, through their sales at the market-stall. A blacksmith and a potter have been helped to set up on their own, and an old-age pensioner sells her loaves weekly. These are only a handful of the hundreds the markets have helped, and, over and above this, there is the friendliness of the market – often the bridge between country and town; a place to meet friends, to gossip and hear news, and a place to laugh.'

Chapter Four
POWER TO COUNTRYWOMEN

*'Now it is up to us to build up again
this beautiful country life.'*
MRS ALFRED WATT

*'The main purpose of the Insititute,' said its first
Chairman, 'is to improve and develop conditions of
rural life.' As the 1983 Parade of the Decades
showed,the Movement soon embraced
concerns of a far wider scope.*

Soon after the war, food production ceased to be a priority. 'It was impossible to lose money in farming just then,' recalled A G Street in his classic autobiographical work, *Farmer's Glory*, published in 1932. All the shoring up that the Government had done to see that farming prospered during the war – fixed prices, wages and so on – made peacetime sweet, at least for now.

Through the '20s, the Movement's work at headquarters focused most sharply on organisation, drawing up plans which would eventually lead to gaining key positions of power in local government for its mem-

bership – an important means for its voice to be heard.

It was for political action that the Movement now prepared itself, political action which was to embrace both the needs of land-based families and of women in particular. At the Movement's second AGM, held in October, 1918, the rules for the institutes were altered. Henceforth they were to be free to take political (as distinct from party-political) action on issues affecting countrywomen. The WI was no longer a non-political movement.

So it was, that on the occasion of the second AGM, a

resolution was proposed – the first of its kind – that all institutes should 'bring pressure to bear upon local Councils and, through the National Federation, upon the Local Government Board to ensure that full advantage is taken in their districts of the Government scheme for State-aided Housing.'

The new houses in question were to replace 'some of the most insanitary of the older cottages as unfit for human habitation'. Some opposition was expected – 'As likely as not some of these man-stys are owned by very "small men", who knowing they will receive no financial compensation, do not wish to see the result of their savings swept away.'

Housing has been an issue for the WI ever since this second AGM. And today, with the explosion of house prices in the countryside and the resulting difficulties which face young people who want to buy a house in their own village, it remains of passionate interest to many WI members. Interestingly, at this meeting in 1918, limits were proposed on who should be able to acquire the new houses, namely those who had lived in the village for three years, and newly married couples.

But the significance of the 1918 resolution went beyond the issue of housing. It was a political resolution; its wording implied active involvement by members in every locality in England and Wales; and it was raised not by Lady Denman or a member of her Executive but by Miss Trenow of Epping WI in a rousing address: 'In rural areas the conditions are absolutely disgraceful and scandalous, and I think we should urge on our councils and everybody to improve conditions, because not only from the physical but from the moral point of view we must do all in our power to awaken people to the scandalous things going on in the rural areas.'

'The strength of this Movement is that it tends to the centre in the home rather than to drive things out from the home under the control of outside bodies . . . to restore that position of real power and responsibility.' F D Acland, MP, 1917.

The next decade also saw other issues central to WI policy being raised for the first time – the preservation of the countryside, education, health, and social issues. There were also major achievements in hurrying along water supplies to rural areas, in making a rural telephone system a necessity rather than a rare luxury of rural life, in campaigning for women police and women jurors. But underlying all the early social and political work of the Movement, lay the strategy for change, namely to get countrywomen into local positions sufficiently powerful to achieve these ends. How Lady Denman would have enjoyed listening to this recent story of the village of Allenheads, by a proud neighbour: 'Quite one of the liveliest institutes around here is the little tiny one up at Allenheads, which has about fourteen members. Allenheads has done a splendid thing over the last year or two. It was a dying village, because it depended for all its employment on two things. One was the big house, Lord Allendale's

shooting box, and the other was the mine and the mining which folded up. Two hundred men out of work at once, a village out of work pretty well, and you see it is so remote. Well, some silly bod (an incomer) wrote a wail to the *Courant* about how Allenheads was dying and how fed up she was, and Allenheads rose in its wrath and said, "We are not dying." One of the local WI members (who is also Parish Councillor, District Councillor, ex-Chairman County Council, a real local powerhouse, as is so often the case) set up a village action committee, got money from hither and yon, got the Manpower Services people involved, and the village is really beginning to live again. It is setting up a Heritage Centre, which will also be the new Post Office and the conference centre. It's got several new ventures – a man runs a freezer van, there is a sculptor, they are going to open a trout farm. It's a wonderful story. They even got to the notice of Prince Charles, bless him, because you know this "Business in the Community" thing he is

'I always reckon that we are often in the forefront of change because we are closer to the earth, we are the people who live in the country and we know the sort of problems that are involved, and we are women, so we know the sort of problems that affect women.' Mrs Elsie Julyan.
Right: *The picturesque scene conceals what in 1918 were described by a member as 'absolutely disgraceful and scandalous conditions in rural areas'. Members campaigned for the 'pulling down of some of the most insanitary of the older cottages as unfit for human habitation', and demanded essential amenities – 'a house containing 3 bedrooms, a parlour, a kitchen and a scullery containing a copper, a good sized shed for prams and bicycles . . . a fixed bath either upstairs or in the scullery with water for it heated off the copper'. In 1937, a Mrs Brown of Lindsey WI looked back '21 years ago [when] many people never dreamt of the possibility of tap water . . . When the question of a water supply was first suggested by some progressive institutes, this was looked upon with great caution by the rest.'*
Above: *The telephone was ever more essential for far-flung communities. The 1927 WI campaign argued for a rural system at a cost fair to all subscribers.*

involved with? Well, they were made conscious of Allenheads and he actually asked if he could come and see what was going on. So, I think we are all very proud of Allenheads.'

Back in 1918, the Central Committee's plan to insinuate itself into the corridors of power moved forward on two fronts: first, by the enlightened engineering of its own political machinery, and secondly, by an extraordinary process of education. To the Movement's 'engineers' fell the task of building the WI organisation and impressing governing bodies with the needs of the rural community; to the educators fell that of raising the consciousness of members and preparing them for local government.

In 1927, members were urged to 'go out as missionaries to increase the number of telephone subscribers.' By 1949 only 701 out of 6,600 institutes villages were without a kiosk.

Chapter Five
THE ORGANISATION

*'An organisation for active people,
the only really coherent body in the village.'*
MISS JOAN CHARLTON

*The Northumberland Federation in 1923, the organisation
which launched the 'Keep Britain Tidy' campaign 31 years later.*

According to the rules of the Constitution each institute is self-governing and elects its own committee annually by secret ballot. The committee consists of not less than eight and not more than seventeen women, including a President, up to three Vice Presidents, a Secretary, and a Treasurer. The institute meets at least once a month.

Groups of institutes are united into County (or Island) Federations, each of which has an Executive Committee, elected for a period of no more than two years and comprising not less than eight and not more than fifteen women, including a Chairman, up to three Vice Chairman, a Secretary, and a Treasurer. Besides being responsible for the formation of institutes, the County Federations' job is to co-ordinate the work of the institutes in their area, to act as a two-way channel of communication with the Executive Committee of the National Federation (NFWI), and to secure instruction, training and other facilities for institute members. At least once a year there has to be a County Council meeting of delegates elected by the institutes. The purpose of the National Executive (NFWI) is (among other things) to foster unity of purpose among member institutes and County Federations and to enter into communication with Government and other authorities on the institutes' behalf. The Executive Committee consists of seventeen elected WI members, four co-opted WI members (including one Welsh speaking member) plus representatives from the Ministry of Agriculture, the DHSS, the Department of Education, and from the Department of the Environment.

Twice a year there is a National Council meeting at which the Chairmen and Treasurers of the County Federations meet with the National Executive to discuss policy, and it is at one of these that the all-important resolutions submitted by institutes or Federations are considered for acceptance on the agenda of the Annual General Meeting. Resolutions are the means by which national policy is formed. They are the political and social issues which may be acted on at local, Federation or national level.

In practice if a member of an institute feels strongly about something she may bring it up at one of the monthly institute meetings. If it is of local significance only, a vote is taken and action decided upon at local

Mrs Rosemary Mackenzie and Mrs Elsie Morris, Alderbury WI, undertake a survey for the Consumer Council.

level. As Miss Joan Charlton explains, 'In Catton we took on the Post Office when ours was closed and battled to get it re-opened. We were successful; we won that battle. We didn't win the bus battle for the late bus, but I think market forces were against us there – too big to take on, but we made our voice known about the awful state of our pavements and got them repaired. I think people in the institute are very aware of what WI can give in the present day, you see it's the only really coherent body in the village.'

If the issue deserves county pressure, an institute may vote for it to be aired at the County Council meeting and put to the vote of the thousands of delegates from all institutes in the region. If successful, action is then co-ordinated at County Federation level and every institute may become involved.

If an institute feels strongly that a resolution merits the attention of the whole Movement, then it can be sent, either through the Federation or direct, to NFWI. Some 200 are discussed by the National Executive each year,

A war-time Council meeting of the Cornwall Federation.

and around fifteen of these are then considered at the National Council meeting. Of these, around four are voted to go forward to the AGM at the Royal Albert Hall, where experts in the subjects of the resolutions are invited to advise and answer questions of delegates, as part of the debate. Should an institute be successful, and receive the required majority vote of the delegates, the resolution becomes mandatory, part of WI policy.

A member of Embleton WI emerged from their seventieth anniversary celebrations to demonstrate the power that the mandates provide at local level: 'We use the mandates as and when we feel it is necessary. Whenever there is a local problem we work through the resolutions that have been passed at the Annual General Meeting by the WI and write on headed paper to all the interested parties to say (as we can as soon as a resolution becomes mandatory) that 350,000 women believe that so-and-so is essential. It is satisfying to be able to exercise the power of the WI, but we also feel strongly up here that we are trying to hold onto a way of life which we feel is right. Some years ago when the village school was threatened with closure we wrote to our MP and the Director of Education. The local maternity hospital was also threatened with closure in Alnwick and we fought to keep that open too.'

Here is how Lady Denman herself once explained the nature of the system: 'I hope today that there are many new delegates from County Federations and from Institutes who have never been to this meeting before. I should like to encourage them by emphasising that the speeches we make and the speeches we listen to at this meeting do lead to practical results. How are these results obtained? Not only by the work of your National Federation Executive Committee but by the efforts of you and of all the institutes in England and Wales which together form the National Federation.

'I want to illustrate this point by reminding you of the way in which the National Federation is helping to save thousands of countrywomen from unnecessary suffering. As you know, some ten years ago a machine was invented which makes it easy for women having a baby to be given a light anaesthetic. At our meeting in 1938 a resolution moved by an institute in East Kent was

The Royal Albert Hall. Right: *AGM lunch-time break beneath the Albert Memorial.* Inset, *the AGM in full session.*

Even by 1954 the AGM was an extra-ordinary experience for village folk. Mrs Mary Smith reads from her diary: 'Travelled to Harrogate by bus, feeling very much afraid. On my arrival at Harrogate station I was welcomed by members of other Yorkshire WIs. Had a very happy journey discussing every subject one could think of. Arrived at Kings Cross at 5 o'clock and immediately separated, the Pannel member and myself going to our hotel. After registering we set out by underground to Westminster and went to see the pier where Her Majesty returned from her travels, but there were no boats on the river due to the coolness of the weather . . . Tuesday morning. Took a bus to the Albert Hall. Nearly everyone on the bus was wearing a WI badge. Inside, at 5 minutes to 11 we were all told to be quite still and 8 trumpets of the Household Cavalry entered and sounded a fanfare . . . The lights focused on the main door and there we saw the Queen Mother, a lovely sight wearing a pale blue hat with a feather and carrying a squirrel cape . . . Then comes the Litter resolution . . . I always say I was there to see "Keep Britain Tidy" started!'

41

carried, asking that this new method of analgesia should be made available to all countrywomen in childbirth in their own homes. The first step, you see, was taken by an institute. At that time there was a regulation insisting on qualified midwives being present when analgesia was given – this made it practically impossible for it to be used in country places. So, acting on the instructions of this great meeting your Headquarters put this point emphatically, by letter, by interview and by telephone to the expert authorities. These representations were sympathetically received and the regulations were altered. Your Headquarters then told the County Federations of the new regulations and gave them details of the machines available; they in their turn became active, many of them got in touch with their County Nursing Associations and discussed the question with them and again with the institutes. Now action lies with the institutes themselves, very many of whom have taken up the matter with their village Nursing Association and, where necessary, are raising the money to buy a machine.'

The system is thus designed to enable any member through her institute to direct the national policy of the Movement in a way that is impossible for a voter in the country at large. Carolyn Green and Katie Anderson describe how the voice of Chalgrave WI in Bedfordshire carried the Movement into an emergency resolution calling for a moratorium on the development of nuclear power until the risks and consequences, following the Chernobyl accident, had been properly assessed:

Carolyn: 'I hadn't even heard of the WI until a short while ago because I am American. But when I came to live in the village and my next-door-neighbour, a long established WI lady and President of the local one at the time, described this organisation I thought, that sounds terrific. And I went along and it was terrific. All different age groups. Because I hadn't heard of it and hadn't had all these prejudices put into my mind I was amazed how everyone mixed and were very friendly.

Katie: 'On a local level it gives us an opportunity to get together and talk about issues that are important to us and participate in things as a group. People get together at meetings who wouldn't normally say more than a few words to each other in the street. We find out more about our community, we do things if we feel things need doing and we can talk about things that are important to us. We all mix together and nobody really minds or bothers where anybody else comes from. But it goes further than that because it actually gets from people what they have to give to the community.

'The Chernobyl resolution, which called for a mori-

torium on the development of nuclear power, came out of the village Post Office. I was there one day and Carolyn, who runs the Post Office, pointed to her field next door and said, "Oh, dear, look at my lovely spinach, I am going to have to dig it all up." And I said, "What do you mean?" And she said, "Well the (Chernobyl) cloud came over on Sunday and it was raining and all my spinach is polluted." And that's what started it.

'That was May, 1986, and we felt very strongly about it. But it appeared to be too late for that AGM in June.'

Carolyn: 'Then one of the old members told us about being granted leave of urgency [permission to put forward a resolution direct to the National Executive]. So we set out and wrote a resolution and sent it in. We then discovered that we needed a seconder, another WI, and we scrabbled around to find our friends down the road who said, "Yes, yes, we agree with it, it's a brilliant idea," and they would be our seconders.

'So, we sent our resolution off to the National Executive and didn't hear any more about it.'

Mrs Carolyn Green outside her Post Office at Tebworth. When her spinach patch was destroyed by Chernobyl, the local Chalgrave institute mobilised the whole village in support.

Katie: 'Then I took to my bed with pneumonia. I had nothing better to do so I picked up the telephone and rang up National and said, "What about our resolution, we want to know whether it is going forward or not," and two days before the AGM they rang up and said, "Yes, we are going to accept it."'

Carolyn: 'They rang the day before!'

Katie: 'The whole village had to be mobilised because I couldn't go, I was still in my bed with pneumonia and Carolyn's husband had to take the day off work and run the Post Office, so that she could go.'

Carolyn: 'It was Thursday, you see, the day of the AGM, Pension Day at the Post Office, that was the problem.'

Katie: 'So we sat down, gathered together various pieces of information and then you went off and wrote it.'

Carolyn: 'I came up in the afternoon, I had taken the

'None of the WI work would have been possible without the contacts.' Mrs Margaret Pike. Below: Mrs Patricia Batty Shaw visits PM James Callaghan in 1977: 'The policeman turned out to be the son of a WI member!

Wednesday afternoon off – it is my half day – and had to be up at the Albert Hall for 9.00 am with it all prepared. They said to me that on the afternoon they would have two experts there to help. One was the man from the Central Electricity Generating Board and the other was Lady Anglesey, both of whom spoke against the resolution. It was passed but not unanimously, about 70/30, but you only need to get a two thirds majority for action to be taken.'

As a result of Chalgrave's resolution, the National Executive made representations to the Prime Minister, the Secretary of State for Energy, the UK Atomic Energy Authority, the Central Electricity Generating Board, British Nuclear Fuels, the National Radiological Protection Board, The Nuclear Installations Inspectorate, NIREX, the International Atomic Energy Agency, the International Commission of Radiological Protection, The Nuclear Energy Agency, the OECD, the Commission of the European Communities, Committees of the European Parliament concerned with nuclear power, and the Associated Countrywomen of the World.

In addition, all County Federations were directed to encourage institutes to write to their local MPs. Influencing decision-making processes in the corridors of power is no easy business. Katie and Caroline, unaware of all the action that followed the resolution, expressed some unhappiness about follow-up, so I asked a number of ex-Chairmen and one General Secretary of NFWI how they felt that the power of the WI was most effectively employed during their periods of office.

Mrs Gabrielle Pike, CBE, JP (1961-1965): 'The thing about the WI is that it has always been one step ahead. The first people to bully the Government about getting women policemen, the first people to bully the Government to say that we must have telephone kiosks in villages, and gradually these things collected and we began to get a reputation for being the sound-box of what women wanted. Since 1966 there has been a national cervical cancer screening service. It was the WI championing that that did it. They were the only co-ordinated organisation. The picture is that in those days there weren't all these pressure groups. We were absolutely the only one, and so brilliantly organised.

'The tradition was for the Chairman of the WI to be the sort of person that met Government Ministers anyway, or people in power at least. My father [who was Bishop of Litchfield] knew all these Ministers well, and he was a member of the House of Lords, so I was in and out of there. We would have very senior people from each Ministry on the Executive because Trudie Denman insisted on having a representative of the Government on the Executive. They were *ex-officeo*, they didn't have the vote, but they would come for the whole meeting from ten 'til four, and they were very senior people, almost Permanent Secretary status. She absolutely insisted on that. I mean she knew the PM of the day, would have had him for the week-end and so on.

'None of the WI work would have been possible without the contacts.'

Miss Meriel Withal, MBE (General Secretary, 1969-1972): 'We were always great on deputations. I was always taking deputations to the House of Lords, the House of Commons. They always met us extremely politely and of course we never went to the Government unless we had (in those days) a three quarters majority vote at the AGM. This meant that there was a recognisable body of opinion on any issue.

'Also, various members served of course on Ministerial committees, and the other link between National and the Government was that we had representatives of the Ministries on our Committees. You would be ringing up someone at the Ministry and say, "My lot want to do this, what can we do about it?" and they might say, "Well it won't be very popular," and we would say, "Well, we have got to do it so how shall we go about it?" You were on those sort of terms with them.'

Countess Albemarle, DBE (1946-1950): 'I remember Stafford Cripps was particularly interested in what the WI was about. Of course his wife was a member. Indeed a lot of the Ministers' wives were members of the WI in those days. Our influence was through the back door.'

Alderman Mrs Pat Jacob, JP (1974-1976): 'The Ministers would always receive you if you had a mandate and you wanted to talk about it. You have to remember that we had great contact, we would have representatives of the various Ministries sitting on our committees. At the time I am talking about, we had the Department of Health and Social Security, the Department of Education, we had the Department of Agriculture on our Agricultural Committee, we had the Department of Trade and Industry or whatever it was called then, we had someone from the BBC – none of these people voted, but the BBC man might join in when we were talking about horror comics or violence on television. They would be there listening, and in fact I think that is how a lot of messages got across – through those people who were on our committees.'

Northumberland, a county inspired to campaign against CFCs. 'It came up because a lot of us in the institute are very concerned about the environment, locally and worldwide.'

The contact between WI and the Government has of course been present since the days when the WI operated under the auspices of the Board of Agriculture, but it was Lady Denman's personality and capabilities which first established the workability of the link.

Lady Brunner, OBE, JP (1951-1955): 'Lady Denman [Chairman, 1917-1945] was a very strong character and dealt with Government Ministeries and that kind of thing in a very powerful way. I should think they were all quite frightened of her. And she had great principles. Every problem or change that came up was dealt with according to her principles. She was a woman of such ability that today, I am sure, she would have been in the House of Lords, and been very powerful in a much wider field. Sadly you don't get the likes of her available to women's organisations today, all voluntary organisations are finding that. All the voluntary organisations share the problems of membership and leadership, though which comes first, I'm not quite sure.'

The Marchioness of Anglesey, DBE (1966-1968): 'The point is that when (in my day) we selected resolutions it was imperative that they should be resolutions that we could do something about, because I couldn't see the point in having resolutions that simply expressed a view. Time and again we encouraged people to put forward resolutions which as members of a particular institute, or as women, we could actually do something about. Consumer pressure, if you like.'

Catton is a beautifully appointed Northumberland village, situated a mile or so from the nearest town. It is not immediately obvious what could drive anyone living there to look beyond its boundaries to the problems of the world outside. Although clearly successful on local issues, Catton WI is far from being inward looking or insular in its political perspective, for in 1988 it put forward a resolution urging decisive action to ban CFCs and protect the ecosystem. 'It came up,' Joan Charlton explains, 'because a lot of us in the institute are very concerned about the environment both locally and world-wide. When we saw that the politicians were ratting out and that the Montreal Agreement was allowing for about 30% production of offending sprays so that the Third World could catch up, I'm afraid I spat! and the WI being the nearest thing effectively to spit to, I brought it forward to our local meeting, and they rose in their wrath too. The WI is an organisation for active people. In Catton there are a number of people who are interested and alert – the WI provides the platform, the forum, an organisation where we can raise matters that concern us like the buses, like the post office, like the CFCs.

'When we saw that the politicians were ratting out (over CFCs) I'm afraid I spat!' Miss Joan Charlton.

'We put our resolution forward to County and got it through there at the Spring Council meeting, but it wasn't actually taken up by National. Instead they chose a similar one from the far end of Somerset – Corfe WI. The President of Corfe then wrote to me and said, "Will you do the seconding and then we will get it from both ends of the country?" So that's how the milk got in the coconut there.

'I think that the reason that Corfe's resolution was chosen and not ours was because Corfe was exhorting the membership to take action, and we were exhorting the Government to take action. Also, it may have been felt that some members might not have voted for a resolution which implied an attack on the Government.'

The point underlines the need for careful preparation and consideration of all aspects of a resolution by the institute members to give it the best chance of acceptance by the National Executive. Federation officers are often consulted as to best wording.

Consumer pressure was indeed the main thrust of the argument advanced by Mrs Audrey Heap of Corfe WI, 'Eighty per cent of household purchases are made by women,' she said at the Albert Hall, 'and our 347,000 members can make a start by stopping buying products which contain CFCs and which are not ozone friendly.'

'It's not like WI to yell at people,' continues Miss Charlton. 'I think the more you yell at people the more they are likely to resent you. I think the WI's line is much more "take the thing off the shelves," or "Haven't you got something that isn't harmful?" – and if not, put it back. Using consumer pressure, using persuasion, changing the climate of opinion, which on the whole you do by individuals talking to other individuals.

'Now there is a ground swell of opinion, which means that places like Sainsbury's are getting rid of their CFCs. How much that is influenced by WI as a body one couldn't possibly judge. It has probably been influenced a great deal by individual people who may have been influenced by WI. What I hope we have done, both here in the village and at County and in the country as a whole, is just to increase slightly the awareness of the danger, and once people begin to think about one bit of the threat to the environment, they also begin to become a little more aware of other threats.'

Communication between the WI and Government very quickly developed into two-way traffic because its membership profile and size make it a readily interpreted worthwhile 'sample' in testing opinion on a subject. Mrs Laverty of Longhoughton WI, now in charge of public affairs on the County Executive, explains: 'We are on the Government's list of organisations to be consulted on any proposed legislation to do with the family and children, the countryside, the environment and education. Recently we did a lot of work on the Community Charge before they decided how they were going to move forward. The Green Paper set out the different types of local taxation that could be introduced and it was discussed among our members. Again, the Warnoc Report on invitro fertilisation and embryo research – came out to every Federation as reports from National, and we in the institutes put our comments on them and sent them back to London. The comments form the basis of a policy which is then pursued by National with the Government.'

What the Movement offers the Government, therefore, is a recognisable body of opinion in the country. The structure of the organisation which was designed to enable local village voices to be heard in Westminster is also well suited to operate the other way. But most important for its own purposes, the Movement's 'bottom-up' structure and its National Council are designed to enable the local institutes to keep control of WI national policy. This is what makes the WI different from other organisations, different too from Britain's national Government, where increasingly, power is vested in the centre, and the feelings of local people may be lost in arguments for what is perceived as the 'national good', as for example in issues concerning planning and development.

The only occasion when major conflict has occurred between the National Federation and County/local members was over the re-drawing of County boundaries following the Local Government Act of 1972. The National Federation, its hand forced by practical consequences of the Act, issued instructions ('top-down', as it were) for County Federations to be aligned with the new County boundaries – a decision which asked some Yorkshirewomen to cease being Yorkshirewomen, some Northumbrians to cease being Northumbrians – and a bitter struggle ensued in these areas.

Chapter Six

EDUCATING THE MEMBERSHIP FOR POWER

*'We are trying to build up a finer England
on a sure foundation of knowledge.'*
MISS GRACE HADOW

Mrs Gladys Morris (left) – *'We didn't
have the education they have today.'*

Gladys Morris in many ways embodies one's impressions of the early rural membership of the WI. She was twenty years of age when the Movement began, the daughter of a farmer in Aber near Brecon in Wales.

'I grew up on a farm in Aber near the Newport resevoir. When we were young we would always help out on the farm, and if it was harvest time or my Dad was doing fencing, I would go with him. I had one brother but he was an express train driver by then so he wasn't home. My sisters were all away at various jobs so it was Mamma and Dadda and I. There was no running water when we

were there, we put it in whilst we were living there. We had to carry it. There was a well in the fields. And in the village they had to get it from the river. Some of them that didn't fancy the river went up the road to the spring. That was gorgeous water. In fact I still get my bottled water from the spring today because I have a few friends that live round there. I don't fancy the reservoir water because sometimes it tastes of the things that they put in to purify it.

'In the evenings, before the WI, we would be busy with concerts and sketches and then there was Band of Hope [a Temperance Society]. There used to be recitations and songs and readings in nearby Talybont school. Then in the winter we used to have competitive meetings (not in the summer because everybody was too busy on the farm), and those would be for different ages and different items according to your age group. And there would be someone to adjudicate. There were four Nonconformist chapels – two in Talybont, one in Aber and another nearby, so we had these competitive meetings all in turn in these four places. Oh, the time was full up, we was never short of something to do.

'Of course one of the problems was that we didn't have the transport that we have today. Today you jump in the car and you are a hundred miles away. We would have to walk everywhere. We would walk to Brecon and think nothing of it. Before the WI, life revolved around the church or the chapel. There were three chapel services on Sunday, and the service in the week, and all these had to be attended. And if we weren't there on the Sunday, then the Minister would be round on the Monday. And we would go up to the church as well by the reservoir, and in those days, the curate up at the church had a tub trap, and if you went up to the church you would get a trip in the trap, so that was an attraction. Some people call them "governess cars", they were low, near the road unlike the usual traps that were high up over the wheels.

'Farming was very difficult. But children were much happier in those days when they had less. People didn't have so many "wants" so they were less disappointed. They didn't have the "wants" because you couldn't get what you might want today. If we had something new we had to look after it because we knew there wouldn't be another one.

'Then there'd be pig killing time. You'd have a couple of pigs to kill to salt for bacon for the year. Most cottages had a pig and chickens. The farms would have two or three pigs and they would be gorgeous – pig meat suppers always appealed to me. There were no professionals then, even the vet was not a professional, but he was a man who had a sort of gift with animals and knew a lot about them, sort of automatically. So, at pig-killing time, the butcher who would see to the pigs would just have the habit of doing this butchering job. On those days I used to go out because I didn't like to hear the pig squeal, because poor old thing he would squeal.

'After I got married and we started farming on our own I never found the difficulty that my mother did in selling stuff, but then I used to go over to the collieries and the steelworks. And oh! those colliers' wives . . . they looked after their husbands! They bought the best food that they could have. All our best farm stuff, there was always good demand for it. Gradually people left the farms and went over there to work because the farm pay was very poor.

'Then our farm was taken by the reservoir. They had taken our place to be flooded by the reservoir. We

Llanrhidian's first bus. In 1919 Mrs Violet Morgan had tramped miles of unmade roads to gather the village's first WI group.

weren't forced out of the farm. We could have stayed there for three years but then we would have had no compensation. So I said, "No," I wasn't going to do that, let them pay me to get out.

'Did I tell you, my husband hadn't been well? We had moved out of the farm and were renting a cottage while we looked for a small place that we could manage. He was up and about again, and we were on our way up to sing at one of those competitive meetings. Yes, we were walking up the hill to the chapel. I think it was a Bible we had forgotten, but whatever it was I said I must go back for it, and by the time I had got back up, he'd gone, he had collapsed . . . So, that finished everything for that night. I was thirty-seven when my husband died and I have been alone ever since.

'One year, not long ago, we went up to the reservoir that was our land and it was very dry that year – no rain. And do you know the water was so low that when I looked across I fancied I could see were we used to be, where we used to farm. And I jumped over the fence and, yes, I could point out all the old farms and the railway station still there below the water . . .'

Having designed the structure of her organisation in such a way that the voices of Gladys and her rural sisters could be heard many miles away – a world away – in

The crowning of the May Queen at Madron in Cornwall.

Right: *Dufton village gala in Cumbria.*
Below: *Traditional arm wrestling at Warcop in Cumbria. Though not a particular speciality of WI members, institutes everywhere foster local traditions and local culture . . . 'A national culture,' wrote T S Eliot, 'if it is to flourish, should be a constellation of cultures, the constituents of which, benefiting each other, benefit the whole.'*

Westminster, Lady Denman set out to harness their spirit to advance her principal aim – to improve the quality of life for countrywomen everywhere. The institutes should not be mere entertainment centres, declared Lady Denman, but a force for social reform. There was no objection to 'half hours of relaxation at the close of an interesting and improving meeting, that precious time when tongues are loosed and ideas and friendliness are freely exchanged,' as one member of Swanley WI put it, but Lady Denman made it clear that 'the main purpose of the Institute is to improve and develop conditions of rural life.'

Fundamental to the well-being of farm and farm-workers in the rural community in those days was work done by farmers' wives and daughters. On this Lady Denman was in full agreement with the 1912 report by the Board of Education (page 8). By 1926 there would be more than 100,000 paid women farm workers, not including farmers' wives and daughters, whose work varied from dairying to kitchen cook.

Appropriately, Lady Denman's educational programme (which she urged both WIs and County Councils to adopt) first and foremost embraced the technical information required to grow produce, milk cows, keep poultry etc, and secondly skills relating to the preparation of food in the kitchen and management of the house. So successful was she in this that in 1925 she was asked by the Government to chair a special committee set up under the Ministry of Agriculture and the Board of Education to 'consider the general question of the practical education of women for rural life'. The result – called *The Denman Report* – espoused her two-fold concept of rural education for countrywomen. Fourteen years later it would have crucial importance for a nation once more at war.

At the start, not everyone agreed that the membership could progress beyond this practical rural education to take up the role of local government that Lady Denman had in mind. Nancy Tennant recalls that 'when the WI started, when members were asked to make a decision about something, it quite put them off. Many village women had come to expect everything to be arranged for them and when they were asked whether they were going to eat scones or doughnuts, they were quite taken aback. They were just not used to taking on any sort of responsibility or making any kind of effort and so on. And that is where the WI came in, that is where the transformation began. Women started being able to do the thing themselves. We had a Secretary who was absolutely shaking when she read the minutes, but later became a parish clerk and pretty well ran the village.'

'It seems incredible now,' adds Lady Albemarle, 'but

In the autumn of the rural idyll – at the turn of the century – there were not the means for rural people to travel far outside village boundaries and there remained a predominantly local perspective, sometimes an isolationism which even found expression in inter-village antagonisms, the cause of which had long been forgotten. The social importance of the institutes was not simply that they drew people together from hills and dales (as in County Durham, below), it was also that by clubbing together they could provide the wherewithal – impossible singly – to arrange outings (as at Durnford and Woodford WI – far right – in 1920). Right: Mrs Worth, by Gayle mill.

some of those women had never even been outside their village. They had a much more limited outlook. You were dealing with quite a different sort of person. You cannot imagine how a woman's self-confidence had to be built up.'

This narrowness of outlook and lack of confidence in the larger world was very much a result of living in isolated rural populations. Mrs Norah Worth of Hawes, a village set in the heart of the Yorkshire Dales, recalls that before the WI 'it was incredibly isolated here. Even

Hawes and [the next village] Gayle didn't mix a great deal. Of course the division of Hawes and Gayle goes back hundreds of years. I'm told that men never went singly from one village to the other.'

Mrs Everitt of Hunstanworth, Durham, recalls a similar isolationism in her village which borders on the Northumbrian village of Blanchland. 'We used to be called "up-byers" and down in Blanchland they were called "down-byers". You know what I mean? You live "up by" somewhere or "down by" somewhere. And

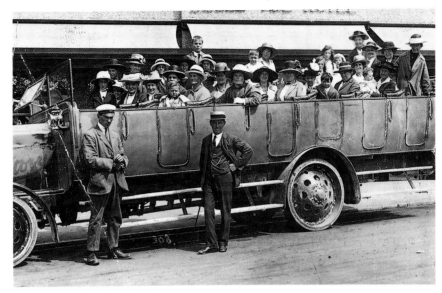

there used to be animosity between the two.'

'People never used to go out of the place,' continues Mrs Worth. 'They had the first coach here in Hawes in 1920 – the Pride of Wensleydale, it was called.' Reading from her WI scrapbook she continued, 'The charabanc was constructed to carry fourteen passengers and the driver, the entrance doors for the passenges were on the near side of the body only. The only door on the off side being for the benefit of the driver. The vehicle had a canvas folding hood, a bulb horn and rear red leather upholstery, the oil lamps were discarded and a complete six volt electric lighting set comprising dynamo, a celluloid accumulator, two head lamps, side and tail lamps fitted: for a time the natives had a feeling of distrust in risking their necks in the Pride as she became to be known, I could relate numerous experiences on this score and canvassing for custom on a trip to the Lakes or the seaside. Such answers as "No you're not getting me into that dithering thing", or "Will we get back today, tomorrow or next week?" were received and so on. Eventually a service was instituted as a result of growing confidence in the charabanc, to adjoining market towns on their market days. Recalled the driver, "I have recollections about the stone bound roads which were not in good shape, and the tracks one could not otherwise term, those loose stone turnpike or bullock tracks snaking their way over the passes to other dales, these were hazards not to be forgotten. I have recollections of one of these journeys over the Buttercups Pass. A farmer sitting beside me asked me to pull up. I promptly did, as he quickly opened the door and dismounted from the vehicle. Inquiring upon the reason for this procedure I was asked, 'Are your brakes good?' To this I replied, 'I hope so.' My reply had a dire effect and I heard the following remark. 'We can't live on hopes,' as he proceeded to walk slowly down the hill.'"

The task that Lady Denman and her Executive set themselves – to educate contrywomen to positions in which they could play an active role in rural development – does seem to have required a fundamental change in attitude. But instead of attempting to break down social and geographical barriers, and straightway attempting to instil wider perspectives into the membership, her strategy was to do precisely the opposite.

De-centralisation was the key principle of all WI strategy – power, in her organisation at least, went out to the countrywomen whom, Lady Brunner tells us, 'Lady Denman believed were the salt of the earth.' From that principle flowed a policy of education which emphasised village identity (through a renaissance of traditional, indigenous crafts and inter-village competitions in craft, drama, singing and so on), rather than a policy which sought to break down boundaries. In itself this proved to be an enormous boost to self-confidence and morale, and was rewarded ten-fold when the individual institutes came together in national efforts.

Additionally, as we shall see, her Executive implemented a new and vital concept called adult education, and as part of the programme trained a cadre of women in the tactics of leadership and organisation.

Lady Denman realised that the strength of the local institutes lay in the values which people held dear in these small rural communities. This was the other side of the 'isolationist' coin. What seems to be narrowness of outlook to the outsider – 'I could write a book about what it was like to come into a Yorkshire village in the 1930's,' says Mrs Hubbard of Follifoot – is, to the fellow villager, an expression of loyalty, trust, solidarity.

'We are used to living in small communities where we have constant contact with our neighbours and where we are all used to playing our part in the life of the village,' said Lady Brunner in 1946. From the start, the National Federation actively encouraged the feeling of belonging to a particular institute village through the renaissance and development of local loyalties and local cultures. Today the efficiency of modern communications has served to encourage a sort of

globalised monoculture, but the WI remains dedicated to the ideal of a national culture as a mosaic of regional diversity. All over the country, villages come alive when celebrating the life of their community in traditional style – left to right: *Gig racing* at Stanhope, Durham; clog dancing at Staverton, Devon; ox roasting at St Keverne, Cornwall; Staverton's Elizabethan Fayre, and, below, the fishermen of the village of Porthallow on the Lizard, race in time-honoured fashion.

As the Movement spread, the WI meeting halls became a vital new focal point in village life. In out-of-the-way villages it acted as a magnate drawing people from outlying farms and homesteads – Miss Mary Rule, of Lowgate WI, remembers: 'The WI meeting had to be the Thursday nearest the full moon. It had to be by the light of the moon because me and my mother had to come across all those fields to the WI hall, and otherwise we would never have got home. This hall was built as a temporary school – Bagraw School, but when they built a new school along the road here we were allowed to have it and it has been ours ever since. I joined the institute when I was fifteen. In fact you weren't allowed to join up here until you were eighteen but I was given special permission to keep my mother company as we walked across the fields.

'In those days there was a great fireplace at one end and another at the other end, and a partition in the middle of the hut to make two classrooms for the school. And these great fires were lit with coal. The first member to arrive was responsible to light the fire and we had to go and get the water to brew the tea. We had to go over the road to the stream, sit there and wait until the kettle was full and then bring it back. It used to sit on the fire 'til we had our meeting.

Above: *Mrs Lilian Seaborn and Mrs Margaret Hitchcock celebrate 50 years of Great Horkesley WI in 1970.* Below: *Miss Mary Rule, and Mrs Mary Douglas, 'The members here, they have a natural affinity with this quiet, lovely place.'*

Above: *The village shop at Dufton in Cumbria; still the news centre of the village, and run by a member of the WI.*
Below: *The Dufton village band at the opening of the village hall in 1912.*

'We used to sit in the school desks, all of us – we all squeezed into these desks! Then a farmer from around here bought the place (after they made the new school) and made hen houses in it. Then, eventually, he sold it to us; we only paid about £25.

'We used to have kern supers. Farm suppers. Mrs Straker [Lady of the Manor, first President of Lowgate WI] used to get chickens, pheasants and all sorts. Eeeh, it was a proper do! And we would cook them and sometimes some of the farmers wives would cook something as well and bring it along, and then someone else would bring something else, vegetables or whatever. That is what we called the kern supper . . . it was grand. And we danced after that. They would sing and someone would play a little squeeze box, a concertina, always a concertina.'

At that point there was a deafening noise from fighter aircraft coming low over the building that drowned out Mary's voice, but she was undeterred, lost in a forest of memories: 'Oh I remember when it was foggy, aye, there was one night when my mother and I really got lost over those fields in the fog. We used to tell my father before we came away to put a light in the window and then all of a sudden when we were walking back, we would see the light. There was no way you could find your way,

however many times you went over it. There was a member that used to come with us, she lived beyond us, she was a person that was always making up poetry. She would stand up and make poetry at anything. Coming over the fields she would be rhyming her poetry and every verse would end, "Mary, her mother and me". Every verse! And then she would start off again. Oh we had some fun in those days.' I said that I had no doubt she had some fun now – 'Oh, we do, but it's not the same.'

In Great Horkesley in Essex, as in countless other villages, the new WI hall became the first meeting place for women. Men had their reading rooms and the pub; now the WI hall was a place for women to meet outside the context of the family, apart from their men and their children. Mrs Lilian Seaborn was born in Great Horkesley 101 years ago. Before the WI hall was built the social focal points of the village were her father's grocery shop, the church, the village school, and the working men's club; there was nowhere for women to gather socially outside their daily rounds.

'We had the grocer's shop in the middle of the village until my father died. Mother and father knew everyone in the village and they'd all come to the shop. You see we didn't have a telephone then. But when the local villagers came in, they'd take their time and talk – nothing hurried. It was the place where both men and women could meet, talk and exchange news.

'The village school was an important centre. I knew practically all the children in the parish and their parents. I think it helped enormously to know the parents so well. People – especially farm workers – would go to church regularly because the farmer was churchwarden so they felt they had to go to church. The men had a working men's club, a reading room, a billiard table – three rooms, it had been a chapel at one time. There was no alcohol sold – but later they had their Christmas dinner there.

'The women had nothing, so when the WI came along that made a lot of difference. We hadn't got a hall so we built one and raised the money with shares. And it's still there today. We had a meeting once a month at least. My mother was a founder member and Mrs Hitchcock (who was on the London Executive from the very beginning), was the one who started it in our village. And later when I became involved I got on the committee. When I was quite young they sent me as a delegate to the annual meeting and I often went afterwards.'

In Llanfair the WI had moved from the shed where the Movement had begun. At a cost of £532-17-4, the institute had bought and transported a wooden hut from nearby Kennel Park to the Old Toll Bar in Llanfairpwll. Blanche Roberts tells just how much a centre of village

Nurse Catherine: 'People sent for me, not the Doctor, because I was born here and most of them had known me all my life.'

The 'new' WI hall at the Old Toll Bar at Llanfairpwll.

life the hall then became: 'There were many, many meetings at the new place where the WI met, we used to have little hops there, the institute hired the hall out for all kinds of things. We used to go to the dances and they had a good band there, but my father used to come and fetch me home at 11.30 pm. They had baby shows then as well. Nurse Catherine, our District Nurse, she was born in the village and became a trained nurse, and they had baby shows. They had a clinic at the hut. The WI fought for that when they had no local doctor. And every so often they would have a baby show and the bonniest baby had a prize. And she taught us as children, we used to meet there after school and she taught us to make little chemises and binders and long clothes, and then we used to dress our dolls as a competition. And whist drives we used to have there. They also had bulb shows. You would bring your plants at springtime, hyacinths, crocuses and daffodils, and there would be a judge there, a county judge. Members taught each other home economics and social welfare. Later on they had plays there and there was a company used to come down here, I remember everyone talking about *Murder In The Red Barn*, but my mother wouldn't let me go near it.'

To these new centres of village activity the WI also brought fresh interest in the traditional crafts of England and Wales – quilting to Durham, lace making to Nottinghamshire, and so on. Mrs Norah Worth, Hawes WI: 'You might think that the crafts and cooking that these early women learned at the WI would have been passed down generation to generation, but although members sometimes had the knowledge and even some interest, the WI provided the focus.'

'Once they came together, they began to produce some really beautiful things. It gave them an incentive – the competitions particularly gave them an incentive and then they began to participate in Group and County competitions – spreading their wings ever outwards from their far-flung villages.'

Mrs Elizabeth Eames of Heddon-on-the-Wall first joined the WI when she was 14, 'My grandmother used to make quilts and she would be on for ages and ages making a quilt. I will always remember her with her white cotton arm sleeves, elastic at the top and at the wrists, so that there was no chance of dirtying the lovely satin material. I can see her now sitting there at these frames making quilts; her fingers would get so sore she would have to leave it alone, and the stitches were so minute that is wasn't good for the eyes (especially with the poor lighting in those days). Now, today, we have members still keen on quilting, though they do the cushions rather than the big quilts. We have a wonderful craft class – you take what you are busy with – hairpin work, bobbin work, knitting and embroidery.'

Betty and Kit Metcalf, outside their home in Gayle in the Yorkshire Dales, 'wapping' and 'shriking' the loop – knitting cycling stockings, in 1904. At one time a considerable number of men were engaged in knitting for the mill, and many a man could boast that 'he cud knit owte ayther cooarse "bump" er t'finest – wussit.'

This then was the wonderful effect of craft work in the village. It gave people an opportunity to pursue excellence in something that came naturally to many; it gave a sense of continuity and pride in their roots, but at the same time – in village, in county, in national competition – it brought people out of their isolated village shells.

Miss Nancy Tennant: 'The two things the Movement was built on were agriculture and craft. There was this marvellous old tyrant called Mrs Heron-Maxwell. She really was Craft, and absolutely terrifying. Wonderful really. She had an old friend and they ruled the roost over handicraft and they set a sort of absolute standard, but she was terribly difficult to work with. I cannot

To the new centres of village activity the WI brought fresh interest in the traditional crafts of England and Wales, which represented a welcome return to old values. Left: *Miss Brock of Little Waltham plaiting rushes in 1948. Below left: Spinning at the Guild of Learners Handicraft exhibition in 1947. Below: The upholstery class of Epping WI. Right: Eight members took 7 months to fashion the Northumberland banner. Far Right: A section of a 30ft by 4ft collage made by members of Clwyd-Flint Federation – 'It was exhibited in London at the Olympia exhibition in 1984 as well as here to celebrate our 50 years,' recalls Mrs Daniels, 'One man returned three times to see and "hear" our history.'*

remember the name of her friend but she had one who ran behind. Heron-Maxwell was very tall, stout and put the fear of death into everybody, but she achieved her ends and set this absolute standard based on very traditional crafts. I was made Chairman of Handicrafts after she left, specifically because I had a certain capacity for calming people down and it was a very difficult boat to row.

'The first full-scale exhibition of WI craftwork was an ambitious and successful affair. It was held in the Caxton Hall, London, in October 1918, and it was designed both to raise money by the sale of work and to show the country how the WIs were helping the war effort. Queen Mary paid it a visit and bought something from each stall.' However, the standard of exhibition was rather severely criticised, and it was then that the redoubtable Mrs Heron-Maxwell stepped in to form the Guild of Learners specifically to encourage and improve craft work in the institutes: 'I have been asked to put

From the start the Guild of Learners established a system of tests: 'A' tests for proficiency in a craft; 'B' tests for lecturer-demonstrators; 'C' tests for teachers and judges. The NFWI also received a special grant from Her Majesty's Development Commission to facilitate the finding and training of its own craft teachers.

In 1922 another exhibition was mounted, this time at the Victoria and Albert Museum. Forty-nine counties sent exhibits and there was a special class for Guild members. It was a grand success and membership of the Guild itself rose to about 1,000 before being transferred in 1931 to the County Federations for administration.

Besides craft, music and drama played a leading role in the harmonisation of the new membership. Country dancing and singing came naturally to country girls, including Nancy Tennant whose love for music led her to start up the first choir that the village of Ugley had known. 'I just sang for the love of it', she says looking back beyond the beginning of the century. 'I suppose my

Far left: 'Nancy Tennant had a sort of essential wholeness, a remarkable personality. Wonderfully fulfilled and wonderfully easy – very complementary to Lady Denman,' says Lady Elizabeth Brunner today. Miss Meriel Withal remembers that General Secretary Frances Farrer (left) ran Headquarters 'strictly on civil service lines . . . she was the daughter of a civil servant. All the Farrer family were civil servants . . . It was a model of government.'

down some notes on the early work of the Guild of Learners. I was elected to the NFWI Executive Committee in 1919 and became the Chairman of the Handicraft Sub-Committee first formed in that year. The idea of a Guild of Learners was first discussed in 1919, and in 1920 the scheme was adopted by our sub-committee. I feel sure that all will agree that the Guild has been, and still is, a great incentive to keen craft workers to improve their standard of craftsmanship . . . "for the exercise of a high skill is a fine mode of life" (Professor W R Lethaby). The main aim of the Guild was to draw together all those members who seriously desired to become proficient in their craft, and from there to select for training those who were prepared to teach (though this was not obligatory).'

interest came from my family being fairly musical. My mother played the piano very well and they both sang; they became engaged singing Gilbert and Sullivan duets, so there was always music going on.' Music indeed became part of the rich pattern of life that her parents wove in Ugley. 'There was always a family party feeling in Ugley in those days, and that has not gone because there are still people who remember the parties and parties for children the villagers had at my parents' home. I met an old boy the other day who said, "You don't remember me," and I said, "Well I do know who you are." And he said, "I've got something what Mr Tennant gave me and I am never going to part with that." And he must have been about 102!'

'Then step by step I got on to the Music Committee in

The village choir – Blucher and Wallbottle WI (above) *and 'The Village Philharmonic' by Stanhope Forbes* (below) – *harmonising the natural rhythms of rural life.*

the counties. I suppose they had heard what I was up to, and then we started arranging different competitions, community singing, that kind of thing. And that was the first time I got into real trouble because I didn't realise that you were supposed to go and organise such things through committees, committees meant nothing to me! So right at the start I was hauled over the coals for not asking permission. Anyway, we struggled all through that and I was on the County Executive and the Music Committee for ages. Then, I don't know why, I was co-opted onto the Music Committee in London, and then to my great surprise I was co-opted onto the Executive. It was a great honour indeed because I was fairly young and about the only person who was not university trained. My education was extremely sort of slap dash. I suppose this was abut 1928/'29.

'We gradually started having choirs all round and competing. It started really with community singing. There was somebody called Ursula Nettleship who was

a very good musician, a professional. I had terrible battles in Essex because I wanted to turn my choirs into mixed choirs. I felt you are so limited without male voice. Then we gradually went on and had conductor schools. It was Mrs Lampson who did a tremendous lot for music, she was from East Sussex, and Miss Farrer (later Dame Frances Farrer, General Secretary of NFWI from 1929 to 1959) who was a tremendous figure. She was very autocratic but immensely clever. I liked her very much. She was very interested in music and a great friend of Vaughan Williams and that is how we got into *Folk Songs of the Four Seasons* really.'

Folk Songs of the Four Seasons represented an extraordinary amount of work. Well over 1,000 choirs competed for selection up and down the country, fifty-nine finally performing at the Albert Hall on June 15th, 1950, with Sir Adrian Boult conducting.

'It was my idea,' recalls Miss Tennant, 'but it was all worked out by other people. We thought, we have got all these lovely choirs, we must try and put them all together. And Fanny Farrer and I talked it over and decided to see if Vaughan Williams would write some-

thing for us and he did this lovely work. Then we started sending out schedules and we got 22,000 people singing (I had reckoned on 10,000) and we held competitions in every county. Then the best from the competitions went on to the second hurdle, and then at the second hurdle, no matter where you came from only the best were chosen. So, Essex got no choirs into the final and Northumberland got three. Sir Adrian Boult conducted the orchestra in the Albert Hall and Vaughan Williams conducted the end bit. *The Times* critic was in tears. Oh wasn't that splendid!'

In a life tragically cut short by pneumonia before the days of penicillin, the person who did most to raise the consciousness of countrywomen – to widen their horizons in terms of a mainstream, especially literary education – was a lady from Gloucestershire called Grace Hadow.

Stanhope WI choir, outside the Albert Hall, preparing to participate in the finals of 'Folk Songs of the Four Seasons' in 1950. Sixteen years later, a musical drama, 'The Brilliant and the Dark', a women's view of history composed by Malcolm Williamson, *was also performed on successive nights in the Albert Hall. Legend has it that so many members were involved in the production that two ladies positioned at the end of the queue of singer/actresses never actually made it onto the stage from the changing rooms below!*

The singing, dancing and drama came naturally to country girls. Below: Eastgate WI, dancing for the sheer fun of it. Left: East Sussex members celebrating in more formal style at their Michelham Priory festival in 1988. Right: Make-up time for 'Scene 80', the biggest theatrical event ever staged by the WI. It involved 100,000 people, 1,300 entries, 62 Federations. The concept was on a regional theme, included dance, music, and speech, and was staged over four days in 1981 at Stratford, home of the Royal Shakespeare Company.

Grace was born on December 9th, 1875, the youngest child of Revd William Hadow and his wife Mary, at the vicarage of South Cerney, near Cirencester. She went up to Somerville College, Oxford, in 1900, at a time when a first class education was little more than a dream even for an able girl. The few women who made it to Oxford University in those days, did so on sufferance, they were allowed to study and were admitted to examinations, but not to the degree. In 1903 Grace was examined in the Honours School of English Language and Literature and placed in the First Class. In 1904, following a teaching engagement in America, she took up the post of English tutor at Somerville and became resident English tutor a year later at Lady Margaret Hall, in 1909 giving up residence there and becoming a visiting lecturer instead. All the while she had worked hard to turn minds in favour of improving educational opportunities for women.

Miss Grace Hadow, pictured in 1917. 'Grace Hadow wakened a surprised intention to attempt something one stage further than before.' Lady Anglesey

When Grace's father died she returned to Gloucestershire to look after her mother. They moved to Cirencester, where Grace applied her considerable energies in support of women's suffrage and became involved in all kinds of social work. When the War came and her plans to do war relief work at the Front were not sanctioned by the authorities, she busied herself instead with Red Cross work, laying lifelines (parcels, clothes, etc) for prisoners of war in Germany, and making arrangements for the housing of Belgian refugees here. Then, when Cirencester was turned into a garrison town, she turned her study into a reading room and taught French to soldiers about to be posted abroad.

As the War progressed she noticed particularly the effect it was having on the status of women. Now, for the first time, they were measured by others in terms of the work they were doing rather than in terms of the men they had married. She began to speak and organise support for women to join professions and occupations hitherto barred to them, to become doctors, to find work in industry and, in the gradually spreading transport systems, to become tram drivers.

In 1916 she was elected to the Gloucestershire Chamber of Agriculture, championing the essential work of women on farms in war-time, and when, on July 10th, the Cirencester WI formed, Grace was the natural choice of President. Then, in mid-1917, she was appointed Director of the Welfare Department of the Ministry of Munitions, where the health and well-being of women munition workers were the priority. 'Women,' she noted of those who fell to her care at the Ministry of Munitions, 'who either had never worked before or had been in the lower grades of domestic service have learned a certain pride.' In the same year she was elected to the Executive of NFWI.

Grace was sister to Sir Henry Hadow, whose famous *Hadow Report* was, in 1926, to pave the way for a revolution in the education of children over eleven. Soon after being elected to the WI Executive, Grace shared a house with Henry who was then occupied in conceiving a sort of educational 'bridge' to help soldiers returning from the War to find their feet in civilian life. She began to relate her brother's progressive ideas about adult education to her own about maximising the potential of women in the changing social climate.

First she turned her attention to rural libraries, the textual background against which adult education could proceed in villages, but discovered an extraordinary indifference on her own doorstep. In 1920 the Oxfordshire County Council actually refused the offer of a Carnegie grant for starting a County Library, its refusal based on the conviction that 'Oxfordshire people didn't want to read!' Two years later, when proposing that the Government use voluntary organisations (like the WI) to further adult education, she was to admit, 'There are, I am afraid, still a few County Councils which consider the kind of education provided by WIs as a sort of luxury. We, as members of WIs realise how important in the whole development of village life these educational activities of ours are.'

Through Barnett house, a kind of information centre for social and economic questions, set up in Oxford as a memorial to Canon Barnett, founder of Toynbee Hall in London, Grace had already begun to generate interest in her ideas with the characteristically practical, 'hands-on' way of the early WI campaigners. A dilapidated black Ford van took books and lecturers (and Grace herself) to groups of villages in the county and readers found their way to Barnett House to utilise their library facilities. In Oxfordshire especially, the WI rose behind her campaign for rural libraries and the Barnett House scheme. They questioned their local councillors on library policy, and canvassed for the election of Mrs Kettlewell to the County Council on the platform of the rural library scheme. A new spirit arose in the Council offices – County librarians were awakened out of a deep slumber, and in 1923 the Oxfordshire County Council adopted the Public Libraries Act, Miss Mackintosh the Librarian of the Village Library at Barnett House, becoming the first County Librarian.

With the backing of the Carnegie Trust, libraries sprang up throughout rural Britain – often in response to active WI campaigns, as Mrs Dorothy Williams of the Worcestershire Federation of WIs recalls: 'One of Worcestershire's first campaigns was the opening of free libraries under the Rural Libraries (the Carnegie Libraries) scheme. They were operated in many places by the local WIs, and the work was co-ordinated by the (WI) Library sub-committee.

Grace had also begun to look at the funding of adult education. In October 1920 she called together representatives of the YMCA, the WI, the Village Clubs Association (then run by Nugent Harris) and the Workers' Educational Association 'to consider co-operation in social and educational matters and to prevent reduplication or checkmating one another's efforts.' The meeting grew into the Community Council, the first Rural Council, and through it organisations could apply for funds – from the Plunkett Trust (Sir Horace Plunkett had begun the Irish AOS) and later the Carnegie Trust. The Council also educated people in how to apply for public grants and as a result many local councils helped finance visiting lecturers to the women's institutes in the days before they ran their own adult education classes. The Essex Federation of Institutes, for example, still continues to benefit from a grant which was first awarded in 1918 by the County Council. And for many years the Cornwall Federation benefited from grants from the County Educational Committee designed to assist the running of classes in villages far away from centres of population. Mrs Elsie Julyan: 'We have always held evening classes in the WI centres, but many

An early list of Nottinghamshire instructors.

'Today,' says Chairman Mrs Jean Varnam, 'we are more and more providing the practical training which women can use in employment, both inside and outside the Institute.'

of the countrywomen couldn't get in to these centres, particularly in the evening. Or if they got in by bus, they couldn't get back again.'

In 1924 a WI resolution at the Albert Hall urged County Councils to 'make full use of the opportunities for the development of adult education in rural areas, afforded by the WI Movement.' It was sent to the County Councils Association and circulated to all County Education Authorities. The resultant action – countrywide – varied considerably and included grant-aided classes, the provision of teachers, grants for administration and bursaries. Through this association with County Councils in the earliest days of the WI has grown organised adult education as we know it today. It is no exaggeration to say that adult education for rural women was inspired by the painstaking work of the early WI pioneers. As Mrs Rowland said in proposing the 1924 resolution in the Albert Hall: 'I wish to emphasise the way in which our County Education Committees were quick to realise that while education is certainly the backbone of our Movement, we were able to discover, and I hope to a great extent we have carried out, the development of a demand for adult education which was perhaps not forthcoming before the days of the WI.'

The WI education policy, designed as has been seen to reinforce the traditional base of English village life and to bring fresh confidence to members on the wings of knowledge, had an additional and most essential purpose, namely to train members in techniques of public speaking and committee procedure so that the voices of countrywomen everywhere could not only be heard but would be listened to. Instructional pamphlets were produced and compiled with the help of Lady Denman's private secretary (and fellow suffragist) Margaret Hitchcock. If recently enfranchised countrywomen were to learn how to use their vote and perform effectively on local and national governing bodies, then they would need to understand how those bodies functioned and how to get the best out of them.

There was a procedural pamphlet about how to run a

meeting written by Lady Denman herself, and leaflets on *The Duties of Secretaries*, on *Planning Work* and *Programmes*; there were Model Minute Books and *Model Account Books*; and later the Movement's *Handbook* – a guide to almost anything.

In 1920, a resolution urged female representation on County Agricultural Committees, and another urged WI representation on Parish and District Councils to deal with health and housing. In 1921, institutes were exhorted to share civil responsibility and to educate members to positions on local Councils, and in 1922 a resolution made it the responsibility of County Federations to secure the appointment of a WI member on the County Council committee dealing with agricultural education. In the sphere of agriculture, members found a natural power base at local level, and in 1926 it became national policy to secure representation on District Wages Committees – 'Who better than a woman knows where the shoe pinches?' said one member at the time.

The success of the WI movement in getting representation of not only women but women members on local Government and other organisations concerned with rural affairs continues today – Mrs Patricia Batty Shaw, CBE, JP (Chairman, 1977-1980): 'We usually find a WI member sitting on the Rural Community Council. Wherever I go, I find a WI member on the Rural Community Council or The Housing Trust. They are always there, it is the story of the WI.'

Mrs Sybil Everitt, ex-Chairman, Gloucestershire Federation: 'First and foremost the WI is a catalyst. For example, the Rural Community Council is concerned with all affairs of the county and particularly concerned with life in the rural areas in all its spheres. In village halls, in the environment, in housing, in art, in local history, all that sort of thing. You have heard of Grace Hadow, and that she helped to found the Oxfordshire Rural Community Council. Well, in 1923, she returned to Gloucesterhsire to influence the then Chairman of our County Council. With one of the Vice Chairmen of the Federation, one Mrs Cripps, (later Lady Cripps), she went to convince him that it would be a good idea to have a Rural Community Council in Gloucestershire. So this Community Council was very intimately tied up with the WI right from the start and on almost all its sub-

committees it had a member of the Gloucestershire Federation Executive.'

Mrs Barbara Darvill of the West Kent Federation sees WI representation on such organisations as the direct result of the successful implementation of WI education policy. 'What we do very well is to encourage women to take part in public life outside the WI with our speech training courses and that type of thing. The whole process of training people to take office goes on the whole time. The teachers are trained nationally. You may think it peculiar that you have to train someone how to stand up and talk in front of a meeting, but you do, and you have to train people how to cope with business as much as how to deal with an audience. They also learn how to deal with the finances of running an organisation like this. For these sort of things, we in the County, organise training days. They may be very small ones, locally, or they may be big ones in a hall like this [I was speaking to her during the 70th Anniversary of the West Kent Federation]. Sometimes we use National teachers and sometimes we do it ourselves. There is no point in getting incensed about things locally if you can't do something about it, and in order to do something about it you need to be trained in becoming effective within an organisation. If, like me, you work on outside committees with other organisations, you realise just how good the WI is at training. So often these outside committees are so badly organised, the structure isn't there, the discipline at meetings isn't there.'

Lady Albemarle stresses the enthusiasm that abounded for this kind of training in the early days. 'Lady Denman had always been very keen on the organisational side of things, that the business should be clearly and well run. The WI offered a very good training on how to run things, and I think she saw the WI as a training ground for women so that when they went into public life they were aware and knew what they were doing and knew how to handle things. There was a lot of training in those days. At that time people rather enjoyed that kind of thing because it gave them confidence. I dare say people would find it dull now, but at that time we were really hungry for it. You see countrywomen hadn't done an awful lot of public work. But when WI members went onto Rural District

Left: *'That's Miss Wall, demonstrating to our two youngest members in 1953. She first suggested that we have a WI at Eastgate,' observes Mrs Kathleen Ward. 'That was the job of a VCO.' Like so many of the VCOs during the great expansion of the Movement, Miss Wall lived for the WI, She had a wide reputation for encouraging the institutes round and about her own home in Rookhope, Weardale (right). She would travel all over the county, often, through necessity, on foot. In order to attend Federation meetings in Durham she would walk the 3 miles or so to Stanhope, catch a bus to a friend's house in Merry Oaks, and walk from there with her friend the last few miles to the Durham office. Twice she was picked up by police for 'hanging about', having missed the last bus after an institute meeting somewhere in the Dale.*

Councils, to a great extent they met the same procedures that they had already met in the WI, so they didn't feel out of their depth.'

Many of those responsible for training WI members hold the office of Voluntary County Organiser. VCOs were Mrs Watt's idea – women in the counties able to work under her immediate personal supervision – at a time (1918) when some twenty new institutes were being formed each week. She ran a residential school for prospective officers at Burgess Hill in Sussex, where practical advice was given on propaganda, programme planning, training of committee members and so on.

Miss Withall remembers: 'In my day in order to become a VCO you went off to a four-day residential school. I believe I went to Scarborough, had a rather dreary time full of rather earnest people, but you didn't argue with it. The thing worked and you had to learn how you could make it work, and it was drilled into us that the rules were the rules and you kept the rules.'

A book published to accompany the course demonstrates the seriousness of the business and the frame of mind of the pioneers building the Movement: 'Talk that does not end in any kind of action is better suppressed altogether,' begins the section on *Aims and Ideals*.

Voluntary County Organisers were mainly responsible for starting up institutes and helping formulate their

Below: *A protest march by Crockham Hill WI to protect their rights of way.* Above right: *Since the Isle of Wight first galvanised members into action in 1927, it has been WI policy to campaign against the pollution of our seas.*

resolutions. In the beginning they had their own uniforms, which June Taylor of the Nottinghamshire Federation describes as consisting 'of a brown corduroy coat and skirt with a white or brown silk shirt, a plain brown felt hat and a brown tie. It was supplied by one of the stores, for sixty-eight shillings; there was also a loose belted overcoat in corduroy and an alternative uniform hat in dark brown straw.' However, uniforms became rather resented in the villages after the war – Mrs Taylor tells of one village where a VCO failed to drum

up enthusiasm for an institute precisely because the women thought that they would have to wear the uniform too.

The confidence that the WI gave its members frequently led to a whole new way of life. Mrs May Douglas of Beadnell WI: 'I am up to here with involvements. There is nothing I am not doing and it's all through joining the WI. I think it is because through the WI you get confidence, you learn how to speak. I have gone to Council meetings, I have gone to London, I have spoken at the Royal Albert Hall. The WI gives you a different perspective on everything. I am a Vice-Chairman of the Parish Council, I am on the Church Council, I am on the Deanery Synod, I am a School Manager, any job that is not paid, I'm on it. Yet years ago, I wouldn't have thought of it. Now I am involved in everything.'

There are two main concerns on Mrs Douglas' mind at present – one is that 97% of houses in Beadnell are second homes, a development which draws the core out of the village, yet still they allow the building of more big estates which are quite unnecessary; the other is the damage being done to the fishing in the area (her husband is a fisherman).

'The last big estate they built looked like becoming a great white elephant, although they are beginning to sell the houses now. But there is nothing here for people who come. If it is not fine weather then there is nothing here at all. There is sailing, yes, and at the moment we are overrun with skin divers. I'm not against that of course, a lot of the sub-aqua clubs are quite genuine sporting clubs, but we depend on the fishing for our livelihood and many of the divers are taking all the lobsters, it's become quite an industry. Our men are limited as to the number of lobsters they can have, but these divers are taking back bags and bags of small lobsters and putting them into tanks, freeing them and then bringing them on. It's a big scale operation.

'In 1978 I spoke on pollution at the Royal Albert Hall. On pollution of our seas. The resolution was proposed by Brixham WI in Devon, but I went to speak because my husband works on the water and it was our problem too. Sadly the problem is worse today if anything. One of the divers sat next to me on a seat just down here the other day, and was telling me the pollution is terrible. They can't dive in Whitley Bay because of the pollution and it's slowly coming up here. The diver said to me, "We haven't seen a fish today," and he said it was the sediment on the bottom – when it is disturbed it just comes straight up.

'There is little I can do about the development I suppose, all the big housing estates, but there is something we can do about protecting our rights of way.

We are the only parish around here that hasn't got new posts depicting the rights of way. We have fought for this for the past five or six years. You see if they continue to build I fear that we will lose our rights of way. You would think they would be safe, but you know what the Berwick Council did with the camping site here? One night we were walking down the fields with the dogs, and came to the gate into the site – a right of way – and it was padlocked. I got on the phone and they said, "Oh, we have diverted it from through the campsite to round the outside." That's all very well, but now the big boats park on the new right of way.

'The trouble with the posts, the sign posts, is that they have just deteriorated. I have sat here with a man from the Council and detailed all the rights of way in Beadnell Parish, and they said they will get around to it, so we will have to wait and see. You see the trouble is that you can't rely on the farmers protecting rights of way like the Countryside Commission recently suggested. There is a farm along here, you can get over the stile onto the footpath that goes through the farm on this side, but behind the vicarage, where you are supposed to get out the other side, you can't because the bullocks have knocked the stile down. Now when I called the farmer, he said it is up to someone else to do that, not him. . .'

Things had come a long way since women 'expected everything to be arranged for them', as Nancy Tennant had put it. 'You see,' she says when we talk about it, 'people through the WI – they blossomed!'

And Gladys Morris? She made it to the Albert Hall too, and made her point: 'In those days we had a two-day meeting at the Albert Hall. Of course we went through more resolutions then but it didn't seem quite so hectic as it is now. Then this transport resolution was discussed, which was a subject near to my heart, living where I did. I can't remember exactly what it was, but something was either said or left unsaid about which I felt pretty strongly. So I said to the member that was stewarding: "Do you think I could go up and say a few words?" Well, she said she didn't know but she would go and enquire. So off she went and when she came back she said I could go up and have a go. So of course I was delighted. I said what I had to say and evidently it was recorded – the next morning it came out on the radio!

'Well, I didn't know that it had because I was still up in London. But back home in Talybont, Mrs Henderson heard it. And I was delighted because only a few years previously I had got up to have a say at a local meeting and when I had finished Mrs Henderson had said, "Oh, I would like to hear you speaking at the Albert Hall." We had all thought it was a great joke and had a good laugh. But, when it actually came off, she was the one that heard it on the radio the following morning!'

Chapter Seven

PART OF A GLOBAL VILLAGE

*'What was happening in Germany
was going to become part of our lives as well.'*
MISS NANCY TENNANT

*Mary Saroja, an orphan 'adopted' by
Follifoot WI. Later the institute raised
money for a brain tumour operation.
She is now grown-up and married.*

With an increasing pride in their work, a strengthening sense of their own village identity and craft cultural background, and with an ever-expanding 'say' in government at local level, the education of countrywomen in the WI began to encourage members to look outside their village boundaries. This was an affirmation of a new and wider perspective which followed in the wake of better education, increasing travel, country-wide competitions with other villages and coming together in the nation's capital to discuss and determine issues that were of more than local significance. But it also reflected a fast changing, contracting world.

Nancy Tennant was Chairman of the first WI International Committee. 'It seemed to me that when events were building up which led eventually to the 2nd World War, you just couldn't live in isolation any longer.' The Committee's purpose – as everything in the WI – was both educational and evangelical, to spread the word of the WI into other countries. 'I remember there was one country in West Africa where members tried to translate into their own language the anthem of the Movement – *Jerusalem* – and found it impossibly difficult. So they told us they'd decided on another song instead, called *Brighten the Corner Where You Are!*

'But most of all at this stage we went out and lectured in the villages, lectured about other countries, tried to make people understand that nations were interdependent, that what was happening in Germany – what was happening everywhere – was going to become part of our lives as well.

'The ignorance in the villages about other countries was absolutely appalling. So many didn't have the faintest notion of where anywhere was. I had an old lady here one day and her son had been sent to the Middle East for something and I said, "Can I show you on the map?" and she said, "Thank you Miss, but I do not hold with maps." And that was that. The foreigner was something rather funny. He wasn't English – that was his misfortune. The idea that something in Germany or France was really going to affect their village had never occurred to them, and that's what I thought we had to get into their heads.

'Our women had no idea what was happening. In this village at least they did not have any idea what was going on. They just did not realise why any of these things that were happening in Europe were going to matter.'

Years earlier Mrs Watt had attempted to form an international association of institutes but it did not get the backing of Lady Denman. Of course Mrs Watt bounced back, this time with an idea of working out an international constitution with movements in England, Wales, Scotland, Belgium and France, but the idea was eventually abandoned due to a diversity of viewpoints among the organisations.

Disappointed but far from deterred, Mrs Watt enlisted the help of Lady Aberdeen, President of the International Council of Women, and with Mrs Drage, the three organised a conference between all the countrywomen associations from different parts of the world. There, the various associations described the aims and programmes of their own associations, and, as Mrs Drage put it, 'We realised that a great moral and spiritual urge towards co-operation and good fellowship had arisen spontaneously among women in different parts of the world.'

Two conferences followed and the association de-

Olive Farquharson, dressed in tribal wear given to her by the Ciskeian Zenzele Women's Association at a meeting in New Brighton, Southern Africa. Mrs Farquharson was honoured with the name 'Nozizwe', meaning 'Mother of Nations'.

veloped a constitution of its own, adopted a new name – the Associated Countrywomen of the World (ACWW) – and as Mrs Drage recalled, 'emerged from their deliberations a free and independent body under the leadership of Mrs Watt as President and Chairman.'

'The actual christening ceremony was unique. After adoption by the conference, the new name was written across a great blackboard in four different languages by four different people. *Associated Countrywomen of the World* by Mrs Watt, *Weltlandfrauenderein* by Countess Keyserlinck, *Association des Femmes Rurales Mondiales* by the Swiss Delegate, and *Verdens Husmoderforbund* by the Swedish Delegate. Thus, constituted and christened, we were, as Lady Aberdeen expressed it, launched upon the world.

'When the Swiss Delegate had written the French name she turned to face the meeting and immediately Princess Cantacuzene, a Rumanian, an old friend of the Swiss lady, rushed upon the platform, clasped her warmly round the waist, but they were both so stout that they lost balance and fell off the low platform. This excess of good will was met by cheers and laughter from the meeting.'

Lady Denman was still not at all sure that the WI should be a part of the ACWW. 'She felt that it was organised on unbusinesslike lines,' recalls Miss Tennant, and the things Lady Denman did were immensely efficient; that was the difference; that was why Lady Denman was not 100% for it.'

The 1939 conference of the ACWW was held in London on the eve of the War. 'I was the conference organiser,' continues Miss Tennant. 'Mrs Watt decided that we were going to have an international conference of the ACWW in England and she started arranging this in 1938. It was simply ghastly because Lady Denman wasn't going to pay and said we were not going to have any money to run it and really didn't want to do it at all. To give you an illustration of the difficulties, we had always said we were going to entertain delegates. I do not know how many thousand were coming but we could not entertain them all in London, it would have had to be done in the country. And on the day that the conference opened, I found six smiling Norwegian ladies in the hall all saying that they had arrived, and where were they going to stay? Mrs Watt had told them that if they came, we'd pay all their expenses, because she knew they wouldn't come unless she said that.'

However reticent the National Executive may have been in affiliating with ACWW in its early days, the institutes had themselves declared their desire for further 'closer relations with similar associations of women overseas' in a resolution way back in 1927, and there had been strong support from individual WI

members who formed close links with ACWW members in other countries. Indeed, since then, institutes have proved to be a generous and vital source of income for ACWW, through the 'Pennies for Friendship' fund and most notably in the campaigns 'Save Sight' (to combat child blindness due to malnutrition) and 'Water for All' (clean water and adequate sanitation in developing countries). The constantly developing purpose of the organisation is to unite countrywomen across the world for cultural and educational purposes, to offer a consultative facility to countrywomen in the United Nations, and to act as an advisory body in respect of grants for educational work and training seminars. It was not until 1971, however, that the worldwide organisation elected its first President from the British WI Movement, as Mrs Olive Farquharson recalls:

'The Oslo Conference in 1971 proved the most momentous for me as I was elected World President of ACWW for the next triennium. What an honour! The first and only English woman to hold the office to date and an opportunity to visit societies and members in such a variety of countries. Re-election in Perth, Australia, in 1974 gave me a further three years of "travelling the world", and though the journeys proved exhausting at times it also meant a wealth of experience gained.

'I chaired my last Conference as President in Nairobi, Kenya in 1977 – again a milestone as it was ACWW's first conference in Africa and the opportunities of helping the women and their families in those countries were boundless.

'Most journeys lasted two to three months and while

While the WI was busy telling its membership that what was happening in Germany was going to become part of their lives as well, German women (left) were actively involved stitching swastikas onto Nazi flags. Right: Healing wounds, post-War, Lady Albemarle chats with the Chairman of the Landfrauenvereine, an organisation that had been launched shortly after the Canadian WI Movement. The meeting was part of a co-operative venture undertaken between the two movements on the suggestion of the Foreign Office. The venture developed into WI trips to Germany on three occasions, and German women made two further visits to England in 1950.

travelling by air gets you there quickly it also means there is little time to have a rest! After about a week of meetings in one place, you are up and away and being welcomed by the next group – privately wondering what different and unusual excitement awaits.

'Sleeping in the pueblo home of an American Indian family was not a bit like the palm thatched hut I shared on a Pacific Island where the land crabs scuttled under my bed, and it was quite different again staying overnight in the Malaysian longhouse where nineteen of us slept on the floor, men, women, dogs and the cat!. . .

'Language presents problems. I spent four days in a Turkish farmhouse (they with no English and me with no Turkish) yet it is surprising how much you can convey with 'sign language', and this helps to build up understanding and friendship. . .

'The phrase "Friendship is a Flowering Tree" had remained with me since the Edinburgh Conference where I had seen it decorating one of the windows of a house on the Clyde and I often felt, as I travelled, that this was a true interpretation of our very existance.

'I see the societies as the roots of the tress, multiplying and thrusting deeper into the soil as our work spreads; I see these societies entwined to make the trunk of that tree, growing bigger and stronger as we work together; I see the branches reaching out, flowering, bearing fruit and sheltering people who seek our help,

knowing that we come in friendship. From the token fruits of our trees, that fall into so many parts of the world, we are giving new opportunities in life to those who are in need.'

Back in 1939, the feeling of friendship made an ironic platform for the carnage that was to follow. One cannot help wondering how different things might have been had these women been in control of our destiny - Miss Tennant: 'The Earls Court exhibition place was absolutely jam packed. The German Landfrauen Verein had been folded up by Hitler, but they wanted to send two women, so two very charming women arrived from a Nazi organisation. They were very nervous, very anxious. All the delegates got up on the platform in turn and gave a greeting, and the moment came when these two lone Germans got up quite clearly nervous and thinking they would be booed. Instead, everyone got up and clapped and shouted. I suppose it was a demonstration of their terror of the thing going wrong. It was very moving and the German women were very impressed. In fact they came down to Ugley for the day – delegates had been sent down from all over the place – and one of them, at the end of the day, I remember her, so charming, she said, "I have admired so much in your country, but what I admire most is your freedom." And I thought "My goodness me, young lady, that is an unwise thing to say." '

Chapter Eight

WOMEN AT WAR

*'Today the place of the countrywoman is
more important than it has ever been before.'*
HRH Queen Elizabeth

*Old Bishop Stortford market, 1933, one of the grimmest
years of the Depression.*

War brought the WI full circle to its founding purpose nearly a quarter of a century earlier, the farmers needing more help in food production than ever before. Bolstered by the Corn Production Act, farming had never been more profitable than in 1918. 'My world went very well then', recalls A G Street in *Farmer's Glory*, first published in 1932. 'The war was over for ever and ever, and farming had returned to its old splendour. Farmer's Glory was then a glory of great brilliance. How were

farmers to know that it was but the last dazzling flicker before the fusing?'

The Government guaranteed the price of grain and the production costs were fixed; the farmer really couldn't lose. But then, in 1921, the guaranteed price became a cash bonus per acre of land on which wheat and oats were grown. It was a subtle change but, as it became plain the following year, only one step away from the repeal of the cash-incentive part of the Act altogether. Incredibly, however, the 'fixed wages' part of the Act remained. No guaranteed price, no cash bonus, but fixed wages all the same. What's more, wages had quadrupled from the pre-war level of twelve shillings per week, and that top wage was fixed to only forty-nine hours, after which overtime was due.

Inevitably, the farmer began a slide into ultimate depression. Every £1,000 invested in farming in the hey-day of 1920 was by 1932 worth only about £250. The result was reduction of farm labour and the putting down to grass of four million acres of arable land. Between the 1st and 2nd World Wars the atmosphere in the farming community had returned to one of defeat and depression, with farmers impoverished and neglected, cottages and buildings falling into disrepair, and with villages still lacking many of the amenities for which Lady Denman's WI had been fighting continuously.

No wonder the WI thrived; it was needed as at no other time. By 1938 the number of institutes had risen to 5,500 with a total membership of more than 350,000. Through-

out the period 1928 to 1938 a major theme of the institutes' programme was thrift. Members adapted themselves to the Depression and welcomed the opportunity – in the face of real hardship – to be taught how to make the most of what little there was. Now, more than ever, the institutes as food producers reaped the benefits of the practical side of the WI education policy. The WI markets' reaction was similarly positive. From 1932, under the leadership of Vera Cox, the first national Markets Organiser, hundreds of new markets were developed up and down the country.

The AGM of 1928 had seen a resolution calling for the special study of *The Denman Report* in the institutes and the result was an extraordinary expansion of this side of WI work. Produce shows and exhibitions abounded. The WI markets went from strength to strength and standards improved dramatically. 'Markets, in conjunction with County Federations and the NFWI, ran their own schools on growing, grading and packing, and all prices at markets were geared to quality,' recalled Miss Cox, and teachers

Henley Market stall – Christmas in the hungry '30s.

and demonstrators were very much in demand. As the depression deepened and the call went out for more to be produced at home, NFWI organised two regional courses in cooking and food values, taught by experts and open only to WI members with previous experience. Before long all the students were employed by their Local Education authorities as teachers.

In 1927 NFWI had attempted to inaugurate a Guild of Food Producers along the lines of the Guild of Learners. But only twelve out of fifty-six County Federations were prepared to pledge support. There had been genuine concern amongst countrywomen that a Guild dedicated to educating people in increasing the flow of produce at a time of depression in the agricultural industry could put smallholders – sometimes members' husbands – out of business: 'One could not really expect Madam President in a district of smallholders to urge her members to till the ground, if thereby she ran the risk of putting Dad or Hubby out of business.' So said members of the Worcestershire Federation, a county that produced less per acre on average than any other county in England in 1938.

However, in 1939, with the war imminent, there was no longer a clash of interests and Lady Denman's Produce Guild was duly formed.

This, then, was the background to the key role that the WI played during the 2nd World War. No less than eight resolutions had been passed between 1924 and 1931, appertaining to the education of women in domestic, agricultural and allied subjects, almost all inspired by Lady Denman herself.

The Denman Report in the late '20s, the enormous activity in the WI Markets during the '30s, and now, in 1939, the new Produce Guild were clear affirmation that the WI remained firmly rooted in the soil of England and Wales at this time. Now, as had happened in the 1st World War, they could show the country what they had learned – Miss Viola Williams: 'Basically, as I have told my women all over the world, you can live in towns, you can have all the amenities on offer, but when the chips are down it's the people that grow food that matter.'

Produce Guild leaders learning the ropes at Sutton Bonington Agricultural College.

A Government grant of £500 helped meet the early expenses of the newly formed Produce Guild which, besides educating members in an intensive cultivation of their gardens and allotments made available fertilisers, seeds and other essential materials slightly cheaper.

During the war 140,000 fruit bushes and 134,000 packets of seeds were sold through the Guild to Institute members. One consignment of bushes arrived at the Durham Federation office on Christmas Eve and had to be delivered around as quickly as possible, mostly on foot, up some very lonely cart tracks. The responsibility of this enormous undertaking fell to Dr Jessie Dixon: 'During the war I was living at Horden, a mining village in the news a year or so ago when they closed the pit. Horden, just south of Sunderland, a main seaport in the North, was a restricted area during the war so we had no evacuees but many bombings and the permanent threat of invasion. The women would come to the meetings with their gas masks. I remember once we were given a drama talk, a recital by a woman famous in County Durham because she had drama groups all over the place. We were in the middle of this "dramatic moment" when some naughty boys, passing by, gave some bangs on the door. Everybody thought it was an invasion, and when we'd got our breath back I looked down the hall and saw that some of the women were sitting with their gasmasks on! Such was the tension.

'I distributed the fruit bushes (blackcurrant mostly) and the seeds (mostly vegetables) which I believe came from America. I lost heart with the vegetables because there were two sizes of packs and in Horden I sent a card round to find which packs people wanted and then ordered them from the committee in Durham who ordered them from London. I discovered that it wasn't good enough to get a list of who wanted what because when they were delivered, women would say, "Oh, I ordered the small packet" or "I ordered the big packet." I soon learnt that when you are dealing with a lot of people it's better to get them to place their own order.

'Being a doctor I had a car and more petrol than most

Miss Thelma Jones demonstrating the art of bacon curing to a war-time WI audience.

people, and I did have some help, a very obliging handyman. I used to drive the car and he would deliver them at the places.'

Encouraged and advised by the National Farmers Union and WARAG (the War Agricultural Committee), the Produce Guild held lectures and very practical demonstrations on all aspects of agriculture – Viola Williams: 'I had done horticulture. During the first part of the War I was growing vegetables for a school in Somerset, then I went on as Head Gardener at Cheltenham Ladies College – terribly superior! Then I went on the Wilts War Agricultural Sub-Committee for the Council. There were four of us doing that, and it got me into WIs. We went all round the country; we were known as the Circus. We had a poultry female, a home economics female, a dairy female and me, and we had a caravan, and we would charge madly all round the country putting up one-day stands and giving demonstrations. We started under the Min of Ag and ended up under the Min of Ed. None of us liked the Min of Ed because it works to a timetable, and the Min of Ag works to nature – a very different set-up!

'Of course, in those days, there was hardly any traffic on the roads, and I covered the whole of the country and the Channel Islands driving with a poetry book in one hand and the other eye on the road. It was so gorgeous (though the cars were cold, there was no heating and they were very uncomfortable, and the roads were awful, but I got to know England as no one else could). I would drive up to Carlisle and then have to do a demonstration, which was fairly tiring.

'You could get a canning machine through the Ministry of Agriculture and you could get cans from the Metal Box Company. This was quite a new thing for England, most of the canned stuff we got in this country was from Australia or America. We were doing fruit and tomatoes. Later on we were allowed to do vegetables, but they are very much more tricky, because you have to do them in a pressure cooker. Meat, I don't think we were ever allowed to do. But fruit yes, and tomatoes, with care, yes.'

Miss Margaret Leech, now a member of Backwell WI near Bristol, was involved as an instructress in both canning and bacon curing: 'I had done a two year poultry training course to get a National Poultry Diploma. I had worked on poultry farms, and I could see batteries coming and I didn't like it. So I became a demonstrator for the Electricity Board. Then I got to know the Rural Domestic Economy Instructor in Buckinghamshire, and I joined her staff. I went from there to Leicestershire where I stayed for fourteen years, and I went from there to Long Ashton Research Station, where I studied on a slightly different level.

'The WI audiences were marvellous. Nothing like a good war to cheer up the WI. We were trained at Smithfield in bacon curing and we taught cheese making too, but the thing was that we were taught at Long Ashton Research Station how to ensure that the produce would be marketable.

'The Americans let us have a whole lot of canning equipment, but apart from that most people had got jam pans of their own. One of the great problems in demonstrating to the WI how to can fruit, revolved around the fact that when you have filled the cans with fruit and syrup, they have to be cooled down very quickly. This cooling process often presented difficulties at the WI. We got quite used to the fact that there wasn't a sink. In fact once, I recall, they had a sink but forgot to tell me that they had no waste pipe, so all the water came down and drenched my feet. But very often you had to take the cans outside in a net and use the water pump, pumping the water onto them. I remember once I was in a rather remote village and I went outside but couldn't see the pump. I asked the woman where it was and she looked at me and said in surprise. "The pump? It's in the brook." And the brook was in a little ravine and I had to slither down the banks of this ravine to drop the boiling hot cans in the stream. It was, to say the least, quite primitive at times.'

In June 1938 NFWI had issued a statement of war-time policy which made a distinction between war work which women might undertake as WI members and work which should not be undertaken by institutes. The reason for making the distinction was declared to be constitutional and harked back to one of the Movement's fundamental principles, that no institute should participate in discussions or actions which might infringe the religious beliefs of other members. The group to be protected by the WI war-time policy was the pacifist Quaker membership.

Some members hailed the refusal by Lady Denman to budge from the principle, as praiseworthy, but there was also 'a great deal of criticism,' according to Nancy Tennant, who has since become a Quaker. 'We weren't allowed to take part as institutes in Civil Defence [specifically ARP, air-raid precaution work] because of the Quaker membership. Whether it was the right decision I don't know, but as a Quaker now, I would have thought that we could have taken part in some of the evacuee side.'

In the autumn of 1938, when the Munich crisis made war appear imminent, it looked as though the WI would be assigned the complete organisation of the evacuation of children from towns to the countryside. Then, the Home Secretary had turned to the WI to draw up an emergency evacuation plan. Lady Denman and the WI

General Secretary, Miss Frances Farrer, immediately responded with plans for the evacuation of children under school age, a plan which made use of the national/county/village 'bureau' structure of the WI – a perfectly designed organisation for the job in hand.

In the end the plans were not used because war was averted until September 3rd, 1939. WI members did become involved in looking after evacuees, but the organisation fell to a new movement under the leadership of Marchioness Lady Reading. In fact the WVS, as it was called (now the Women's Royal Voluntary Service), took on much of the organisation work which had been forbidden the WI by its Executive. As a result WVS membership prospered at the expense of the WI, and some WI members were not at all happy when, at the end of the war the WVS was not disbanded. By September 1939, the WVS was some million members strong while the WI showed a decline of roughly 12% between 1939 and 1943.

Although many members worked co-operatively with the WVS, Meriel Withal, Assistant Secretary to the General Secretary at the time recalls that while 'the WVS worked alongside the WI during the War there was always slight rivalry. Perhaps Lady Reading and Lady Denman were not exactly compatible.'

The WVS had in fact been called into existence by the Government prior to the WI statement of non-involvement; apparently the call to the WI for an evacuation plan had come only because Lady Reading's movement had yet to find its feet. Whether its formation prompted WI war policy as much as Lady Denman's commitment to the 'non-denominational' biass of the constitution is not known. But it is certainly true that Lady Denman's defence of the constitution was absolute, even in the context of compulsory religious instruction in schools, an issue of passionate interest to some members in West Kent, but one which she refused to discuss nationally.

'The basis of the institutes since the foundation of the NFWI has been the inclusion of countrywomen of every

'The Americans let us have a whole lot of canning equipment . . .' Miss Margaret Leech.

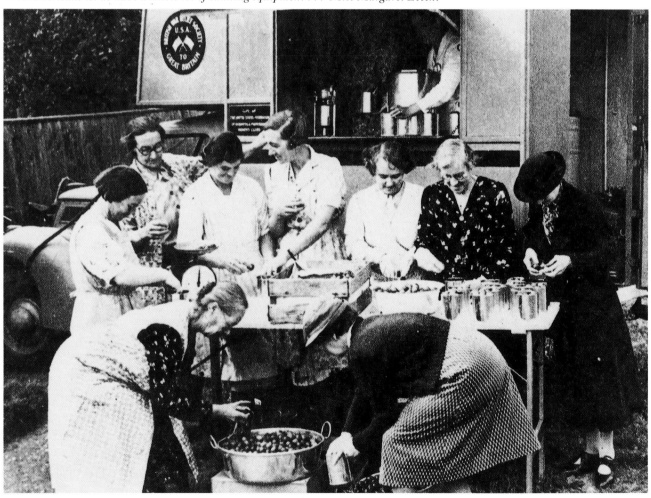

religious belief, political persuasion and social and economic status, who are ready to be good neighbours,' she wrote to West Kent Federation.

WI policy notwithstanding, we find the same personalities deeply involved in war work across a wide spectrum. On April 9th, 1938, a month prior to the official formation of the WVS, Lady Denman was herself handed responsibility for the Women's Land Army – if the appointment had come as a sop from the Government it could not have been better judged. In the 1st World War Lady Denman had gained invaluable, personal experience in recruiting for the Women's Land Army. With her friend Nellie Grant (with whom she had devised the domestic egg-producing enterprise), she would drive through the Home Counties dressed in Land

Above: *Digging for Victory under the camera eye of Niton WI.* Right: *The Land Army in action.*

Army uniform, stopping the car in the middle of some market square. She and Nellie would then get out, work an ear-splitting wooden rattle to attract the undivided attention of the townsfolk, and when they had it, one of them would stand on the running board of the car and deliver a rousing recruitment speech through a megaphone. The close contact between the WI and the Women's Land Army, originating as it had from the fact that both organisations at that time came under the auspices of Dame Meriel Talbot's Womens' Branch of the Board of Agriculture's Food Production Department, was now re-newed and developed during the national emergency.

'The approach of the Second World War, and the realisation that it would be necessary to have a nation

self-sufficient in food, led to the setting up of WARAG,' writes a contributor to the Llangernyw village scrapbook, North Wales, 'with chosen representatives organising the effort throughout the country. A percentage of the grazing area on each farm had to be given up to be ploughed for the planting of potatoes and wheat. Compensation was paid by the Government for the loss of income from that land. Ploughing was carried out by men or by Land Army girls, using tractors and ploughs supplied for the task. Help was also given with the harvesting of the crops and the potatoes were stored to await collection in an earth covered pit close to the main road at Pentre. Grants were made available for land drainage, which was carried out by prisoners of war, thus helping to reclaim hitherto uncultivated land and increase the productivity on many farms. Wool from sheep shearing was also bought by the Government at a nominal cost and taken to make clothes for the forces.'

The same story might have been told of land work anywhere in Britain. Even where the land was not obviously good, agriculturally, it was to be cultivated. Women travelled the country to wherever they were needed to help on farms whose workforce had been diminished by the call-up. Lady Denman was in the ideal position to make use of the same women who made up the nation-wide network of WI County leaders and VCOs, in organising this Army of Women which would literally dig for victory, and this she did.

Lady Elizabeth Fraser: 'My mother [the Hon Mrs Anthony Methuen] was the County Chairman for the Women's Land Army in Wiltshire. She had been on the National Executive of the WI, and my father actually sat in on that very first meeting that was held at Colonel Stapleton-Cotton's house in Wales. He had been very badly wounded in the 1st World War and gone up there to spend some days to convalesce. My mother married him in 1920 and she became involved in the Wiltshire Federation and then became a National Executive member in the early 1930s. She was on the National Executive for thirty-one years – thirteen years as National Treasurer, a year as Vice-Chairman, and a Trustee until her death in 1972.

'I was brought up in a village in Wiltshire, and one of our dailies, whom we had for twenty-one years, was an Eastender, half Austrian, half English; her mother died when she was quite young. She was learning to be a milliner, but with the war she became a land girl in our village and later married a farm worker. There were hostels for the land girls. They wouldn't necessarily live on the farm; a group of land girls might live in a hostel with a warden. I think it was Lord Eccles who was MP down there and got the money to turn an old barn into a

Mrs Liz Keast and her husband, whom she met while she was a land girl during the war. 'I did so much ploughing that I dreamt about ploughing straight furrows.'

hostel, and it was done out most beautifully, and my mother opened it, I remember. She had the responsibility of the girls, making sure they were living in decent conditions and, if they were ill, to see that they were looked after. I remember there was one girl who was quite young, and had suffered an appalling accident. She'd had her neck broken and was in plaster and was going to be paralysed, and my mother would spend hours, you know, going to see her, seeing that she was all right. Then there were the naughty girls who got themselves in the family way. Mummy used to have to go and talk to them quietly and look after them. So she had a lot to do and she took it all very personally; they were her extra children that she had to look after. A lot of the girls coming from towns found it very difficult to adjust, and this is where my mother came into her own.

'She used a lot of the WI's Voluntary County Organisers to help; she would parcel out the county. If she had a good VCO around (they were very carefully hand-picked in those days), then she knew she could rely on someone to help. In those days the VCO would have a patch of the county and look after the land girls; they were the shepherds, if you like. But if there was a crisis my mother would be over there like a flash. I think this was how it was done in most counties. Lady Denman, who was Chairman of the whole thing, would call upon her County Chairmen to be responsible for the Land Army girls in their area and if they couldn't do it they would suggest someone who could.'

As a member of the Land Army, Mrs Liz Keast travelled from her home in Yorkshire to work on a farm in Cornwall, and never left the county: 'I just thought I'd like the Land Army and I wanted to come south. Yorkshire was so cold and I'd never been south. I didn't say what part I particularly wanted to go to. I was thinking of Sussex or Surrey perhaps. But in the end I was sent to Cornwall. It seemed to me a foreign country. I came down to replace a farmer's son who'd gone to join the RAF. The trains were very dicey then. Although I left quite early in the morning it got later, and later and we got to Plymouth in the midst of the most abominable air raid. We got off the train and I just didn't know where I was. So I got a taxi and asked him if he would take me somewhere where I could stay the night (in those days it was perfectly safe to do so), and he took me to a house and they put me up. As I recall I slept on a billiard table! They were full up with people in all corners of the place. I asked them where I was in relation to the station and would they call me early so I could find out and catch the next train to Cornwall.

'The next day I came down, had breakfast, got on the train, got off at Lostwithiel and there was the farmer! He didn't know I was on that train. He just took a chance.

He'd heard the raid and worked out when I'd be likely to arrive – which train.

'I lived on the farm with the farmer's family. I found it difficult at first. People were a bit different and I was a bit lonely. This was 1939. The family was very nice to me. I found some of their ideas a bit odd but then they'd probably have thought the same about some of mine if I'd given them.

'I learned to drive a tractor – I had seen a tractor before, but that's all. I'd had no training at all. There were no self-starters in those days, you had to "crank" the engine. It was an Allis Chalmers, I remember, an American make. It was like a two-stroke bike, you know? I liked the bigger tractor best. I was pulling a plough behind the tractor. At first the farmer stayed with me, on the step at the back, to see how I would behave. He taught me to plough. If you can plough in Cornwall you can plough anywhere because the fields are all sorts of shapes. I ran into a wall once. I didn't say anything. I wasn't frightened; a trifle stunned but I didn't make any comment and we carried on. It was awfullly hard on the steering and I had more bruises than I have ever had in my life before or since.

'I did so much ploughing that I dreamt about ploughing straight furrows by night and by day endeavoured to do it as well! Oh I slept all right, I just couldn't wake. The latest we were up was 6 am. The farmer's wife milked by hand (they didn't have many

School dinner for evacuated children. 'They had never heard of God, except as a swear word . . .'

cows), but that wasn't my job. I went purely and simply as a tractor driver, though I'd do all sorts of odd jobs too. Sometimes I'd go into the shed where all the bits and pieces were, clean the plugs, that sort of thing. Or I'd take some hay down and feed the bullocks. It was barely light and I'd call and they'd all come up once I'd cut open the sheaves.

'Breakfast, as near as I can tell you, was at 8 o'clock. It was a full breakfast with cream and syrup and jam to round it off. The cream was a high treat for me; I hadn't had the Cornish clotted cream before. Then I'd work the tractor, ploughing, rolling, whatever was needed to prepare the ground, depending on what time of year it was. And I'd be in the fields until lunchtime. Sometimes, if the weather was good, they'd bring us lunch out and we'd sit in the hedge and eat pasties which were home-made.

'They had – I wouldn't call her a servant, she was part of the family – she was called Odessa. She made the pasties and they'd bring them in a huge basket with a lovely cloth, and I'd enjoy that very much. And then I got back on the tractor and carried on until I'd finished or until I hadn't finished, and the only indication I had of the time was that a certain bus would go by. I didn't have a watch. Then I'd take the tractor back and put her away and clean her up and have tea. After tea I was free to do as I wished. I used to walk about three or four miles into Lostwithiel to the cinema, sometimes.

'I was at that farm for about a year and then went to a bigger farm in a place called Anthony near Torpoint. There I did milking as well as tractor work.'

Mr Keast interrupts – 'And she did a milk round into Torpoint and I was working for an agricultural tractor machinery company, and she used to deliver milk to us, and that's how we met.'

By the time of the 1939 AGM, it was obvious that although the WI, as an organisation, wasn't to be in charge of the evacuation, ARP, or indeed the Women's Land Army, WI members were very much involved. In her AGM speech, Lady Denman said, 'It is obvious that Women's Institutes can give and are giving the most valuable help with regards to plans for the reception of city children in the villages. It is also obvious that if the great disaster of war should overtake us, the authorities will look to the Women's Institutes to give their help in increasing food production and in looking after members of the Women's Land Army in addition to caring for evacuated town dwellers.' And in a letter issued afterwards, headed 'War Time Plans,' she explained again the important role of the WI in evacuee work and in looking after the welfare of land girls, as well as in the production and preservation of food.

In some areas, organisation left much to be desired: 'During the war, I had moved from Sevenoaks, and we were involved in taking in evacuees in East Malling where my father, a parson, had retired,' remembers Miss Vera Thompson, now 92-year-old member of Brenchley WI in Kent. 'We had a school evacuated to us. Any rate, this school that was evacuated to us took over the infant school and when we arrived we realised they were all sixth formers. We had arranged a lunch for when they arrived, but expected them all to be small children and it really was very difficult because they found it impossible sitting at the desks. They were all billeted all round the village, but they didn't stay many months because it was quite unsuitable, partly because it was an infant school, but also because it was much too near London for the evacuees so they were moved out pretty soon, I think they were moved on to the Midlands somewhere.'

Elsewhere, preparations were made but the evacuees didn't turn up. On September 4th, 1939, the day after war was declared, WI members of Linkinhorne village in Cornwall, recall that 'the school [Upton Cross] closed for one week to allow for preparations to be made to receive evacuee children from the areas most likely to be devastated by bombing. In October, instructions were received concerning the darkening of windows to give an effective blackout, the use of gas masks and the obvious need for economy. It was a gloomy winter, not helped by the exceptionally severe weather in January 1940, with twelve degrees of frost and a snowstorm. Numbers were down to less than half.' Not until the following June did the long-awaited evacuees arrive: 'One hundred and seventy-four children with twelve teachers found themselves transported from Denmark Hill in London to scattered billets in the decidedly rural parish of Linkinhorne. What must they have thought about it? Language was a problem for a start, so initially a double shift system was operated with Upton Cross children having lessons in the morning and Denmark Hill children in the afternoon. Both schools played games together, no doubt with a healthy rivalry. The shift idea was too clumsy to operate for long and was replaced within a month by full time instruction for both schools, with Denmark Hill using the north side of the main partition and Upton Cross the south side.

'The evacuee children were later joined by a smaller number from Plymouth and they probably had the most difficult time of all. The Upton Cross and London children were in two well-defined and often hostile groups, but the Plymouth children felt that they belonged to neither and were rejected by both, as one of them remembered many years later. But even before the Plymouth children came on the scene, the tensions were there. In July 1940, the log records that a parent came into the school and boxed the ears of a boy who had quarrelled with his son. The quarrels were common enough. If not the method of dealing with them! But a real effort was made to help these at least temporarily orphaned children. The school stayed open through the summer holiday that year, for informal lessons and games. In August most of the children went on a trip to Polzeath for a cricket match . . .'

Three months after the first, September '39 evacuation of town dwellers to the countryside, the National Executive issued a questionnaire to every institute asking for particulars of the evacuee children and adults received in the village. Broadly, the responses from 1,700 institutes concerned three subject areas: the condition of the evacuees when they were received; the misconceptions planted in the minds of mothers encouraged by the Government to accompany their children; and lastly the 'education' that resulted for both town and country folk alike.

In many villages, by the end of the first week, beds were ruined, cottages stank, pots and pans were burnt and the village children had lice for the first time in their lives. Mrs Joy Foot lived near Weymouth in Dorset during the war: 'We had them in the first year of the war, we had three evacuees and they were just slightly older than me. Whole schools were evacuated down and they took over the Baptist Chapel and other places, they would take them over as schools for these children. I can remember they came down with head lice and I can remember having one's hair washed every day, and then there was something else, impetigo or something, and we had to go and be publicly bathed in that awful purple stuff. There was an allowance which my parents would have been given to help them look after the children, but it was not a very big one. It was very difficult. I can remember all the butter being cut up into little portions, making do with what we could. But the hair washing was particularly bad. I can remember it well because I had very long hair at the time and all that going through one's hair, that was all down to the evacuees.'

A London school teacher, one of many responsible for organising a block of children to be evacuated from London, recalled how she had been encouraged to persuade mothers to evacuate with their children. She had been told to tell them that it would be a nice holiday – 'We'd never have got them to come, if we hadn't!' So the mothers left for the countryside in the gloriously sunny month of September 1939, and presented the countrywomen with yet another shock – Mrs Ward of Eastgate WI, County Durham: 'I can tell you about one evacuee here. She came with her nice long red-painted nails, and she said, "What can I do?" Well, the milking had been done, so I said, "If you like you can put my clothesline up out here." "Oh," she said, "I'd break my nails." So I said the best thing she could do was to get the train straight back down the Dale.'

Stories abound of town mothers leaving their children to be looked after by their country hostesses and coming rolling home after closing time, and of others being billeted down the road from their children, by choice! 'It was felt,' responded one institute to the survey, 'that these mothers came as much as anything for the novelty of a country holiday and did not try to settle down.'

But what an education the evacuation afforded. *Punch* magazine published a drawing of a little girl who said as she skipped down a lane between flowering hedges, 'They call this Spring, Mum, and they have one down here every year.' Mrs Maureen Wall of Rookhope WI, tells of over-hearing one evacuee child asking why,

'They couldn't understand anything about country life and we understood very little about them.' Mrs Maureen Wall.

when it rained, the cows weren't brought in from the fields. 'They couldn't understand anything about country life and we understood very little about them.'

A sense of inferiority had long been bred in countrywomen by their urban neighbours – their rough clothes and broad speech comparing unfavourably with the more fashionable town dweller. Now having experienced for the first time the ragged appearance and street-wise persona of some of these urban children, old preconceptions began to disappear and were sometimes replaced by outrage: 'like little heathens' was a phrase used at the 23rd Annual Meeting of the West Kent Federation of Women's Institutes to describe evacuaees, and a resolution deploring the lack of spiritual knowledge among urban children was carried: 'The reason for this resolution,' said a speaker from Matfield WI, 'is that like other villages in Kent, we have had evacuated children. The foster parents were shocked that the children were like little heathens . . . they had never heard of God, except as a swear word. It will be for them to build the new world that we are all hoping to see arise. But they cannot build it except on a God fearing foundation. I think it is up to us to see that they get this foundation.'

Some of the later evacuees were rather different, however, as three members of the Cornwall Federation remember: 'The trouble with the later ones,' recalled Mrs Elsie Julyan, 'was that some of them had had some very bad experiences due to the war. They had been in the bombing you see. After the first wave, after the first great enthusiasm about evacuating children, they all went back. Well then of course, when the bombing started, some of them came that had had some very bad experiences.'

Mrs Joyce Donnelly: 'When our lot arrived, the train drew into St Austell station and about ten minutes later we had the only stick of bombs on St Austell during the whole war, and they went up parallel to the railway line. The poor kids thought they had come from bad to worse.'

Mrs Julyan: 'So many of them were in a shocked state, a very poor state. Of course some of them stayed at the end. Mrs Arthur of Whitemoor, her daughter married a fellow who was an evacuee. They still live down here. So some of them never went back, or if they did, they soon came back again. As soon as they were old enough to get a job, they would come back and stay.

Mrs Joy Foot: 'That happened with a neighbouring farmer of ours. She used to joke with me, that as a child she had had a label on her saying Lillian Rhodes and another saying Coombe Farm. Now she says: "Just think, if I had been put into another farm, I might have married so and so!"'

Collecting fruit and making jam. Mrs Joan Boucher recalls that 'during one of the perfect summers of the war, East Kent members were boiling up vast quantities of the famous jam, and the heat became unbearable so they stripped off! And continued their task. I have often wondered if the general public would have appreciated the Movement more if the press had heard of such goings-on and had publicised the WI as made up of Page 3 Girls, who also made excellent jam!'

The war-time enterprise for which the WI is remembered best is of course the making of jam. What began as a WI Produce Guild project in 1940 became a Government-sponsored, nationwide effort of women everywhere. Jam work provided a perfect solution not only for the 1940 harvest glut of plums, but for the tensions that were felt in the WI following NFWI's decision to hand over other work to the recently formed WVS.

As Cecily McCall recorded at the time, 'Here was the longed-for piece of war service . . . Jam. It seemed the perfect solution. Jam-making was constructive and non-militant . . . It accorded with the best Quaker traditions of feeding blockaded nations. For those dietetically minded, jam contained all the most highly prized vitamins. For those who were agriculturally minded, the scheme saved a valuable crop from literally rotting on the ground, and it encouraged better fruit cultivation – though not, one can only pray, of plums only. And for the beligerent, what could be more satisfying than fiercely stirring cauldrons of boiling jam and feeling that every pound took us one step further towards defeating Hitler?'

Jam-making was a spontaneous WI effort, and was, as ever, marvellously organised by its membership – Viola Williams: 'A lot of what I would call the non-Ladies of

the Manor came into their own with the jam centres, because they were the ones who knew how to make jam. You would start at the crack of dawn, probably on primus stoves, and go on all day with great cauldrons of jam, and then bottle it. It was like a small factory.

'I was inspecting. I had to check on cleanliness, on packaging, on labelling, and although we weren't in a position to (because we didn't have saccharimeters), we were supposed to check on sugar content too. A "selling jam" has to have 60% sugar in it (this applies to the WI now) and this is one of the things we had to check out. You can work it out by quantities: if you knew how much sugar was available to make into a jam, then you could work out – almost to an ounce – how much jam should have been produced with a 60% sugar content. The reason for checking was that we were given the sugar on trust. There was utter and complete honesty, but it was a temptation to syphon away the sugar and use it for yourself during those days of high rationing. I think people did used to go home with a saucer full of scum, which is almost as good as jam but which you couldn't possibly have put into the bottles. But I would say that there was almost 100% honesty in those jam centres.'

On December 31st, 1940, Lady Denman received a letter from Lord Woolton, Minister of Food:

'I have just seen your Agricultrual Organisers report on the results of the co-operative fruit preservation scheme which was carried out last summer at 2,600 centres set up and managed by your institutes.

I have been very greatly impressed both by the quantity of preserves made and by the enthusiasm and determination with which the members of these centres . . . undertook the formidable task of saving the exceptionally heavy plum crop. . . This was work of national importance, demanding administrative ability of a high order at the Headquarters of your organisation . . . a fine example of democratic action at its best. . .'

The letter was sent by Lady Denman to all Chairmen of the Fruit Preservation Centres. She wrote in an accompanying one: 'The winning of the war depends enormously on the country population. We must all be ready to undertake any job which comes to hand. We countrywomen are fortunate that, owing to our peacetime Women's Institute organisation, we have the machinery through which our efforts can best be used in this time of national crisis. I know that you will not slack in your efforts this year and that as there will be longer time for preparation, the results will be even better than those achieved last summer.'

So it was that Lord Woolton decided to turn this highly successful WI action into a Government spon-

sored scheme for the whole nation. The project fell under the the auspices of the Ministry of Food, but all the central administration work was done by National WI staff, and in the counties by County Federation staff. On Friday, June 6th, 1941, Lord Woolton broadcast a call to the countrywomen of Britain. It was an extraordinary broadcast, presumably delivered in a fairly jaunty manner, but somehow it is difficult to read without hearing an oddly patronising tone:

'I am going to talk about jam, and I can imagine a vast number of women in the towns saying: "I do wish you would get some jam for us instead of talking about it." Well, it isn't to the townsfolk I want to talk, but to the countrywomen – and I want to ask them to join in a great national effort to help us to get a bigger jam ration for everyone. Of course I know that you were all looking forward to making your own jam in your own way, in your own homes. Those of you who have been able to save some sugar will still be able to put a few pans of jam into your store cupboard.

'As Minister of Food I have to be careful to save sugar in order to see that there will be enough to keep up our ration even though the Germans may sink more of our sugar ships. This year I can't do this and give every householder an extra ration for making home made jam. Now that is a fact and we have to except it.

'But nature will produce fruit in your gardens and in many cases the crop will be more than you can use in your homes. I want you to sell this so that we can use every pound of it to make jam for the nation. I have heard of people who have said that if I won't give them the sugar to make their own jam they will let the fruit rot rather than collect it. Well, well, I know they are just feeling disappointed and annoyed – they haven't been bombed as much as some who live and work in towns, and they just haven't thought what they were saying.

'Ladies, come on, we are fighting for our existence; all of us are in this war and we must pull together, sharing our resources. If you are among the fortunate people to whom God has given an excess of the kindly fruits of the earth, so that, as the prayer book puts it, "in due time we may enjoy them", then be thankful that you may take a real part in helping our country's food supplies. Collect the fruit, don't let the sin of waste lie at your door; collect all you can and take it to the communal jam making centre in your area; you will be paid for it and paid quickly . . .

'Last year 2,600 village centres worked under this scheme; already we have 4,500 centres ready this year – ready with their workers, ready with their jam jars, and the covers for them; everything ready for your help in bringing in the fruit.

from old stockings and rags, and even something useful from the tails of their husbands shirts. At Bude, Mrs Julyan quickly became involved: 'I'll tell you what "make-do-and-mend" was, it was making the most of anything – coupons were required for everything then. So we would show people how to make a blouse out of an old dress. When my brother came back from the war, he had grown two inches and put on two stone, so my sister and I moved into his wardrobe. I've still got a grey flannel shirt that was made out of his suits.

'"Make-do-and-mend" was how I came into the WI. We had got married a bit earlier than we intended because my husband was going to be called up, actually he was deferred for sixteen months partly because he was a teacher and partly because he was short-sighted. Anyway, as soon as he had gone, I joined the WI in Bude. It was very difficult to get speakers during the war, so I was asked, as a new member, what did I do. I said I had been a domestic science teacher and was asked if I could do a demonstration. I said, "I can't do a cookery demonstration because a: we have got nothing to cook, and b: we have got no facilities." I think we only had a boiler or something like that.

'"Well, could I do dress-making?" I was asked. Nobody had any material, although dress-making was my second subject. And then I had a brilliant idea! Well, everyone wants to make the most of everything, so I will do "make-do-and-mend". So I gave a "make-do-and-mend" demonstration. It was a phrase which was used all over the country. It started as a naval phrase. They had "make-and-mend". They used to make or mend their clothes or sails.

'I didn't realise at the time, but one of the people present at my demonstration was a member of the County Handicraft Committee and the next thing I was invited to a two-day exhibition, helping the war effort to make the most of everything. There was war-time cookery, war-time jams, and my "make-do-and-mend", and that's how I got onto the County Executive. After the war we made the boys' shirts out of black-out curtains. "make-do-and-mend" was a great thing, but after the war when the "new look" dresses came in – I got mine in London – they were down to the ankles and we were thrilled to pieces about them – they had lots of material, a real luxury.'

Angela Jones writes in the Bryn-y-Maen village scrapbook that her 'first memories start during the war when it was all "make-do-and-mend". In the evenings Mam and Nancy knitted by hand using Welsh wool from Llanwrst. This was coupon-free so we caught the bus on market day. There were two shops in the town and one belonged to Trefiw Woollen Mill and the other to Penmachmo Mill. There were so many ounces per

It was a time to make do, there were coupons for everything. The only war-time exhibition was for 'make-do-and-mend'.

'I spent last Sunday going in to see one of these centres in a remote country village. I saw there the eagerness of good patriotic people, full of enthusiasm because there was a very practical piece of war work for them – and the next day I saw in one of our most bombed cities, heroic women and children who have lost so much and who stand up to the dangers and disasters of war so heroically.

'They want more jam; you women of the country districts can give it to them from the surplus fruit in your gardens. I appeal for your help and I applaud all those who are unselfishly giving their work to increase our food supplies. Good luck to all of you for helping in a grand piece of work.'

Another important contribution to the war effort derived from skills learned in the thrift classes of the pre-war Depression era, which in many villages took the place of craft classes at that time. We see from meeting minutes that members learned how to make felt slippers out of old felt hats and odd remnants, 'not horrors of slovenliness but blockheeled and well fitting, fit to catch the fancy of the most fastidious'. They made 'thrift rugs' person allowed so Mam would go to one and Nancy and me to the other. We had to stand in a queue to get our allocation. We then met each other in the square and checked our shades. As my sister was blind I had to see that the colours matched. We then swopped shops and got another allowance each. Result, enough to knit a twinset, fashionable at the time.'

As had happened during the 1st World War, knitting parties became one of the favourite WI activities, when all sorts of 'comforts' for the troops were made. For example the Handicrafts Sub-Committee of the Durham Federation distributed wool, allocated by the National Service Association, and collected the finished articles. 'By 1942, 2,223 articles, including balaclava helmets, sea boot stockings, scarves and sweaters, as well as a further 1,284 pairs of 'mine sweepers' gloves had been completed. We knitted for ourselves and our families too. Old sweaters and cardigans were unravelled, the wool washed and straightened and reknitted into fair isle jumpers and dresses. Warm woollen stockings in all colours became fashionable and some even knitted vests and knickers. Crocheted curtains appeared at the windows, though owing to the weight of the knitting cotton, they sagged sadly in all the places where we didn't want them to. They disappeared very quickly when terylene curtains came in after the war.

'When Russia entered the war on the allied side and the Baltic Run was one of the most dangerous and uncomfortable duties of the navy, Mrs Churchill opened a fund for "Aid to Russia" to provide fur garments for our own sailors, airmen and also for our allies. We were urged to keep rabbits, eating the meat to supplement our meagre rations and curing the skins which were then to be made into fur jackets, hats and gloves. Classes on "The Curing of Rabbit Skins" and on glove making were held, whilst other skins were sent to National Headquarters for further processing.'

And in villages where troops were stationed, country-women found plenty to keep themselves occupied. Mrs Enid Burden was a schoolgirl at the time, living in a house right on the village railway station at Gainford, near Barnard Castle. The picture drawn by her (from her own memories and her readings from the minute books of the local WI which she later joined) colour a wonderful picture of good will and sheer energy sustained by the tensions of war: 'No bells rang during the war, for the bells were to be a sign of invasion, so our school bell didn't ring all through the war. I remember when it rang for the first time again, it was lovely – you see we'd always had our school bell rung at 9.00 am and 1.00 pm – and even today the whole village listens for it. In those days we lived on the station platform. I loved it,

the station was our garden, though we had a proper garden behind. They took a pride in their stations in those days and won prizes for best-kept station. How I remember it – all the pictures on the wall would be skew wiff, due to the vibrations from the trains. I loved trains. It was noisy I suppose, but you got used to it and there weren't trains through the night except in wartime when there was a lot of activity. I had one brother, two and a half years older than me – we used to put pennies on the line, but we were careful; there was never any worry about safety then.

'The troops were entertained in people's homes at the beginning of the war, before rationing had bitten. Father being the station master had a lot to do with them, a train would come in and he'd get to know who was on it. The village gave a wonderful welcome to the troops.

'Of the soldiers that came to our home, one was a teacher, one was a banker. They used to help me with my homework! and they've kept in touch – mother still gets cards. One of them played the piano. Quite a lot of village girls married troops. I can think of half a dozen girls who married troops in the village. It was nice, you see, there was no aggro – these were boys who were dying to get into a home having just left their Mums – and sit in front of a fire. Now, I see from the war-time WI minutes that we had a committee for the evacuees and a committee for obtaining clothes for evacuees if they'd been bombed out. They would come to us from Teesside, Wearside and Tyneside. But by then I was at my grammar school. And we had a First Aid Post, a whist drive for wool to knit for the army boys – how much do you think it raised? Twelve shillings, a lot of money in those days. Then of course the Produce Guild was formed.

'Here are some of the 1940 evacuee survey forms. Something about the WI working with the WVS – they helped with whatever was needed. We had two ladies collecting salvage all the time. They had a horse and cart – cans, whatever they could get and they didn't care what it was provided it could be recycled. In 1940, sugar was made available by the National Executive for communal jam making. Again in 1940 we held a stirrup pump demonstration – a bucket of water and a pump for dowsing fires. Having troops here meant we were at risk – everywhere there were buckets of sand. But we were very sheltered. You could hear the planes flying overhead and one or two crashed on the hills, but we didn't have any bombing. Now, Christmas 1940: twenty soldiers were invited to a party, provided with sweets and cigarettes – music dancing and carols. Then a YMCA started in the village hall and they could get rations so lots of us helped with that and it became a

Left and above: *The station master's house at Gainford – then and now.*
Right: *Mrs Victoria Peart, the station master's wife, would watch the soldiers arrive at the garrison town: 'My son was abroad and I knew people were being kind to him, so I thought I'd be kind to the soldiers here . . . As time went on you didn't have the food. I used to bake everything – four out of five days in the week the table would be full of home-made things.'*

NAAFI. There were bandaging competitions. Refreshments at meetings abandoned in 1941 because of rationing. Tea to be reintroduced at meetings but supplied by members. Another party the next year: twenty soldiers invited, double came. The following March members held a sock darning competition for servicemen's socks. The report doesn't say whether the socks had to be washed but the lady who won the competition was my mother! 1942, the Land Army were invited to the meeting. 1942, another soldiers' Christmas party for twenty-four soldiers . . . 1943, a blood donor's scheme, food demonstrations, "make-do-and-mend" schools.

The winner of the soldiers' sock darning competition, Enid's mother Mrs Peart, is now in her 90s and still lives in Gainford: 'I was born on Diamond Jubilee Day, that's why I'm called Victoria. At the start – in the station house – we had no light in the bedrooms and there was just gas downstairs and the toilet was at the back, right past the offices. And the bath was in the kitchen, and we had a very old-fashioned fireplace with a plate along the top and we would cook on that. And there was a crack in the bottom of the oven and you had to bake in that, but you would have to allow for the crack – it used to take me all day to bake. And when the man came from the rail company that owned the house I asked him for a proper range. I'd been baking that day and I had all the things I'd baked on the table top over the bath. The man said, "I think there can't be much wrong with the old one," as he looked at all the baking. I could have cheerfully hit him. Now my son, he wasn't a bold little boy, but he said, "Well, my mummy doesn't tell lies." I remember that. They didn't relent, though they replaced it later.

'During the war I'd go down to the YMCA to help cook for the soldiers. We did a lot of work for the soldiers. I used to bake everything – four out of five days in the week the table would be full of home-made things. We had some glorious times, mind you it was a busy time too. My son was abroad you see and I knew people were being kind to him, so I thought I would be kind to the boys here.

'I used to go in for all the WI competitions. I loved darning and the soldiers socks. Well, that time I got 1st prize, I was thrilled! You had to take your own soldiers' socks along. I also won a competition for bandaging – I was so keen on First Aid I went to private classes in the village, but if anyone started talking about bones I'd be on the floor. If a saw a skeleton I was all right, but as soon as they started talking about bones I was on the floor. I could work on things but I couldn't bear hearing about them. I'd always have to sit at the end of the bench in case the bones came in. I couldn't overcome that.'

Ernest Bevin and Winston Churchill acknowledged the institutes' war work at a special conference in 1943. Nottingham County Federation's delegate was one Mrs Herbert. This is her report, an excellent expression of the atmosphere and spirit of a day: 'Saw nine Land Army girls and sat next to the Vice-Chairman of the Dorset Federation. Commenced with "the King", Mr Bevin welcomed us on behalf of the Government and said it was an historic gathering, the first in history. The sun of victory was rising and he must ask for greater effort. Women tipped the balance between victory and defeat. There are two million more people in industry than at the beginning of the war, all because of the women. They had confounded our enemies. In 1939 we stood alone, forty-six million against two hundred million. We had won the respect of the world. They had called the conference first to thank us and then to tell us of their difficulties. The last great effort had to be made. Tell your friends that we shall not do anything that is not absolutely necessary. More buses on the road meant more clippies – help these girls all you can. Lord Woolton has a difficult task, the coming autumn and spring will be the toughest part of the war.

'Mr Churchill said the enemy hoped we would grow weary but no community in the world was better organised than ours. We were ready for any form of air attack, ready to grow more food, make more munitions and more ships, care for the sick and wounded and maintain civilian life. This would not be possible but for the women.

'Miss Dorothy Elliott proposed a vote of thanks saying to Mr Churchill, "For many years your voice has called us to heights we never believed we could attain. You have taken us into your confidence and set the seal on the status of women in the war effort. We are grateful to you for letting us see you and you have our full support and affection. Women never took kindly to the saying, "men must work and women must weep" but, Sir, you men must not say after the war, that women are too old at thirty-five. We women hate war and we shall find our fullest opportunity for service in the peace for if you cannot win the war without women, neither can you win the peace.'

And this was the hope of countrywomen everywhere. As in the first War, women had taken on roles previously held only by men, not just in factories, but in those seats of local Government that the WI had been pressuring to fill with their members since the early days of the Movement. Women had filled vacancies on Parish Councils and similar bodies and they had dominated many of the committees and temporary organisations that the upheaval in everyday life had made necessary.

'If anyone started talking about bones I'd be on the floor.'

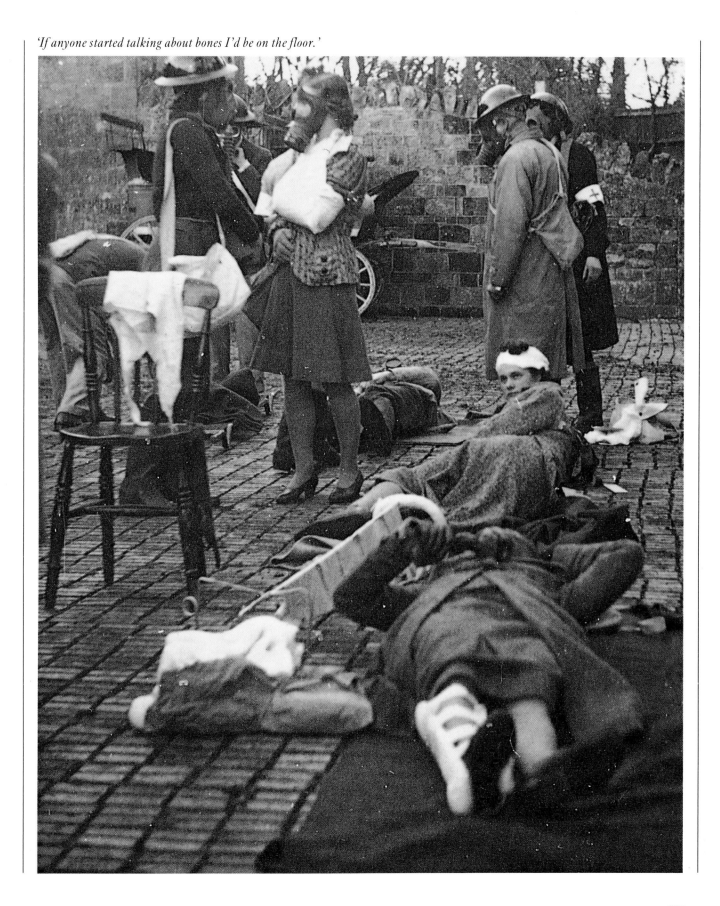

Chapter Nine

PLANNING FOR A NEW AGE

*'Some planners believe that the
ordinary small village has no future.'*
LADY DENMAN

*Countess Albemarle. 'Lady Denman was determined I would
be her successor because I stood up to her, and she loved that.'*

'The women who started the WI had enthusiasm, originality and organising ability, and they were slightly idealistic . . . There was a feeling that if you had the privilege of education, and the privilege of position, you wanted to give it back, you wanted to give other people the opportunities you had.

'Lady Denman was a splendid person but terrifying! I had had no education, left school at sixteen, so I was absolutely stunned when I found myself side-by-side with these people on the National Executive. I remember Lady Denman looking down the table at the first committee I attended with a friend of mine, Joan Yeo – we had both been elected at the same time. She looked at us and said, "Lady Brunner and Mrs Yeo, to what do you attribute your success in getting onto this committee?" It

absolutely flummoxed me, I can't remember how I got through that one.'

Lady Elizabeth Brunner, Chairman 1951-1955

'Mrs Watt? I admired her, but I could not bear working with her. She was just too woolly where Lady Denman had clear judgement and great precision. What I find interesting is that I don't think Lady Denman would ever have started the WI; you had to have some darling old bumbler like Mrs Watt. Lady Denman would have frightened village people. They wouldn't have understood anyone of her stature. She was immensely respected, but she was not loved in the way that Elizabeth Brunner was loved, as a person, as a warm person. She was looked up to enormously and was very valuable.

'Miss Hadow was an academic. She looked like a bean pole, very tall and angular with pince-nez, but attractive and funny, and gay, and sweet. I would love to have known her better.

'Lady Denman and Mrs Watt worked in totally different ways, but they were both absolutely necessary, and I think that Miss Hadow was a sort of king pin in between, because she was more approachable than Lady Denman by a long chalk, but had all the precision of the academic.'

Miss Nancy Tennant, Vice-Chairman, 1940-1948

Now, at the end of the War and nearly thirty years after first being elected to the Chair, Lady Denman decided it was time to step down, her resolve strengthened by the belief that she had found, in Countess Albemarle, the right successor. At the first AGM after the war, which took place at the Albert Hall in May 1946, it fell to her Vice Chairman, Nancy Tennant, to announce her retirement – 'Two things I must say, first, that although Lady Denman would wish the success of the Movement to be attributed to the work of the members as a whole – and in that she is right – yet I am certain that it would never have acquired the character it has without her . . . Secondly I must say something about her influence as Chairman of the National Executive Committee. She has not always suffered us gladly if we were foolish, but her criticism has been of the kind that not only left no sting, but spurred us on to do better; and no one has been more generous with praise where praise was due . . .'

'I had to say that she had not suffered fools gladly,' recalls Miss Tennant today, 'but one could say that to her. She didn't mind. She was quite ready to have that. She laughed. I did, I hope, say it in an ungrudging way, but I thought one had to take her as she was and I had immense respect for her gifts and her qualities.'

The immediate adminstrative problem to which the new Executive turned was the war-time fall-off in membership. As Miss Meriel Withal, then Assistant to the General Secretary of the WI (Dame Frances Farrer), recalls, 'A lot of the WIs round the coast had been suspended – it was simply too difficult for them to carry on.' But now there was a huge effort to expand and welcome back into the Movement women who had joined the forces or left to become more directly involved in the war effort than the WI allowed.

'I take credit for the fact that after the war there was a great influx of new members because after the war when Lady Albemarle was Chairman of the organisation, we hatched between us a plan. We wrote to all the Counties saying would they please review all the institutes that are suspended and make plans to get them started again as soon as you can. And this they did, and the membership increased dramatically.

'During the war and towards the end of the war Headquarters was run on strictly Civil Service lines. Dame Frances Farrer, as she became, was the daughter of a civil servant. All of the Farrer family were eminent civil servants. Her sister was married to the Secretary to the Cabinet at that time. It was a model of Government. At the end of the war the VCOs were kept particularly busy starting up all these new WIs, or restarting the WIs, and with a shortage of petrol many went round on bicycles. There is one celebrated VCO in Cambridge who is reputed to have bicycled 1,000 miles a year.'

Post-war England was an exciting place. Relief at the cessation of fighting mingled with anticipation of great new things in the future. 'Before the war people hadn't moved away from the village,' one war-time member recalls. 'Then they were called up, they went somewhere else, they saw different things, different standards, everything was moving, and I think it was that that sparked off a move to modernisation.' Again, evacuation, Land Army movements – all had jogged people's minds into making comparisons between the conditions and lifestyle of different villages and towns.

The remarkable thing about the 2nd War was that people were planning for its end almost as soon as it began: 'Government plans for the land and for building are already in progress,' Lady Denman had written to the Counties on August 27th, 1941. She wanted to be sure that the institutes would be wholly involved when the time came – 'Our members have ideas on what sort of houses should be built and how they should be arranged on the needs of the water supply, drainage, sewerage and electricity.

'We shall be finding answers to many questions.'

In 1944, 3,500 institutes responded to a survey which brought to the attention of Parliament and other public authorities the sometimes horrifying conditions that obtained in villages as a result of poor water supply and lack of proper sanitation. Besides questionnaires, residential schools were held to consider and discuss 'the Future of the Village', and in 1950 a pamphlet was published called *Your Village* which summed up the results of a yet more comprehensive survey of conditions of village life carried out a year earlier; nearly 7,000 institutes participated.

The 1949 survey posed twenty questions on a variety of subjects such as bus services, water, sewerage and electricity services, village surgeries and village halls, telephones, midwifery and 'home helps' services – all issues on which institutes had campaigned in the pre-war years. The responses indicated great differences among villages. For example in two counties –

Anglesey and Radnor – the majority of institutes put a better electricity supply at the head of their list of priorities, while the vast majority of villages now had a supply of some sort.

Ten years earlier Mrs Bailey of Blackdown in Dorset had complained that Britain was a backwater by comparison with other members of the Commonwealth: 'It is funny to think that my sister who lives in Australia, is more in touch with things than we are. She can call the flying doctor when needed to her house by wireless in no time and has her telephone, whereas we have nothing up to date except our wireless.

'For us who have no gas substitute, electricity would be an enormous boon, first for making an early cup of tea, then for preparing breakfast, heating hot water for washing up, and preparing the dinner, perhaps an electric fire in the sitting room, an electric boiler for washing, and not by any means least, the electric iron. As it is we light a stick fire for our early cup of tea, the copper for hot water, then the range for breakfast. That is three fires to be lit. When I have a good fire for cook-ing and could heat my irons, I have no time for ironing . . . Think how nice it would be not to have that hot range in our room, especially in the summer weather.

'And when night comes, I have seen my house burnt and most of my treasures perish by fire: and now that the children are grown up and go to bed as late as we do, many is the time I have gone along to make sure they have not gone to sleep and left their candles burning. Think what a joy it would be to know that the light could not fall over.

'Our farm is down in the fields and though our WI meetings are at full moon, there are many other occasions when we have to grope our way home. As I come stumbling through those fields, I think what a difference it would make to have a light outside the house to make for and to light one the last bit of the way . . . Surely the first need is to see that those who live in the country in outlying districts are not penalised by having to pay such a huge price for electricity.'

Thanks to information gathered by the institutes and pressure exerted on the Government by the National Executive, conditions had much improved by 1949, but as

The old village pump at Dufton in the shadow of Dufton Pike, centre of the Pennine Way, a favourite spot for walkers.

Mrs Jeffrys of the Glamorgan Federation, speaking in 1952 about the vital importance of electricity in the agricultural industry, pointed out, there were still great differences in conditions between one place and another: 'There is a farm high on a ridge overlooking a river estuary; twenty miles of twinkling lights face the farmer night and morning as he carries his oil lamps across the yard to the milking shed. His farm is one of a group left stranded in a narrow gap between two terminal points. Between them, from an area of about 800 acres, they supply 1,500 gallons of milk weekly to the Milk Marketing Board. Most of them have Attested herds with all the extra attention that this involves – and no electricity – "feather-bed farming" indeed!

'Contrast this with the lot of the farmer who broadcast recently on what electricity does for him. It lights his buildings, milks his cows, washes and sterilises his bottles, and dries off grass and cereals for his stock. It saves him the wages of a farm-hand. If he had taken us into the kitchen I dare say we should have seen all those domestic helps which are invaluable to a busy woman.'

Again, it would be some twenty-five years (1962) before members of Llangernyw in North Wales could boast of an electricity supply: 'No more oil lamps to be filled or wicks to be cleaned or lamp glasses to be washed. No more candles, no more ironing with the old flat iron. No need to hand pluck chickens, turkeys and geese, except wings and tail feathers. No more beating or mixing of cake ingredients by hand. No more sweeping of carpets and staircarpets with hand brush and tray. No more warmed bricks heated in oven and covered with flannel, or hot water bottles for cold feet (electric blankets instead).'

And it was not until three years after this that electricity was brought to the church, and farms and houses lying on the fringes of Dufton in Cumbria. Even then it was recorded in the village scrapbook that 'there is not a complete sewerage scheme. Although all the houses have water laid on, some have not got water closets.'

There were some encouraging statistics in the *Your Village* survey, however. For example, by 1949 only 701 villages out of 6,600 were without a telephone kiosk, a statistic for which the WI could justly claim credit - but basic amenities, such as mains water and sewerage systems, had barely improved at all from the shocks of the survey five years earlier.

In 1949, out of some 6,200 villages, 4,097 were without a sewerage scheme, and the reports given of conditions in some of these villages do not make pretty reading. At Kingsland in Herefordshire, sewage ran into an open drain down the village street. The same was true of Woodborough in Nottinghamshire. In the flat county of Lincolnshire, contaminated water from cesspools lay in pools in and round the village of Willingham. At St Buryan in Cornwall, with a population of 1,200, there was no sewerage scheme and some houses were even without a garden or land in which to dispose of the contents of earth closets. In Bowburgh, Norfolk, there were nine cottages housing twenty-five people with a piece of ground not eleven yards square where garbage and latrine contents would be buried and sink water emptied. Stilton in Huntingdonshire had no sewerage scheme and no night soil cart – the sewage from twenty-two new Council houses ran down an open dyke at the side of the road and 'the smell is dreadful'. Snaith in the West Riding of Yorkshire, with a population of 1,500, reported that in part of the village 'ashpits and earth closets are emptied periodically by day; the contents are wheeled in a barrow to the top of a street, leaving its trail on the way. This is dumped in a heap and eventually piled into a wagon. The stench is terrible for days after and houses round about swarm with flies.'

Mrs Gilgannon, who now lives in Amble in Northumberland, in those days lived nearby in a village called Radcliffe, now no more than a name on a map. 'Radcliffe was a mining village for years and years. They knocked it down because they wanted to open cast mine the coal. All the people were moved to a new estate in Amble (but we still call ourselves Radcliffe WI). For the first time in their lives (this was in the early '70s) they had proper bathrooms and inside toilets. I lived in Radcliffe; I knew what it was like. We had come from Scotland, and believe me we hadn't seen anything like it before. We had an outside toilet with an ash pit – there was an ash pit between two toilets, back to back as it were. A man used to come along once a week or once a fortnight and shovel everything into a cart and away. It was horrible. They called them netties. But funnily enough, Radcliffe was one of the most healthy places to live, though in summer it was a bit nifty!'

Lady Brunner recalls how ordinary countrywomen in the Chiltern villages valued proper bathroom facilities: 'I remember Mrs Johnson, up Rocky Lane – her husband was an agricultural worker – saying, "An indoor WC would be worth five shillings a week on my rent." Well, her rent was probably only five shillings!'

In the same year as the '49 village survey, Perranuthnoe and District WI, Cornwall, made a special plea for proper sanitation in rural schools, and today Mrs Pat Jacob JP (Chairman, 1974-1976), recalls that the problem was widespread: 'When I joined the WI in 1948 – Hallen and Henbury, just five miles outside the boundaries of Bristol – I was a school correspondent in the village. One of my jobs was in the infant school. They used ordinary buckets to go to the lavatory, and my job was to get a village man to collect the pails once a week, dig a hole in his own garden, upset the pail into his garden, cover it all over and take the bucket back – this was in 1948! Even at that stage, so near a very large city! I had to pay this man so much a week to take the bucket, dig a hole in his garden and empty it all in. If you had had it in the middle of Northumberland you might not have been so surprised, but this was a few miles from Bristol in Gloucestershire.' One can only add a word of sympathy for the poor man whose garden ended up as repository for the waste.

As a result of Perranuthnoe's 1949 resolution, which called for emergency measures (immediate small-scale schemes as stage one of a comprehensive scheme), the Minister of Health, Aneurin Bevan, agreed to examine specially urgent cases as reported by the WI. Too often in the past ministry officials had tried to justify action only on a platform of economic efficiency. This was the fundamental problem in providing services of any kind to outlying rural areas. For example, in 1930, a Mr Taylor from the Ministry of Health (an engineering inspector) had stated at the AGM that people who lived in isolated areas should have to pay whatever it cost to link them to a supply of water. The unfairness of such a policy had shaped the WI response, which was to call for the adequate provision of water, sewerage and electricity services in both country and town. The resolution,

proposed by the Essex Federation in 1943, made provision of these services a national responsibility – just as earlier they had called for a re-definition of the rural telephones service as an 'essential amenity'. Miss Christy for Essex used the analogy of the postal service: 'This plan will very likely be termed nationalisation of these services, and to the Faint Hearts who fear that means Domination and Dictatorship, I would point out that it is simply the same idea as our Postal System which has stood the test of time for almost a century.'

Inadequate supplies of water had been a constant feature of AGM resolutions since the late 1920s. In 1930, the villagers of the Berkshire Downs had complained that during the dry weather of the previous summer they 'had to pump for several minutes and pump hard before they could get a single bucket of water, besides being faced with the perpetual anxiety that the supply would fail altogether.' And in many similar districts – the Chilterns, the Cotswolds – we know that the same sort of conditions prevailed and people often had to pay as much as threepence for one

bucket of water at that time.

Frequently, the emphasis of complaints was on the health hazards of supply. A Cornish member recalls 'a story about an old man who lived in a village near St Austell and he had his own well in the garden, and he always drank that water. Then one day he was rushed into hospital and all the time he complained about the water there, he hated drinking the water in the hospital. And when he went home, in six weeks he was dead, because the well water was actually contaminated and the spell in hospital had deprived him of his immunity.'

In 1930, the lack of an adequate water supply could seriously affect a farmer's livelihood, as Mrs Griffiths of Anglesey pointed out – Mrs Griffiths: 'I am here to speak for Anglesey. . .The supply of water is almost altogether wells, and it is carried in buckets. It is carried very far. It makes the work of the farmer far more difficult. It makes the work of the farmer's wife far more difficult. It makes the work of the women who make their living by laundry very difficult. It hinders the work of the district nurse. It holds up sanitation and the absence of sanitation in the schools is a menace to the children's health. I do not know how the women of Anglesey have such spotless homes. It is a wonderful tribute to them and to their hard work. We believe in Anglesey that cleanliness is next to godliness, but I think the want of a water supply makes it very difficult for us.'

In one Cambridgeshire village, a Mrs Stacy claimed that 'brown paper is used largely in maternity cases to save washing, a very insanitary state of affairs.' And Mrs Adams of the Yorkshire Federation, speaking at the 1930 AGM stated: 'I have had concrete cases where the women used the water for washing one day and had to pass it on to their neighbour the next day for her washing. . . the housewife has to go to that awful thing the village pump to get her water, the pump round which there is so much of story, song and gossip; that is what we want to do away with. . . I thought there would be no opposition to this resolution [which urged WIs to press County Councils to form Regional Water Committees] and yet yesterday I came across a delegate who told me that at a village close to her they would not have a water scheme. When asked the reason, the reply was, "Why, it's only parson and doctor that wants a bath!" It rather

Far Left: *The site where the village of Radcliffe once stood.* Right: *Water and sewerage 'cheek by jowl' at Eastgate – these services were far and away the worst supplied to villagers in post-war Britain and had been so for a long time. By the '30s some people had even become convinced that a proper sewerage system was not necessary – Mrs Methuen, Wilts Federation, 1937: 'We do not want you all to go home and think that every village should and must have sewage taken away in pipes . . . There are many, many places where it never can be done, and where very old fashioned and simple disposal methods work admirably.' But when the WI nation-wide survey of 1949 showed the truly dreadful conditions that obtained in many places, the WI campaign reached new peaks. By 1956, the institutes were able to turn attention* (left) *to other, related matters. The resolution by Littleham WI in Devon led to the removal of turnstiles from public lavatories on the basis that they 'deny access to those most in need of access (the blind, the near blind and the aged). Then,' added Mrs Clarke of Littleham, 'there are the stout. . .'*

reminded me of that good old Yorkshire story of the Yorkshire woman who was told by the inspector she must not use the water from a certain well, it was contaminated. She said, "Well, I think nowt of new water: it has neither taste nor smell."'

By 1949, 1,468 villages out of 6,470 surveyed, were without a water supply of any sort, and among those villages which had a supply, many were still inadequate.

Many reports spoke of taps which ran dry at certain seasons of the year, certain hours of the day, or certain positions along the pipe-line; of villages where only a few houses were connected and where most housewives had to fetch water from a stand tap which often froze in winter. At Hawkesbury Upton in Gloucestershire there were no taps or sinks in most workers' houses: water had to be carried from street taps nearly a mile to some houses; dirty water was thrown outside. In Dorset there were several villages with mains water where almost all women still carried water from street taps because the cost of connecting to the mains supply was so high. Braunton in Devon found its main water supply totally inadequate when summer visitors added to the population; in 1949 the supply failed and the village, without warning, was supplied from the river into which sewage was drained; an immediate epidemic followed and one village doctor had to look after 300 patients alone.

Villages without a mains water supply depended mainly on wells, often inadequate and rarely pure. Langham in Norfolk spoke of 'vermin infested wells'. The wells in the village of Hardwick in Oxfordshire were all nearly dry, and Sykes Junction near Saxilby in Lindsey (Lincolnshire) had to rely on a well which was 'appalling' and from which every drop of water had to be boiled. Ripe and Chalvington in Sussex depended on shallow surface wells, unfit for drinking and often situated in gardens where 'night soil must be buried'. Breconshire commented that 'it is curious that we export millions of gallons of water to other counties but our own villages are badly served and even where there is a main supply, it is often inadequate.'

Having helped take these basic amenities into the responsibility of Government, by way of nationalisation, many members of WI now look with some concern at Government action to privatise them again, especially the water supply. The principle of responsibility is, after all, the same now as it was in the '40s; there remains the feeling that essential services should not be subject to market forces, and there are additional worries in their ownership by foreign companies – Mrs Batty Shaw: 'I think that water is such a basic commodity and the care of water and the care of land drainage and all the things that are connected with the environment are things that are so important that it is dangerous to let them out into private ownership of companies abroad. . . I would suppose that the present membership of the WI will be expressing their concern.'

In June 1989, NFWI's position is described by Mrs Joan Davies, Chairman of Environment and Public Affairs: 'We have to be realistic about how to tackle this issue – we are unlikely to be able to change this Government's mind about privatisation. However, we have been invited to put forward nominations for representation on the Regional Water Authority Consumer Committees, and once we have WI members on these committees you can be sure that we will work the system to the benefit of users. Members' concern is in the area of health and the possible unequal division of costs for improved supply among users in different areas, however isolated they may be.'

In the 1940s there was a two-fold concern – first that a line should be drawn for 'adequate provision', a line below which supplies and amenities would be absolutely unacceptable. 'Adequate provision' was evidenced in the WI house. This was a house designed to suit the basic requirements of a rural family consisting of father, mother and three young children, and 37,000 WI members travelled to the 1951 Daily Mail Ideal Home Exhibition in Olympia to see it.

The second concern was that the post-war planners soon to become engaged in huge building programmes for new houses, new estates, even new towns, should proceed with an eye for conservation.

In those days 'planning and development' had an optimistic ring about it; many needed housing as never before – Mrs Ellis, Avelon, Gifford: 'I come from a blitzed village. We lost eleven houses in the blitz and we have waited a year and still not got a site. The first site in mind, the Council wanted for a by-pass in twenty years time. The next site the farmer wanted as valuable agricultural land. The respresentatives of the Minister have paid various visits to this village, rushed from one hill-top to another, or should I say they meandered, that is a better term; they go back to their headquarters and ponder over it, and it seems to take months when they ponder.'

Mrs Black, East Suffolk Federation: 'We have one of the most fertile strips of land in East Anglia, and our farmers are working hard against very great odds of labour shortage with no chance of getting more help until we have more houses. One of the cottages was demolished by a bomber crashing on it and now this one is about to become derelict . . . We are determined to leave no stone unturned until we do get our workers' houses built in our own village.'

Miss Sylvia Gray, who had a hotel in Burford at the time was also Chairman of the Housing Committee, the

Planning Committee, and Vice Chairman of the Whitney Rural District Council and became closely involved with post-war planning, as well as being active in the WI, of course: 'In those days new houses were being built all the time, and I was also organising the modernisation of properties and amenities at the same time. You see nothing had been done through all the war years. It was a time of catching up. This was also the time that the big Council house boom was going forward. There was a great shift and change in population brought about by the war. A lot of people who had gone into the army now came back here and wanted homes. Many used to arrive at the back door of the hotel in those days saying how absolutely "done" they were for accommodation – could I get them on the housing list, what was their chance of getting a house, and so on. Being on the Council I was forever going to

Reading to try and get an allocation of "houses to let" – getting allocations, that was the great thing. And then we had the building programme itself – we had the job of getting builders to build Council houses. If the builders wouldn't co-operate, you had a problem. But as Chairman of Housing I had control of building licenses of course – I remember I held a meeting in Whitney and invited all the builders in the area and said that if they wouldn't co-operate and build their share of Council houses then I wasn't going to give them a licence to build anything else. I got the MBE for that at the end of the war, for working on the Housing Authority. We brought a new generation to Burford, and to the WI.'

Despite – because of – all the excitement there was a note of caution in Lady Denman's final address as Chairman, which in the context reads as an extraordinarily perceptive vision: 'Just one word about the future.

Blanchland, Northumberland: the beauty of the old with all the convenience of the new – no wires, no cables, everything piped in.

Planning is the order of our age – and some planners believe that the ordinary small village has no future and that people can only be happy if they live in a community with a population of two or three thousand.

'Some of us, on the other hand, believe that a village with a few hundred inhabitants is a good place to live in – providing of course, that water and electricity, which farms must have, are taken to the villages as well, and that the children can get to a good school. It is of the utmost importance that institute members should realise that within the next few years, or perhaps within the next few months, plans may be made for the future of their village. I believe that this is the moment for country people to consider this problem from every point of view – the needs of agriculture, the employment likely to be available in the future, the demands of the cities, the advantages and disadvantages of living in a small community – and then to make their views known to all the planners, in the district, in the county, in the region, and in the national Government. For after all, we country people have experience behind us; we have enjoyed a great heritage, and we must do our share in ensuring that in years to come the value and the delight of the country are not lost to our successors.'

Lady Denman was only re-iterating a strongly felt principle in her organisation. Even in 1938 there had been concern expressed about the planning of new developments – 'We are countrywomen and our home is the countryside. We live there and bring up our children there . . . A small development in the wrong place can destroy a whole district of many square miles.' And even this expression of concern by Mrs Granville Streatfield of the West Kent Federation had a precedent, for conservation had been a theme of WI planning policy since 1928 when members called for the use of natural resources of a locality when building new houses – 'in Westmoreland, stone and slate; in Oxfordshire and Warwickshire, red brick and thatch; in Cambridgeshire, half timber, in order [that] houses may harmonise with their surroundings.'

Conservation is a concept that goes to the core of the WI Movement. It is not simply an in-built resistance to change, it harks back to 'the green and pleasant land' of its anthem – William Blake's *Jerusalem*. And if, in the business of planning and development, the WI looks to nature for aesthetic guidance, there is also a sense in which a desire to preserve natural beauty lies at the heart of all WI policy, a primitive prompting if you like of an organisation born of the soil and dedicated to preserving its heritage. Let that go, and the values enshrined in the WI constitution — truth, fellowship, tolerance and justice — will very soon follow.

So it is that issues such as the preservation of wild

In 1938 the WI called upon the Government to start a Ministry of the Environment. Fifty years later, members of Caster and Ailsworth, two villages whose history had been linked since Saxon times, stood firm over a development which threatened to turn their villages into one. 'On the development site stands the oldest house in Castor, already on the list of ancient buildings. To the left stands a very fine dovecote complete with lantern tower and nesting place for 300 birds. Linking the two is a perfect example of old English walling studded with wooden blocks, once used for the training of fruit trees. Rising majestically behind the house is a magnificent 200-year-old walnut tree.'

flowers and footpaths are as important to local institutes as the big international pollution issues or the national campaign in 1954 – perhaps the WI's most visible success ever – to Keep Britain Tidy (now the Tidy Britain Group), which began as a resolution from the Northumberland Federation and went on to become a nationwide effort involving the giants of industry.

Back in 1938, the organisation's first big planning success was built around the theme of conservation and the preservation of natural beauty. Mrs Granville Streatfield had been talking in support of a resolution which served to spearhead a campaign that eventually culminated in The National Parks and Access to the Countryside Act of 1949. The Act helped to preserve large swathes of countryside as areas of special beauty. There are now seven National Parks in England and three in Wales, and developments in these areas are subject to special standards. In addition, a number of Areas of Outstanding Beauty have been designated by the Countryside Commission, and Local Authorities are expected to protect these against unnecessary and unsuitable development. Increasingly they are under pressure to maintain them as sacrosanct.

This is what she said: 'The land is our national heritage. But during the last few years much of the beauty of it, many thousands of our agricultural food-producing acres have been destroyed or converted to uses which are not always for the welfare of our nation. The object of this resolution is to prevent ill-considered interference with the essential needs of the countryside . . . For instance in my own county, it is proposed to drive a huge arterial road right through one of the most beautiful valleys in the south of England, cutting up the farms separating the farm buildings from the land and stock, when a good alternative is available . . .'

The upholding of the long established policy on the protection of the Green Belt was of particular interest to Bricket Wood WI when members proposed a resolution at the 1987 Autumn Council meeting of the Hertfordshire WI. The Resolution was supported by an overwhelming majority and forwarded to the NFWI. The

resolution read, 'This Institute welcomes the Government's increased support for Local Authority policies concerning Green Belt and Green Field Sites. It urges the need for further strengthening of these policies, particularly for developments adjacent to the M25 and other Motorways.'

Bricket Wood lays no claim to being a picture postcard village, but has a strong sense of its semi-rural identity. This is where Sunday schools would once come in special trains for their 'days out'. The village is surrounded by some of the oldest woodland common in England, but over the past few years has suffered major upheavals due to the widening of the M1 and the building of the M25 motorways. The piece of land threatened with development as a huge shopping centre is farmed agricultural land (though not top grade), and there are two public footpaths which are used by residents frequently – one would have had to be diverted to skirt a huge car-park in the proposed development.

'There had been a village meeting in 1983 to inform residents about the proposed developments,' recalls

A desire to preserve beauty lies at the heart of all WI policy . 'Conservation is a positive thing.' Mrs Greensmith, Mount Rayleigh.

Mrs Harrington, 'but as time went by, the urgency faded.' In January 1988, Mrs Vera Green invited members to her house to discuss a campaign and to alert villagers to the fact that the Enquiry would take place in February or March, and time was running short.

'Five WI members and one non-member met at Mrs Green's,' continues Mrs Harrington, 'and within two weeks leaflets were ready and a public meeting had been called to inform, and lead the opposition to the developers' plans.' They called the campaign SOCEM – 'Save Our Community from Environmental Mess'.

'Much to our surprise, people flooded to the meeting, and some had to stand outside; the windows were left open so that they could hear. One or two other village representatives spoke, but mostly it was SOCEM members – each one concentrating on a particular

aspect, for example road congestion, pollution, over-development, and erosion of the Green Belt. We were taken aback by the overwhelming support, and donations to pay for more leaflets, and coaches to take people to the Town Hall to picket on the first and last days of the Enquiry. During the six weeks of the Public Enquiry someone from Bricket Wood was in the public section every single day.'

In 1989 Mrs Harrington's good faith and the work of the WI was rewarded: 'We won the case. The developers are now appealing to the House of Lords, but we have been told it is almost certain that the original decision will not be reversed. The major reason for their appeal is that costs of about £200,000 were awarded against them. That is what it cost the Council. Apparently this is the first time such an award has been made and this is

Cornish hedgerows, buttercups and wild honeysuckle. Since 1937, the WI has waged a campaign against the destruction of wild flowers. In 1975, with the passing of the Wild Plant Act, they were successful.

the reason for them going to the House of Lords.'

A year earlier, village members living near the Berkshire boom towns of Newbury, Reading and Bracknell, the M4's 'golden corridor' – the 'high-tech' industrial belt that is the subject of massive development due to its proximity to London, and to Heathrow airport in particular – share the views of their predecessors in the Movement and are no less vociferous in championing them. Here, in Berkshire, the County Council plan to allow a further 36,000 homes to be built by 1996, and the Department of the Environment wants them to plan for 7,000 more. In the village of Winkfield, members of the WI meet in a hall adjacent to an estate now being developed by Ideal Homes. 'Two hundred and eighty houses on twenty-eight acres just across the road. If you're going to have that sort of development it is going to be sheer hell to live in,' says one member. 'Villages have a tradition and once that's gone and there's only towns left I think there's a lot that people will miss in life,' says a second. 'I'm very very in favour of the green and pleasant land that we've been singing about. And if you're going to build thousands – and I mean thousands – of houses on this green and pleasant land then the villages have now gone.'

Their worry, the worry of conservationists up and down the country in areas of new development, is that there is no morality implicit in a policy of development left to market forces. Yet it is largely 'the market' which is in control. The market decides that areas around the M4 'golden corridor' will be developed fit to bust, while other areas far to the north ache for the opportunity to build houses, factories, offices and attract work to old industrial landscapes.

Such a policy of land development puts an impossible burden of trust upon developers and local authorities. As one of the speakers in 1938 had said, 'The Town Planning Act is all very well for councils of millionaires with hearts of gold.'

Again, the voices of early WI campaigners find clear echoes in that of Mrs Barbara Darvill, present Chairman of West Kent, a county that has had to contend with more development than most since the end of the War:

Dartmoor, protected since the passing in 1949 of the National Parks Act, for which the WI campaigned from 1938.

Far left: *Two ladies from Ketton WI clear a stream. The 1954 'litter' resolution was developed by Lady Brunner into the 'Keep Britain Tidy' campaign, now called 'The Tidy Britain Group'.* 'They gave me the OBE for keeping Britain tidy,' recalls Lady Brunner. 'Lord Attlee was a great support, and we got Butlins and coach companies and members of industry in on the thing.' Right: *The Bricket Wood site.* Below: *The Settle-Carlisle rail route, saved in April 1989 by the 5-year campaign of Dentdale WI.*

'We are very worried about Kent becoming a concrete corridor and we have become very involved. We are members of Kent Rural Voice. Rural Voice, both nationally and at county level, is an amalgamation of a number of different organisations interested in rural communities. We come together as Rural Voice, and we have been present at many meetings and our concern about the Channel tunnel has been made known. In the early days we opposed the Channel tunnel; then when we realised that it was a *fait accompli* we started to look at how it was going to affect the county. We have lobbied members of Parliament, we have done all we can to try and see what we can do to make it as least damaging as possible. If you spend much time in Kent, you will find that our roads are virtually at saturation point already. As you know, the M25 was obsolete before it was opened practically, and the M25 has brought a lot more people into the county, and because of this, property prices have escalated. And what we are finding, if you live in rural areas, is that developers are knocking on doors if you have a garden even half an acre. I mean, we only have a a third of an acre and they've already been at our door.

'Our biggest arguments are on behalf of the people who have to contend with living in the area during the daytime, and it is a fact that the infrastructure is not keeping pace with development and this has been our biggest worry about the Channel tunnel. The Government was head over heels in love with this idea about the tunnel, but there was no evidence of whether government money was going to come into the county. There was a lot of talk about the employment it would bring, but in fact a lot of that employment wasn't coming from our own county, it was coming from outside, it was coming from France.'

The Movement has never been opposed to development for its own sake. 'Housing is necessary. Roads are necessary. But, for goodness sake,' Mrs Granville Streatfield had said in 1938, 'let us feel confident that our sacrifices are not unnecessary, and that the muddle and the chaos which is daily devastating our homeland shall give way to order and to foresight.' Where development is necessary they want its careful integration into the countryside and, as important once the decision has been taken to go ahead, they want a

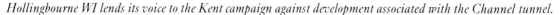

Hollingbourne WI lends its voice to the Kent campaign against development associated with the Channel tunnel.

well-planned social infrastructure so that people may be happy living there.

In 1988 WI policy on planning and conservation, made up of mandates accumulated since the 1920s, provided Anne Jones of Winterbourne WI with sufficient power to defeat developers over a site of great beauty at Hicks Common in the Frome Valley: 'North Avon is in siege from the developers. But we have got a strong conservation lobby there. We started to mount a campaign of which the WI was spearhead, and I was on that action group. When the barristers arrived from London they said to us it was no good saying we didn't want the development, we had to prove a case at the three-day public inquiry. There were six or seven organisations lobbying through the action group, of which the WI was one. The Preservation of Rural England and the Local History Group were among the others. At that point, when the barristers said that we had to prove a case, more than half the group melted away, but I realised that a detailed document had to be produced so I decided to do it. What I did, in fact, was to use the resolutions listed in our handbook – *Keeping Ourselves Informed*. These are resolutions which had been voted by more than two-thirds majority in the Albert Hall over the years. They were WI policy and I applied them where I could, to the case in point.

'I think this approach had a great impact on the inspectorate at the inquiry and we did in fact win the case. But now, alas, the builder, Mr Bayliss, is putting it through the House of Lords. In order to keep him on his toes I am constantly having to ring up the press and leak little bits of information about what the WI in Winterbourne intends to do. I have also sent an emergency resolution to National. It reads, "This meeting urges her Majesty's Government to produce legislation which after failure of appeals by developers seeking planning permission would refuse further repeat appeals (either in part or whole regarding the original site) until a period of five years has elapsed."

'You see, even though Mr Bayliss has lost his fight, he can go on appealing and appealing and appealing *ad infinitum*. But once we have lost, we have lost for good. It is heavily weighted in his favour. I don't know what it has cost him, but it's cost us £16,000, all raised locally.'

The Hicks Common site in the Frome Valley.

Chapter Ten

EDUCATING AND EXPANDING IN THE NEW AGE

'At the back of our minds was the
thought that we could lose touch with our roots.'
LADY BRUNNER

Ellen Wilkinson: 'I know you agree with me that young life
must not be sacrificed to the merely picturesque.'

'Planning and development' was but one of the subjects which the Executive encouraged the institutes to discuss in their monthly meetings at the 1946 AGM – education, international affairs and health were others. In both education and health in the 1940s, major changes would have far-reaching effects upon village life.

The Education Act of 1944 changed the whole nature of village schools and laid down the guidelines for the development of education thereafter. Some schools were closed, the children grouping with those from neighbouring villages, all became primary schools for the five to eleven year age group. No longer would a child complete his or her education at one school under the tutelage of teachers from the village.

Two years later, Lady Elizabeth Brunner pointed to the social purpose of the village school, something at the heart of village life, implying that more was at stake than the academic education of children: 'The strength of our Movement is largely that we are used to living in small communities where we have constant contact with our neighbours and where we are all used to playing our part in the life of the village. In our villages we are brought together by a variety of common causes, and where the school is taking its right place in the community, it is a valuable focus, both social and educational. Without its own school, a village will be bound to lose much that is of inestimable benefit to the community. The teacher, who lives in the village with her pupils and their families, can have far greater understanding of the characters with which she is

Lady Elizabeth Brunner – 'Without its own school, a village will be bound to lose much that is of inestimable benefit.'

Below: *Church and school at Madron in Cornwall, working together as a unit to promote the social and spiritual health of the village.*

dealing, if she knows the background of her pupils.'

The WI wanted well-equipped, adequately staffed junior schools in the villages, and where grouping was absolutely necessary, to place the new schools in rural areas. Many felt that the new Act threatened to remove an important part of village life and also threatened the security of village children at a time – immediately post-war – when they should not be up-rooted from the home environment.

'We rural parents love the village school and its interests, and take part in all its festivities; it is more of a family affair,' said Mrs Cook of Farrington Gurney. 'The backward child gets a better chance, for the teacher knows its home background, and its limitations are understood. We have seen so many little "vacs" suffer through parting from home surroundings, and in a small way our tots will suffer the same.'

On the second day of the 1946 AGM, Ellen Wilkinson, on behalf of the Ministry of Education, espoused a new 'scientific' approach to education, more efficient she felt than the traditional, cultural comforts of a village environment. She indicated that the old form of

village education was as outdated and unscientific as the image of the village school was spuriously picturesque: 'From what I have seen of the archaeological remains of Roman Britain, they were a great improvement on the sanitary conditions of most of the villages in which you and I live. I know you agree with me that young life must not be sacrificed to the merely picturesque. It is not enough that a building should be beautiful or merely old outside. I am sorry, but from an educational point of view, one of our good, well-designed prefabricated huts is better than the best medieval building you have got . . . The new type of secondary modern school is to be a type

of school which is to teach the children to live in the world in which they were born, and not in the world as it was when Julius Caesar came to Britain.'

Had Miss Wilkinson simply missed the point of Lady Brunner's earlier speech? It really must have seemed to 6,000 countrywomen gathered in the Albert Hall a quite extraordinary response to their way of life. That she got away with it suggests that she rode in on a wave of public optimism for the new post-war era. Everyone, enthused by victory, waited for the promised post-war 'new life' to be unfurled before them. There were going to be big changes – didn't Ellen Wilkinson know best?

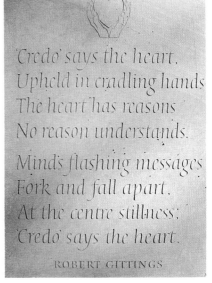

'Credo' says the heart.
Upheld in cradling hands
The heart has reasons
No reason understands.

Mind's flashing messages
Fork and fall apart.
At the centre stillness:
'Credo' says the heart.

ROBERT GITTINGS

The maze at Grey's Court, near Henley, home of Lady Elizabeth Brunner, seemed to me to symbolise a great deal of the striving within the WI for Absolutes – values upon which new directions, campaigns and involvements, are based.
'At the Archbishop of Canterbury's enthronement,' Lady Brunner explained, 'he gave a sermon in which he likened the search for truth, to finding your way in a maze . . . Robert Gittings, who wrote "Out of This Wood", five verse plays for our 1957 National Drama Festival, provided the inscription for it, which you see as you enter the maze.'

But what of this new science based education? 'Some of you say, "Well, and when my boy is going to follow the plough, what is the use of his knowing about the larvae of dragonflies?". But these boys have been so tremendously excited; they have really found something new themselves by using their eyes. They have learnt scientific method, and as a result they are just ready to get interested in agriculture as a science instead of as a bore . . . May I say we are getting some wonderful new stuff in these young men and women coming back from the forces, whom we are putting through our intense teachers' training course, and will be available for that extra year's schooling when we raise the age to 15.'

It must have occurred to members to wonder where Ellen Wilkinson had gathered her information that village boys considered agriculture to be a bore. She was right in that post-war Britain was about to embark upon a new scientific age, that nothing after the war could be like it was before. But she had raised fears among the audience that profound changes were afoot, changes that would alter something fundamental about village life, and somehow the examples the Minister called upon to illustrate her case – like the dragonflies in the pond, above, or this young bomber pilot put into a class to show children the purpose of education – seemed inept and extraordinarily condescending: 'This young bomber pilot started to tell them the sort of arithmetic you had to know, and the sort of trigonometry and algebra you had to know before you could take up flying really satisfactorily. For the first time, apparently, it had begun to dawn on those boys that there was some use to mathematics. . .'

Mrs Vernon of the Executive Committee closed the issue, gently reminding Miss Wilkinson of the members' deeply felt love of the traditions of village life, of which the village school was an integral part, while also stressing that the villagers of England and Wales were not idealists disinterested in progress: 'We country-women like to feel that we are important. We are proud of our heritage, and like our ancestors we love to serve the land. I do not think we are so proud of our old beautiful buildings and of our schools – anyway not of some of them. We want many new things in that direction. But we do love tending the land, cultivating it, making it more fruitful, helping to beautify it, and we do want our children to love it too. We know they will only do this if they have a fair share of the advantages of the modern world, and above all in the opportunities offered in education.'

As for education in the institutes, interest continued to develop following Miss Hadow's tragic death in 1940. As Life Trustee of the Carnegie Trust, the new

Lady Brunner, Lady Denman and Sir Richard Livingstone – 'he set a spark going which struck the right ground.'

Chairman Lady Albemarle became directly involved in training adult education teachers and utilised the particular experience of the institutes in doing this: 'The Carnegie Trust, in 1948, were trying to do two things, to assist those organisations that were trying to rebuild a community life, and to meet the great demand for further adult education. There was this extraordinary hunger after the war for adult education. Institutes had always had their interest in handicrafts and traditional crafts and so on, but the interest now was in informal adult education, a more liberal education. The local Governments were themselves developing their adult

Denman College as purchased in 1947. In 1988 Chairman Agnes Salter's £1,000,000 appeal ensured its future.

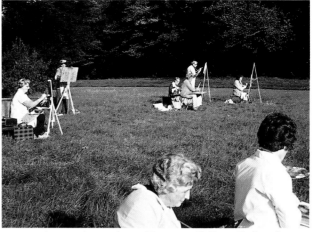

Midnight feasters? A far cry from today's comforts at Denman.

education but they hadn't got people trained to teach, so they gave us money at the WI to do the training of teachers, and then they were employed generally, not just in the WI but in the general adult education in the counties. They wouldn't have found people with the right background if it hadn't been for the WI.'

Earlier, in 1945, the WI had conjured an idea which would crystallise their plans and hopes for adult education in the institutes. The institutes' own college, at Marcham in Oxfordshire, was the brainchild of Lady Brunner: 'As soon as the war broke out, everyone had begun to plan for its end, and I think that because of the unemployment in the '30s there was a great feeling that nothing like that should ever happen again. Naturally, we all became very interested in education. Just as we had a questionnaire about housing, so we had one about education. We knew what the members wanted. We already had summer schools at various venues, and one particular one at Somerville College in Oxford. But we'd got rather tired of always finding ourselves in rented accommodation, and students accommodation being, even in those days, singularly uncomfortable, the idea was produced that we should aim at having a college of our own where we would provide the sort of courses that we were organising for ourselves in other people's premises. Richard Livingstone planted the seed. He was a great man, lovely man, he was Vice Chancellor of Oxford University. His sister married George Bell, Bishop Bell. He set a spark going which struck the right ground. To understand what the whole idea was about, you have to go back to Richard Livingstone, and read his book *Danish Folk High Schools*. When Richard Livingstone was talking to us at the summer schools on education, he spoke of these folk high schools which were organised at the time of the Schleswig/Holstein business, during the German occupation. The idea behind them was to keep young people in rural areas aware of the traditions of their country during the occupation. The schools gave courses for boys working on farms, farmers' sons and farm workers, courses in good husbandry in winter and in the summer they gave courses to farmers' daughters. They were good courses for practical farming and domestic economy and that kind of thing, but into every course they introduced something about the history of Denmark and the culture, so that they kept it alive, and they began all their sessions with a hymn so it was church based as well. And that is what these Danish Folk High Schools grew out of. I think, possibly, at the back our minds, was the thought that the essence of a

An art class in the gardens of Denman College. Before the 1960s, art had never been singled out in the institutes as a subject for exhibition, but 'in 1963 we had the first ever Art exhibition – "Painting for Pleasure",' its organiser Lady Anglesey recalls. 'It involved a lot of people who had never painted before. Since then there has been a large growth in amateur artists and the WI Art Groups have gone on ever since.'

rural community, would, after the war, need fostering, although it was being given every possible service, electricity, housing and so on, we could nevertheless, lose touch with our roots.

'The courses that the college was to run were enormously varied, but into each of them we cunningly inserted, rather like the Danes with their own history during the German occupation, cultural subjects – literature, art, drama and so on, and then we sort of canalised people who enjoyed a touch of literature or whatever it might be to take a literary course and this was very very good. it was all purposeful, done by people who valued education.'

The new college thus became the jewel in the Movement's educational crown. It embodied, at its inception, the full character of an organisation dedicated to fostering, elucidating and developing the cultural traditions that are at the root of English rural life. It was everything that Ellen Wilkinson's concept was not. Hundreds of thousands of women have since benefited from the college. Taking a course has been called 'participating in the Denman experience', for appropriately, upon Lady Denman's resignation at the 1946 AGM, her successor Lady Diana Albemarle dedicated the college to her. At the end of the second day of the meeting in the Albert Hall, she rose to say: 'All this afternoon suggestions have been coming in of ways in which we can keep Lady Denman's name in perpetual association with the work of the Women's Institutes. . . The most popular one is that the Women's Institute College should be known as Denman College. We want this to be a memorial, of the sort that would appeal to her.'

119

Chapter Eleven
WIDENING HORIZONS

'I beg you to let Foreign Affairs
be constantly on your agenda.'
LADY LLOYD GEORGE

A choir at the 1988 International Eisteddfod at Llangollen,
where the WI promote their international theme.

The 1946 AGM was extraordinary in that it laid down so many of the lines along which the second generation of WI leaders were to pass. 'Many institutes are trying to learn something of the points of view and difficulties of other nations,' Lady Denman had said in her opening address, and the West Sussex Federation developed the international theme with a resolution to study the United Nations Organisation and work for the promotion of friendship between nations by making contact with individuals and organisations in other countries. The Movement's interest and active involvement with international affairs through the 1950s and '60s reflected a general post-war widening of horizons throughout the nation. Lady Anglesey, Chairman of the

WI from 1966, stresses the complementary role played by the greatly improved media channels in enhancing discussions in the institutes. 'You could go to a WI and talk to anybody about subjects which they would not have known about before, but when television began it opened up whole avenues of discussion. The educational effect of early television was enormous from the point of view of current affairs, social issues and things of that sort. In those days of course television was quite different. You were seeing one or at most two channels, and there was a requirement to show serious programmes at peak viewing hours. There was an enormous widening of horizons and there was more awareness of international affairs. The positive effect of television was that when you did go to a WI and came to consider resolutions, people were very much better informed.'

Television of course had an enormous effect, but in the first place, as Lady Megan Lloyd George said at the time of the 1946 AGM, it was the war that had broadened people's perspective. 'Our job was to look after the homes, the children, to concern ourselves with their education and to secure their future. And what happened? Those problems forced themselves into our homes, turned them upside down, and we found that the future of our children, which we were so busy safe-guarding and securing, was in greater peril than we had ever imagined possible . . . I beg you to let Foreign Affairs be constantly on your agenda. . . . Make up your minds to follow what is going on in the world . . .'

The Movement took the initiative and the Carnegie Trust provided 'launching grants' to spread into the Channel Islands and subsequently the Isle of Man. And the new spirit of internationalism took Miss Viola Williams into the jungles of Malaya. Her account of her adventures in helping secure the organisation a foothold in the East provides a wonderful sense of the spirit of exploration and adventure which accompanied the Movement's resolution in days before air travel was commonplace. She had followed in the footsteps of Miss Margaret Herbertson, who had launched the WI there with the help of Lady Templar, wife of the Commissioner.

'As I went out of the door of the committee meeting at Eccleston Street in London, one of the Executive said to me, "Well, Miss Williams, I hope you have a lovely time in Africa!" which gives you an idea about how small most people's world was in those days. I had gone out there during the war as a "Fanny", hopping about all over the place in aeroplanes, and I had done my first flight in 1932, so it wasn't new to me.

'This was early '52 I think. Heathrow Airport consisted of two Nissen huts beside the road, and my father drove me up to the Nissen huts and I got out of the car and I said "Goodbye Daddy," and I got on the plane and when I came back there he was, with his car, outside the Nissen hut door, and I just got in and said goodbye to the other people, and came home. There were Customs, but can you believe, Heathrow – two Nissen huts? I went out BOAC, it took nearly a week; we stopped at Zurich, Beirut, Karachi, Calcutta, Singapore, and then I went off to KL [Kuala Lumpur]. Lady T met me and she found me lodgings with a police inspector, and from then on I was her sort of *aide de campe*. At that time there was a very strong, slightly pro-communist movement and we had to be frightfully careful what we did. What we were trying to do could be very easily misconstrued. Security was very tight, the day I arrived I got yanked into the Military Attaché's office and he said, "Now look Viola, I don't care where you go in

Miss Viola Williams walks with a new spirit of inter-nationalism through the jungles of Malaya – 'I don't think we had time to be scared.'

Malaya, you can go where you like, but if I have to send a regiment of soldiers in to get you out of trouble there is going to be hell to pay." A lot of the plantations were barricaded. There was a lot of barbed wire and alarm systems, dogs, God knows what – half the roads had notices on saying, "It is dangerous to stop here", "Do not stop on this road." Even when one was there, people one knew got murdered.'

Was she scared?

'I don't know whether I was scared or not. You had a job to do, sometimes you had to go in by helicopter if the area was very bad, several times I went in with a lorry load of troops behind me and on one occasion I went in with a field gun because they thought it was necessary – into a village with a field gun behind me! I remember coming into one village one night, I came round the

'Members' shoes, left outside, indicate a meeting in progress - everyone would sit on the floor.'

corner and there was a tiger fast asleep in the middle of the road. Well, the road was warm and he was asleep, and I retreated slightly so I could see where he was and waited until he had gone and then I went on. No, I don't think one had time to be scared.

'We had different set-ups. We were dealing with the Chinese, who were basically communists, and had been herded together in what were called new villages, new towns, and it wasn't always easy to get through to them. I can remember on one occasion addressing a meeting standing on a table because that was the only place where there was room for me. And I think I had four

'When they saw that in an institute village they were better clothed and fed, the Chief would get in touch with us.'

different interpreters because we had three completely different nationalities there. So, we had the Chinese who were difficult, we had the Indians who were on the make – they saw the WI very often as something which ultimately they might be able to profit from. There were perks – when we had sugar over after having tea, that was considered one of the perks – also being in the WI meant that they probably came to Lady T's attention, and therefore they came to the Government's attention and therefore that was good for their husbands. On the whole, I wouldn't say that the Indians went into it altruistically, though a lot of them did a very good job, there is no doubt about that. I remember one lady who belonged to, I think it was eleven different organisations, and she had a handbag with all the badges inside and when she went into a meeting, she looked round to see which meeting it was and then found the appropriate badge and put it on. Now the Malays themselves were absolutely marvellous. Completely feckless, absolutely charming to deal with, tremendous fun, desperate to learn anything. At one of the meetings, a very nervous District Officer's wife decided that she was going to start in on birth control and they had a quiet meeting in the village on birth control. And the next time they had a meeting on birth control they had about 200 there, and the next one was cancelled because all the men came down against it because of course it was a Muslim country. So, that was the end of birth control.

'The meetings were absolutely hilarious because nobody had a watch, nobody had the time. You might have been able to get a message through the District Officer's wife, that you were going to arrive at a certain village at a certain time on a certain day, and you would arrive and you would park the car in the centre, in a clearing in the middle of the village, and the message would sort of go round the village that you had arrived, and in about two hours you had got a meeting. A lot of them would have to come in quite a long way through the bush, and they weren't going to come until they knew that you were going to be there. So, you just sat and waited until they arrived. Sometimes we would have meetings under the trees, sometimes if it wasn't safe we would collect members in an armoured vehicle and they had to lie down in the bottom of the vehicle.'

What was taught?

'They were passionate about knitting because it was quite cold at nights and it was a practical thing to learn. In fact, the WI was almost entirely educational. We did have some flower shows, largely to see what they were doing and what kind of things they wanted help with. You see most of these women couldn't even read or write, only the school mistress would be able to do that.

'I remember one day I received a round robin from a village right up country, about 150 miles away, a real round robin, with the little note in the middle and everybody's thumb print all the way round, and in the middle it said, "Please come and remove our President, we do not like her," and they had all signed it with their thumb print, and I drove up there and all the way up I was thinking, "How the bloody hell am I going to remove a President?" She was presumably elected, so what on earth do you do about this. Anyway, by the time I got there I decided it had to have been my fault, and so I said to the meeting that I was terribly sorry but the last time I had been there we had had an election and I am afraid I hadn't done it quite correctly, and would they mind terribly much if we had another election. And so we had another election which was, as usual, completely democratic. That is to say we had a collection of papers and we had palm trees and alligators and crocodiles and tapirs and tigers and black panthers and ginger trees and things, and each member who wanted to be elected would stand up and say, "I am an elephant, I am a palm tree, I am a crocodile," so that everyone knew who they were voting for, and they had to put their cross, which all of them could manage. They only had one pencil but they could manage the cross against the appropriate picture, and we counted them all in afterwards and do you know what? They had elected the same woman again, unanimously . . .

'When I went out there in 1952, we were involved immediately with the Queen's coronation. We decided that we would have a WI float, it was the first time that we would go absolutely public, so we had this float for the procession in Kuala Lumpa. The procession was about six miles long, and we decided we would show all the things that we were doing. We would show child care, cooking, sewing, agriculture, we would have all the nationalities on the float, we would decorate it, marvellous! Then it was a question of the personnel and I should think the WI came nearer to foundering on trying to pick out half a dozen people to do that than it ever came in it's life, because everybody of course wanted to do it, except the Chinese. And we were determined that we were going to have a Chinese on that float but we could not find a Chinese that would come. The whole atmosphere was anti-Chinese at the time because they were the communists. But in the end I found a most attractive Chinese woman who would come and be part of the float with us. As it happened she was the one who would be dealing with powdering the baby, bathing the baby and so on. The procession started and we had been going for about an hour when the procession stopped because it was Ramadan and therefore all the Malays wanted to have their evening meal. So we stopped for an hour while the Malays had their evening meal. We then started off again and I noticed that our float was especially popular. There was no doubt about it. Then we discovered that the men were enjoying it just as much as the women; there was a great deal of applause and a great deal of excitement. It was the following day before I discovered why. The Chinese woman I had got was the number one prostitute for Kuala Lumpa!'

Activities in international affairs took many forms and were regular features of the programmes drawn up by many individual institutes. But ever since the first jumble sale or Christmas bazaar, the WI has been pre-eminent as a fund-raising force, and it was in this area of its business that the organisation proved spectacularly successful in helping meet the needs of the emerging Third World nations. It raised £185,000 for the 'Freedom From Hunger Campaign', launched in 1960. The moving force in this was Mrs Barbara Santo of the Cornwall Federation. The money was spent on

agricultural projects designed to enable a country to maintain its own food production and learn about nutrition. It was not a measure undertaken for temporary relief, but one aimed at underpinning the long-term livelihood of communities in places such as Bechuanaland, Karamoja in Uganda, India, Pakistan, Trinidad, Sarawak, the British Solomon Islands, Tristan da Cunha, and outlying districts of Southern Rhodesia.

Previously, in 1943, the WI had committed itself in a resolution proposed by the Essex Federation, to the relief of post-war Europe. Over 250,000 garments had been made by WI members before the scheme came to an end in 1945. The 'Freedom From Hunger Campaign', post-war relief, and a commitment of £75,000 to World Refugee Year in 1960 were the visible tip of an unquantifiable mountain of activity in the institutes.

It seemed a fitting, though still somewhat surprising, mark of the Movement's international achievements, therefore, that in 1961 upon Mrs Gabrielle Pike's election as Chairman, she received a telegram from the

Bottom left: *Porlock WI in money raising session. The raising of £185,000 for 'Freedom from Hunger' was but one – albeit an exceptional one – of the many fund raising successes of the WI which take place all the time for local, national and international causes. Institutes tend to devise their own, often quite idiosyncratic, activities – for example, the major fund raising event of the year at Brampton Bryan WI in Herefordshire is the Christmas Pudding Mix-In* (right), *organised last year by Mrs Norma Dark.*

Shortly after the War a Government Minister attempted to deny WIs the profit from one of their most traditional fund raising events, as 'The Daily Mail' of March 13th, 1947, recorded, 'The village jumble sale is under sentence of death by Sir Stafford Cripps!' Pangbourne WI had been caught trading goods at a jumble sale without collecting clothes coupons from the purchasers. A five-page memorandum from the Board of Trade was issued, and when WI member Mrs Alice Ponting asked, 'Why on earth should coupons be surrendered for an article made through our ingenuity?', the response from the Board was – 'You mustn't think that I and my officers sit in some ivory castle of isolation.'

As fate would have it Chancellor of the Exchequer, Sir Stafford Cripps, was guest of honour at the AGM that year. As he came onto the platform, Lady Albemarle, who was in the Chair, detected a groundswell of booing from the floor – 'Startled, I felt, "My God, how can I stop this?" – what I said was, "Well, of course we are also equally delighted to be welcoming our fellow member Lady Cripps, who is also here," and there was never another sound!'

Kremlin. It read, 'Many congratulations on being elected Chairman of the National Federation of Women's Institutes at the Albert Hall STOP Cordial invitation to visit the Soviet Union, and bring a friend.'

'So I put this to the Executive,' Mrs Pike recalls, 'and I said I would take a Russian speaking member, and a letter was sent to every WI (with others of course, to save postage), saying, "Have you got a Russian speaking member?" And there were literally hundreds, 800 or something. We chose Marina Bloxam. I was about forty-six and she about fifty-four. She was much more gutsy than me, we had a great time making arrangements.

'Of course Khrushchev was in power then. The minute Marina and I arrived at the airport, we were met by Nadia, my interpreter, and she stuck to my side the whole time. She was very interested that I was the great grand-daughter of Elizabeth Fry, because they are all Elizabeth Fry mad. It is interesting because she, of course, was a social reformer and so they thought, "Ah . . . ", and that very first evening we made friends a bit. I had said to Nadia, "I want some money," and she had said "Why do you want money? We pay for everything." I said, "I might want to buy some presents," and she said, "OK, we will buy you some presents," but I insisted, "No, I want some

Lady Anglesey – 'Following the "Freedom from Hunger" success I went to visit these people in Columbia to see how our money was being spent . . . our aim was to do something about the malnutrition amongst these people.'

money." The next morning, there we were in this hideously uncomfortable, meant-to-be grand hotel, and I said to Nadia, "We must visit the British Embassy, because we always write our name in a book when we go to a foreign capital." And she said, "No, no, no, you can't go there," and I said, "Yes, I can, come on, you had better come too." And she did come, and if you could have seen this Russian sidling into the British Embassy!

'I was very interested – once inside, I caught sight of a note on this man's desk, I could read it upside down, it simply said, "Gabrielle Pike might call today." Wasn't that fascinating? I said, "I want some money, they won't give me any money." The British Embassy said, "Here's £50, but hide it and whatever you do don't leave the country with it

because if you were found taking out £50 worth of roubles you would be shot, it's as simple as that."

'We had a fascinating time. We were in the hotel for only two or three nights, and then we were taken on a propaganda trip through two villages and then we went riding. That was marvellous because Marina could talk Russian, and she chatted away like mad with the groom that came with us. I shall never forget, as we were climbing on our horses, she said, "Do you realise you are mounting a grey Arab stallion?" And I said, "Oh, Marina, I wish you hadn't told me that." And then after about ten days, Nadia said, "Gabrielle, I'm going to have to leave you. You are going to have a new interpreter in the morning when you go to Leningrad.' And I said "Oh Nadia what a bore, we have just got to know each other." You get used to your interpreter and I could chat to her as easily as to you, so I said, "Tell them we have got to stick together." And next day, sure enough, she turned up. When I asked her how she'd fixed it, she said, "I told them I'll never have another Oxford accent again!" – she was an English teacher at the university.

'It was all quite dotty, I gave her all my rather lovely clothes, maps off the aircraft and that kind of thing.'

Maps off the aircraft?

'Oh yes, all the bumph you get in the aircraft. One day she just said to me, "Have you got all the bumph that you get in the aeroplane, can I have it?" So I gave it to her.'

What were the country folk like that you saw?

'They were absolutely delightful, and completely different. I went to Kiyev and we went 200 miles down the Dnepr and then ten miles in-land, because the Dnepr is as wide as the sea and you can't see the other side, and when we arrived, there was a little Edwardian village, nothing had really changed, because they hadn't got a cent to do anything with, and there were these little Edwardian houses, wooden with steps, and there was a nice woman to say hello, and she had a white handkerchief on her head and a white cotton blouse and skirt to the ground, a gathered peasant skirt. A complete peasant, no shoes and socks. She held out her hand and I jolly nearly gave her my bag. I was thinking she was a servant, which you would have done! But she wasn't, she was our hostess, and she was a wonderful woman, and somehow Nadia had fixed it so that we should stay in this place and I had said to Nadia, "Now, honestly, I don't mind how uncomfortable it is going to be but I do want to visit a village." So we stayed in this little house. The bedroom was perfectly good, simple, the bath was

rather quaint, you collected fir cones and lit a fire beneath. Frightfully good, actually, because you got such good hot water, and when I said to them, "This is marvellous; such a good system, just what I want for my bath in Wales," (because Georgie and I have a wild house in Wales), they said, "Oh, I suppose you can't get hot water or baths where you are." They were all so misinformed. They said things like, "Oh I hear you can't get a doctor in the country unless you are rich," and that sort of thing.

'As to the food, the food was tiresome to me. For example at breakfast we would have beef stew and much too much of it, and it was very difficult not to eat it. And then they would just eat again when they were hungry. You didn't have lunch and tea and dinner, you just ate at odd times. They drank a certain amount, they didn't drink with us at first until I said I thought we were going to live on vodka and I see we don't get any. And after that we had too much!

'They were mostly farmers. They were picking blackcurrants, but Marina told me they were incredibly inefficient. The whole thing was laughable. They will never get crops while they work like this. And of course they didn't care a damn, because even if you do get a crop you would have to give it away, and anyway, anyone who knew anything about farming had been killed off by Stalin. There were no women's organisations that I could find, and I kept tackling them on this. They said that they wanted something like the Institute but I told them that if they had it they'd have to be democratic – the secret ballot is the secret of the whole thing.'

What about religion?

'Nadia was very annoyed with us when I said that we wanted to go to church. But we insisted on going to that wonderful church in Leningrad which was then the only one open and therefore packed. Marvellous choir. But up to the gallery there were women sitting on the steps feeding their babies. In the village, they would often take me aside and say, "Do you believe? Are you a believer?" and they would show me an icon behind the stove. And there was amazing Christianity, but underneath. Nobody admitted, because if you did admit you didn't get a job. You couldn't be seen to be a believer. If you went to church you ran the risk that you wouldn't get a job as a teacher or anything, you had to be an atheist. Nadia didn't even know the story of the Nativity, and of course if you have three generations of anti-teaching it doesn't get through. That's very much the same here. I have got a nephew who is a parson outside Liverpool, and he says it is fascinating, the children have never heard of Jesus Christ, let alone "Thou shalt not steal".

'Of course, when we came back we were met by so many of the press. And the Foreign Office asked me if I would go and see some very senior people, who said, "How on earth did you get asked to this?" I explained that I had just got this telegram. And they said, "But you stayed in an ordinary Russian home, 200 miles from Moscow, how did you do it?" (It was unheard of, in 1962) and I said, "When I was in Moscow seeing hospitals and things, I said to them, 'Look here, I am not interested in hospitals, I am a countrywoman, and I want to meet countrywomen. I don't want to stay in Moscow, if I have got to do that, I may as well go home. I have got plenty to do there.' And I said, 'We would have you to stay right in the country,' and added, 'I hear your plumbing is shocking, but I don't mind a bit.'"'

It did seem extraordinary that the WI, in the year of the Cuban missile crisis, should have been issued with an invitation to visit Communist Russia. Then, as we continued to talk about how she had first joined the WI, Mrs Pike mentioned that 'when I joined the WI, I was in MI5; it was during the war and, don't faint, I worked for Anthony Blunt.'

Had it not occurred to her, since then, that Anthony Blunt was an active agent during the period of her trip to Russia? That she might have been invited on the recommendation of the KGB, as a possible recruit?

'Oh well, of course, I had no idea . . . I suppose they might have known that I worked for MI5. I suppose they must have done, yes.'

But was there never an approach to her while in Russia besides the handing over of BOAC's maps? 'No, though the only thing was that at one stage, a woman did say to me, "You are the sort of person who could be tremendously helpful and useful among the women of Russia and we would like you to stay here always." And I thought, "Oh my God, no!" So I said, "I have got a perfectly good husband, thank you!"'

The contact between the WI and the USSR did not cease with Mrs Pike's visit in 1962, as I discovered in corresponding with Mrs Jane Jenkin of Bowerchalke WI in Wiltshire: 'In 1984, a link with a women's group in the USSR was sought – the voting of the WI for this purpose gave consent, just! It was the time of President Reagan's oft repeated reference to the "evil empire". But, already, the Foreign Minister in the UK was urging informal contacts to improve relations. However, it was difficult to establish the link. Our final attempt was to write to Mrs Gorbachev, c/o The Kremlin. Success was finally achieved in March 1988. One day, it is hoped, visits may take place in both directions. The letters we receive are full of interest and details of the life in

Tonya and Nana at the Black sea.

Moldavia. So far, thirty-one WIs from all over England and Wales are also seeking correspondents. We try to show how the WI has helped improve country life; how such a body of women is influential to our Government on many social issues.'

Here are some extracts from letters from Tonya, a teacher in Moldavia, which provide a fascinating insight into the lives of women across the great divide. On June 6th, 1988, Tonya wrote, 'Dear Jane, Thank you for your most friendly and interesting letter. It contained so much information! This very kind of information is of greater value than that taken out from newspapers and magazines because it's the first-hand one! I studied carefully the items devoted to the Women's Institute and its history. They contained very interesting things. As far as I understand, the WI enjoys the support and recognition of vast majority of country-side women. We can't boast of having anything similar, I'm afraid. You see, our women's Council isn't numerous at all. There are over thirty thousand people inhabiting our district. Half of them must be women (to be precise, over 50% belong to the fair sex). And there are only thirty women in the W's Council. They are elected by women working in different branches of economy, health service, educational establishments. The Council is attached to the District Soviet (Council) of People's Deputies.

'It's main task is to co-ordinate supervision over the fulfilment of different programmes aimed at the improvement of living standards of certain families in need. The Women's Council also organizes Solidarity Markets. The money gained are usually sent to the Soviet Peace Fund or to the Soviet Children's Fund. Women in trouble can apply to the W's C for help. And the Council tries to do something for them, if possible.

'So, you see there's fundamental difference between W's Institute and W's Council. Although there are no restrictions for organising informal women's associations. And they do exist in many places. But we've got nothing of the kind. Maybe some of us (if not the majority) lack time. Practically all our women have to work, they can't afford themselves to be house-wives only. They used to go to work at 7.30 – 8.00 in the morning. We've got an 8-hour working day (plus 1 hour for dinner break). So our women used to come back home after 17.00. Add to this doing shopping, which isn't a quick thing here. One has to stand in long queues. On coming back home we are busy preparing supper, doing other things. The only dream is to wind up with the whole business and to go to bed! Mothers have little time to communicate with their children. It affects seriously the youngsters. The only way out here is to let mothers spend more time at home! . . .'

Later in the same letter, Tonya speaks of the attitude to religion in her community: 'Dear Jane, it might amaze you, but there are people in this country who fully share your religious views. The thing is my father and mother belong to one of the Protestant streams. When I started telling them about the Quakers and their principles, they said that to their mind they couldn't see any difference as far as their own religious views are concerned. So, I was brought up in the family of Protestant Christians. They are absolutely independent from the Russian Orthodox Church which was an official one before the 1917 Revolution. Protestants of all streams have been in less favourable conditions than the former official Church. They were severely persecuted in pre-revolutionary days, under the tsar, as well as during the Stalinist regime. Today Protestant Christians enjoy much greater freedoms. Thus they have been given an opportunity to build a beautiful modern building where they can assemble to pray and to preach The Living Bible. (It's in our capital Kishinev). So my parents greet you as their Christian sister, and send their good wishes to all of your family and to Salisbury Quakers as most dear and tenderly beloved in Christ.

'Dear Jane, they would like to address you these lines from Philippians 1: 23,24: "'May God give peace to you, my Christian brothers, and love, with faith from God the Father and the Lord Jesus Christ. May God's grace and blessing be upon all who sincerely love our Lord Jesus Christ.' Sincerely, Pavel (Paul) and Victoria (Victory)." These are my parents' names. They are sixty-two. You see in this letter of mine I tried to touch upon some aspects of our everyday life.'

Three months later, Tonya having received news of the '88 AGM from Jane Jenkin, replies: 'I enjoyed the view of the famous Albert Hall and the women sitting here and there having their lunch waiting for the Assembly to start. Looking at the magazine cutting I felt the spirit of Fellowship you live with. God bless you in all your deeds! . . .

'And now about my family life: Two months ago we were very lucky to buy a car. You see it's not an easy thing to get one in our country. Before getting a special paper which makes it possible to go to a special car-shop to buy a car, one has to apply to the Town Administrative Committee for one's name to be put on a list. Then you have to wait for many years for your turn to buy a car to come. Our family had to wait for nearly seven years. The car we've bought cost us about 10,000 roubles. We had to work hard (often doing extra jobs) to accumulate the necessary sum. The fact is an average income of a Soviet family (a wife and husband working) doesn't exceed 350 roubles in a month. Half of it is spared for food. Consumer goods are rather dear. This woman's boots cost 100-150 roubles, a good coat cost 300-500 roubles. I've given these figures for you to better understand what it means for us to have reached the goal. . .

'My dear friend, I wish you and all your women from the WI to be always energetic, healthy and in good mood. Thank you for the trouble you take.

'Love, greetings from all of my family. Yours Tonya.

'P.S. I'm enclosing a photo of mine taken at the Black Sea where I was together with Nana.'

Chapter Twelve

POST-WAR BABIES AND SOCIAL REVOLUTION

'We all had a concern;
it was the concern of a mother.'
LADY ANGLESEY

Teddyboys, juke boxes – something was happening amongst
the youth in the mid-1950s . . .

The late '50s and '60s were dominated by the 'bulge' generation – the post-war babies that had been born to a nation in victory. Many WI members were mothers to the new generation, a generation with a morality which often so bemused its progenitors that the Government actually sponsored a committee to be set up (with a WI member in the Chair) to determine how to cope with it.

The media – now truly a mass media – leapt at the chance to fan the flames of a generation war that would sustain publishers, film makers, and television companies for decades to come. 'The reason for the "youth problem",' wrote Keith Waterhouse in a mould characteristic of the times, 'is that people who aren't teenagers

don't like people who are teenagers, and spend a lot of time saying so. Old women want to get teenagers flogged. Retired colonels try to get teenagers gaoled. Magistrates try to make them get their hair cut. Headmasters stop them wearing fancy clothes. Cinema Managers stop them snogging in the back row. And all – all because they have committed the criminal folly of being young.'

Mary Smith, member for Ripley recalls travelling to the 1958 AGM and listening to an address by Lady Ravensdale in which she pleaded with her WI audience to 'discuss in your meetings what you can do about Teddyboys and girls and juvenile delinquency . . .' and concluded with an appeal to God – 'Give us a good digestion and something to digest, give us a healthy body Lord.' At the WI there were also particular concerns for the health of the younger generation, for example a campaign was launched to make crash helmets compulsory. When a certain Mr L Barrett learned what they were up to, he wrote a letter:

'Dear Madam, I have just read an account of your members' intention to ask that crash helmets be made compulsory. Frankly I cannot understand how the matter can possibly concern them. Are they under the misapprehension that the wearing of helmets can in some way prevent accidents? At the most the helmet can only minimise the injuries to the wearer, if/when an accident occurs. This is a personal risk – and it is for the rider himself to decide whether or not to wear a helmet. To make it compulsory is an unwarrantable interference with individual liberty.

'I am in no way opposed to the voluntary wearing of helmets, but as a motor cyclist with over thirty years of accident-free riding to my credit, I would not wear one myself. I find that it causes headache, and which is more important, interferes with my hearing and thus to some small degree tends towards making me a potential danger towards other road users.

'Despite the vicious prejudice which exists against motor cyclists, I insist in believing that your members have the welfare of us riders at heart, and I thank them for the kindly motive which lies behind their very much mistaken action.'

Whole industries grew up to give the new generation the distinct identity which it demanded. A fashion industry and a record industry crowded round the new consumers and transported them into the pleasure-filled '60s. It was a time to be young, to live dangerously, to have fun, and if you weren't part of it you weren't living.

Lady Diana Albemarle, by this time retired as Chairman of the WI, was called upon to help advise the

Hastings, when pitched battles were as common as deck chair tickets. 'Despite the vicious prejudice which exists against motor cyclists,' wrote a biker to the WI, 'I insist in believing that your members have the welfare of us riders at heart.'

Government what to do about 'the youth problem'. She collected into a Committee a member of the TUC, a Director of ICI, a vicar, two 'proletarian authors' and seven others. The purpose of the committee was to study what was going on, and draw up a report for the Minister of Education. Eleven months later, on February 4th, 1960, the report was published proposing a massive spending increase by the Government in the area of The Youth Service: better training for Youth Leaders, better Youth Clubs with facilities that youth wanted, more Youth Clubs and the doubling of the number of trained Youth Leaders. It was called *The Albemarle Report* after its Chairman. On its publication, the Countess received a bouquet from one London Youth Club with a card which read, 'Best wishes, we are cheering for you today, The Sewerside Mob.' But in 1960 the 'youth problem' had barely begun.

This was the decade when the WI, representing the rural mothers of England, expressed their concern about the sexual revolution – the new permissive society. For example in Kent, more than 11,000 housewives declared war on pornography 'which is threatening to undermine the family life of this country.' Mrs Patricia Henson from Sevenoaks said that the sexual revolution in Britain had led to an increase in and an irresponsible attitude to sex, which was having a dangerous effect on children: 'Children need care, affection and stability and these conditions cannot exist in a society which is in a state of sexual anarchy. In a society in which the pursuit of sexual gratification is regarded as the highest goal, it is our responsibility to see that children in their most impressionable years are not put under pressure by people who are peddling obscenity for financial gain.' Mrs Henson cited the spate of 'X' films, sex on TV plays, displays of erotic paperbacks and magazines, and she criticized the popular magazines in their treatment of sex subjects. 'Most of all we resent public figures of so-called liberal or progressive views blandly assuming in the press and on TV that this is the way to a better and happier world and that anyone courageous enough to disagree is just an absurd figure of fun. The new persuaders would have us believe that what is private is furtive, indeed they have inverted the standards of good and evil, so that public indecency is now paraded as a virtue, modesty as a vice.' Mrs Radvan of Hilldenborough Evening WI told a conference, 'We have always promoted beauty so can we allow this tide of filth to engulf our young people?'

'We all had a concern,' recalls Lady Anglesey who was Chairman between 1966 and 1968, perhaps the key years of the 'sex and drugs' revolution. 'Don't forget that I have five children and two of them are '60s generation. We all had a concern; it was the concern of a mother. Look at the resolution at the 1966 AGM,

Lady Anglesey – 'We all had a concern; it was the concern of a mother . . . Two of my children are '60s generation.'

designed to make all members, all parents aware of the dangers and availability of drugs . . .'

'A new disease is starting in this country,' the Albert Hall audience heard in 1966, 'a disease which will potentially age people before the age of thirty and a disease which has to a certain extent affected the problems which were being discussed . . . of over-population, because it is said that some of the more arid and uncultivated parts of the world are so because the local population are rendered incapable of thinking or moving around by drug addiction known as hashish, which is smoked by our children at parties in the form of reefers . . .'

In contrast to this, almost comic-book picture of a world over-populated by an addiction to hashish, came forward members with real knowledge: 'I want to urge you not to be smug like I was,' said Mrs Darke, 'not to discuss it as "something that could not happen to me", because it can.' We hear of 'the daughter of one of our East Sussex members during her first term at a University who, before an examination, was approached by a fellow student who assured her that "everyone takes amphetamines (purple hearts, pep pills) before exams". She did so, and collapsed at her desk.'

The call came for the spread of information through teachers as well as parents; booklets to be made available; a more limited availability of drugs at chemist shops; prescriptions to be written in words not numbers, as numbers could too readily be altered and increased. As one delegate pleaded, 'Couldn't mothers be made more aware of the early symptoms of this? I know a mother of a fourteen-year-old boy, unable to find out what was wrong with the boy. His temper was very frayed during the week; halfway through the week he was nearly going mad, and every week, and it was some time before the parents discovered what had happened.'

Concern about 'the permissive society' was concern about the welfare of the community, for its health and for the values that members knew were vital for its survival. But though most members could not be said to belong to the youth generation which threatened these values, it was characteristic of the debate (and the times) that an extraordinary honesty attached to its flow. It was the honesty of personal experience and by all accounts it had an electrifying effect upon the meeting, as when Mrs Meigh of Frensham WI admitted that she had herself been tempted on the downward trail: 'I myself have worked amongst the drug addicts and people who take drugs and I wanted to try and, if I may point out, it only says "parents" to beware and "young people" but do, parents, please remember that so many of you do take drugs; so many of us are given tranquillisers . . . when we are depressed and ill . . . and you know that young people become conscious of the fact that their parents are using these things.'

If the 1960s brought out the social concern of a Movement dedicated to maintaining stability in a fast changing world, it was also a time for rejoicing in the constancy of the WI itself, for in 1965 the WI turned fifty years of age. High point of the Jubilee Year celebrations was an invitation from HRH Queen Elizabeth – herself a member of Sandringham WI – to a garden party in Buckingham Palace, an event which members and organisers alike recall with vivid clarity:

'I started it and absolutely did it,' recalls Mrs Margaret Pike, then in her final year as Chairman. 'I said we had to have a garden party at Buckingham Palace in the Jubilee Year and I wrote to the Royal Household in 1962. Word came back that "We don't plan as long ahead, but we are very glad you have told us." But then when I got in touch nearer the time, I had a letter saying, "We are terribly sorry but we can't have a big party at Buckingham Palace on the week of your Albert Hall meeting (which was when we had planned it), because

the Queen is going to be in Germany." So I thought we are going to have to think about what to do about this . . . I remember being in a telephone kiosk in St James's Street, and I rang the Lord Chamberlain – I didn't know him – and I said to him, "Will you come and have lunch with me tomorrow at Pruniers," and he was so surprised that he said, "Yes, I would love to," and I said to him, "This is really to convince you that we have really got to have that party the day after she comes back . . ." And of course we fixed it, and it was an incredible occasion.'

Invitations went out to the village institutes – the youngest Member to go was thirteen-year-old Janet Bearman, a schoolgirl from Gloucestershire – and plans were laid in the most far-flung village halls. In Cornwall, as elsewhere, it brought out the best of the Federation's organisation skills: Members of the Cornish Executive realised that 'the people who were coming from the west of the county were going to have to leave at 5.30 am and not get home again until 3.00 the following morning.' So it was decided to hire a train and share it with the neighbouring Devon Federation, the carriages a hive of activity when members changed into their best outfits as the train approached Paddington.

The finances were naturally carefully worked out, and the enterprise actually showed a profit for Federation funds: 'The train was to start at Penzance, so we contacted a representative from British Rail and said, "Now look, what about food?", and he said, "Yes, you can have a meal," and eventually, it was arranged – we had a three course roast beef lunch for fifteen shillings on the way up, and a turkey dinner on the way down for seventeen and sixpence. We ran a "pooling of fairs" scheme; there was an invitation for every institute in the county and there were three for the Federation, but the fairs were pooled so it could be either the person going or the institute who would foot the bill. And the total cost per member was £2 10s. That paid for the railway journey from a member's nearest railway station to London, coaches to meet us and take us to the Palace, and back again. It paid for our half of the train and covered a tip to the engine driver, who had never had one in his life before. We also tipped the dining room staff, it covered that, and also the coach drivers, as we had three coaches. When we came back there was enough money left over to buy two clocks for the office.'

Upon arrival, excitement ran high, as Mrs J M Hill of Mablethorpe WI in Lincolnshire remembers: 'As a child I was taken by my parents to see the Changing of the Guard and wished so much to go through those Gates . . . Crossing the square to the steps leading into the Palace itself, footmen were waiting to collect our invitations, and we then entered the Reception Rooms, where one could see all the beautiful porcelain and

China tea and dinner services – it was a case of just looking as you slowly filed by, there were so many of us to pass through . . . At last we reached the Terrace and went down onto the lawn – it had taken forty-five minutes from entering the gates outside.

'We spent quite a time strolling between the flower beds and trees, and came to a lovely round summer house; there were lounge chairs and stool with exquisite embroidered seats and backs. Here too were children's toys, an indoor slide, a heap of sand, buckets and spades. Then, at 4 o'clock the band played the National Anthem and the Queen appeared accompanied by Prince Philip . . . [then] the Royal party split up, each taking a lane, but owing to the large crowd they were soon surrounded. The lawn was just a sea of gorgeous coloured hats of every size and shape.'

Gabrielle Pike, accompanying the Queen and unable to find a way through the crowd, said to her hostess, 'I am so sorry Madam, it is such a squash.' 'And she replied, "Oh, don't worry, we had a party like this after the war and it was such a squash that my parents walked out through a door in the garden wall, down Buckingham Palace Road, and back into the garden again without anyone recognising them!"

'. . . Oh, and I remember so well when my stiletto heel got stuck in the grass, and there we were – the Queen and I – sort of grovelling around trying to find my shoe . . . We had a very good tea: Lyons, the Caterers, produced eclairs and sandwiches and so on, but they didn't reckon on countrywomen – it was gone in a second and they had to go off and provide a whole lot more. At the very end, when I had seen the Queen back into the house, I was walking around with the Lord Chamberlain and we met a whole group who, like so many, hadn't been able to meet the Queen. So I said, "Oh well, here's second best, here's the Lord Chamberlain." And one darling old Yorkshire member dropped a curtesy just like that, and the Lord Chamerlain told me

Chairman Mrs Gabrielle Pike, a member of Marcham WI, with the Queen, a member of Sandringham WI. A French magazine report of the Royal Garden Party was headed, 'La Bataille des Chapeaux.'

C Day Lewis at Litton Cheney, guest of Mrs Pike. He wrote a poem to commemorate the WI's 1965 Jubilee.

'I do beg of you to live more dangerously, not recklessly, but to accept the challenge and tackle it.' Miss Sylvia Gray.

afterwards, "Do you know, it brought tears to my eyes, I have never had anyone drop a curtesy naturally like that before."

It fell to Miss Sylvia Gray, an Executive of NFWI, to escort Prince Philip: 'I had to escort him all round the crowd, it was a terrible job. You can see what a crush it was from the pictures. In fact he was getting a bit cross towards the end, saying he wished they would let us get on. He kept saying, "Stand back," and some members kept on calling out all sorts of silly things to him. One called out, "I've just had a son and I have called him Charles," and he called back and said, "Quite a good name too," and then another said, "I saw you when you were up near Hull last week," and he said, "Sorry, I didn't notice you," and he went on through this crowd of people (your feet being trodden on the whole time). Eventually we got inside the tea tent where we were due to have tea with the Queen. At that moment, the Queen's party came up on the left so I started to slow down, and he said, "Go on!" and I said, "I can't, the Queen's going in!" But he said, "I don't care, Push on!' So we did push on and eventually we got in and had tea . . . As we came out, one of the Yeomen of the Guard – all lined up - leaned over and said to me, "I bet you've never been in an operation like this before!"'

Appropriate to the meritocratic ideals of the times, in 1969 the Movement elected its first Chairman from the ranks of working women. 'I have worked my way through the rank and file and I am sure that others will do so in the future,' said Sylvia Gray upon her appointment. And one newspaper commented, 'This is obviously a big change from the days of the Lady of the Manor being in charge.'

Sylvia Gray came to the chairmanship as a Governor of Burford Grammar School, a member of the Post Office National Users Council, a member of the Executive Committee of the Keep Britain Tidy Group. She had also been involved in local government work, having been involved as Vice Chairman of Whitney Rural District Council, Chairman of Finance and Housing Committees and Vice Chairman of the Planning Committee. She had also served on the management committee of a mental hospital and an old people's home. But much more interesting is her own story, one of self-motivation and great enterprise: 'I haven't always lived in Burford. I grew up in Rugby in Warwickshire. When I left school my parents had this idea of my staying at home and I wasn't so keen. I saw an advertisement in *The Times* for a job as an *au pair* or companion help at a country house at Stratford-upon-Avon and I applied for it. It was very, very valuable experience; I was there for about four years and helped generally. They did a tremendous lot of entertaining and had a big farm which I helped at as well – even nurtured pigs on a bottle and so on – and I taught the family's youngest child. It was during this period that I first joined the WI. I was only eighteen at the time but my boss there was the President of the local WI, and suddenly she said to me one afternoon, "It's the WI this afternoon, do you want to go?" I had never even heard of it. Anyhow, I went. This was around 1929/1930. The WIs in those days were wonderful. They had many sub-committees and many interests and what made it especially interesting was that most women and girls weren't doing anything else, they weren't in jobs so they had the time to be very active on all the sub-committees. We also did many theatrical, craft and cookery courses.

'When I left that job I went off to London and did a Domestic Science course. Then the family asked me to go back again to help them out a bit, so I did and it was while I was there that I made up my mind that I might like to have a hotel or guest house to run myself.

'Eventually I found this house in Sheep Street here in Burford which I took with no experience. I realise now how very good my family were, that they didn't try to stop me. I had no capital behind me at all but the house I bought was a beautiful one called Tandfield House. It had been occupied by the Tandfield family since Elizabethan times. But when I took it, it belonged to a young man called Anthony Alexander who was up at Oxford. The family was very wealthy and Anthony Alexander had this house to come to in vacations (if you please!). He had spent a lot of money on it. It was very well done. I couldn't afford to buy it of course, but eventually he rented it to me on a sliding scale rent, starting on a very low rent and going up with an option to purchase. He wasn't a friend of mine but he travelled a lot and I think he was anxious to get it off his hands, and he knew I would look after it. It was very small and I started with only four bedrooms. I couldn't afford to furnish the whole thing. I rented it at the end of 1933 and opened it in the Spring of 1935, and it really took off very well.

'I also got very heavily involved with the WI. I became Secretary, Treasurer and President of the institute and was co-opted onto the County. I think the first committee I served on was Agriculture, which was

'It was a bit like a WI organisation . . . All my businesses were run entirely by women. I had no men at all.' Miss Sylvia Gray.

cookery and all that kind of thing. Eventually (1955) I became Chairman of Oxfordshire County Federation and then I was co-opted onto the National Executive.

'By this time I was handling three businesses – The Bay Tree Hotel at Burford and then a little bit later I had the Manor House Hotel at Moreton-in-Marsh. The third was one I started here called Hufkins, a homemade produce and catering business. Hufkins is actually the name of a Kentish tea cake. I had a tea room there too. I wanted somewhere where I could have homemade jams and marmalades and sell them, which I did, as Hufkins marmalade and Hufkins jam. It was a bit like a WI organsiation. Quite a few of the staff were members. My manageress at Hufkins was a President here eventually so quite a lot of them who were making the jams and so on were involved with the WI.

'One thing that has interested a lot of people is that all my businesses were run entirely by women. I had no men at all. You see I started by doing a lot of the cooking myself, but soon I realised I could not go on doing it, and when the war ended we were asked by the Government to offer jobs to girls coming out of the forces. The first two that I had were a couple of Wrens and that was very successful, and then a couple of WAAFS. Then as my businesses were growing I decided I would run a kind of training scheme which I did throughout my time in the hotel business. A lot of the girls I had, came from domestic science colleges. They'd come for at least a year and go through all the branches of the business.

'When I knew I was going to be National Chairman of WI, I consulted my senior staff who had been with me for a long time and said if I take on this job it's going to mean that I will have to be away three or four days a week. A lot of these staff had been with me a long time (I had a secretary for thirty-five years and my head cook for forty years, and a number of the manageresses for fifteen years or so). They were all long-standing staff and so we made them directors. We had no secrets – they knew exactly what I had out of the business and so on. That business principle I tried to put over when I was Chairman of WI – that you have got to give people responsibility and due credit if you want them to contribute. I couldn't possibly have done what I did if I had not been backed by the staff.'

Sylvia Gray was very much 'the new countrywoman' and in striking contrast to those who lived their teens at the turn of the century and been handed the Vote. This fact was not lost on Miss Gray; indeed she made it the thrust of her chairmanship: 'I think women should have equal opportunity and that is our major aim. It is a fact that 85% of administrative jobs are held by men. We think something should be done about that but it is lunatic to antagonise men by marching around burning bras which are used very little. I am sure things will improve for women but we have to keep up the pressure, but it all takes time. It is a question of the best way of doing things.'

Chapter Thirteen

WOMEN IN A WOMAN'S WORLD

*'I think women should have equal opportunity
and that is our aim.'*
MISS SYLVIA GRAY

*WI members in the late 1960s – at long last,
old battles could now be won.*

Freedom of choice for women was of course no new aim for a Movement whose whole strategy had been to get ordinary countrywomen into positions from which they could exercise control over their lives. But in the late '60s, public opinion was such that at last old battles could be won. Three years before Sylvia Gray's election to the Chair, Frenchey Evening WI in Gloucestershire had called for an investigation into maintenance payments to separated mothers. Then, two years later, a resolution calling for proper maintenance for divorced women prompted the gathering of evidence from WI members which was heard and helped shape the Divorce Reform Act of 1969.

Mrs Gooding of Three Stones WI in Essex argued the resolution, echoing the feelings of many in the late 1960s on divorce reform: 'It seems to us that the financial arrangements after a marriage has broken down are of immediate practical importance to the wife

and children. The emotional stress may be great, even grave, but very often the greatest hardship arises from the financial anxieties. . . We do not claim divorced women ought to have priority over all categories of women under the law; the position of widows, married women and single women could also be improved, but if all women are second class citizens under the law, divorced women are even further down the scale. . . On the day a woman becomes a divorced person she is automatically deprived of rights she enjoyed the day before as a married wife: she gets no widow's pension, either from the state or private pension schemes; if the man she married dies, she gets no old age pension without instantly starting to pay in contributions from the day of the divorce.'

The point was that a divorced woman had to do all the agitating while the man could sit and wait: 'The key word in our resolution is "security"; we wish a divorced woman to know for certain what her financial rights are, that they are hers by right and not by condescention of administrators.'

Mrs Kingston of the Essex Federation pointed out that widows were partially insulated to loss while the divorced wife was not: 'She is dependent upon the goodwill either of the state by supplementary benefits or the goodwill of her ex-husband, who perhaps deserted her. And she must fight it out on the employment market, where her opportunities are largely unequal.' Additionally, as Mrs Blemkiron of Hudswell WI, York-shire, pointed out, 'there was no way to ensure that maintenance payments will indeed be maintained. If the wife is deserted, why not make him pay a lump sum, assessed as damages to her earning capacity? If she trained for a job, gave it up on marriage for any length of time, then was freed by divorce to take it up again, she would have lost seniority, be out of practice, and in many cases age would be against her. Damages could be assessed as after a road accident. . .'

Then, characteristic of the times, the final word came as personal testimony, and clinched the argument – Mrs Kinch of North Wraxall and Ford WI in Wiltshire: 'I am a deserted wife: my husband left me twenty-two years ago, soon after the war – possibly chiefly because we just had not got a home and could not get a home – leaving me and a son, four years old, to fend for ourselves. My doctor advised a divorce . . . I always thought he would come back. Several years later, because I had a very bad nervous breakdown, he said until I cut my losses I would never be any better. Then I had all my own divorce costs to pay – everything – I never got a penny, although the costs were granted against him. I did have a mainte-nance order made out for the boy up until he was sixteen, and I had 10 shillings a week; I spent possibly more than I ever got in trying to get them . . . I am obliged to work full time, despite a major heart operation a few years ago. I have to pay full rate insurance, income tax, and no pension unless I keep up my full payments of insurance, so life really is a problem and a great hardship at times and it really is time something was done to make things easier . . . Anyway, thank you for listening to me.'

Never could it be said that WI policy is made in an ivory tower. It was, however, in a wider context that the new Chairman Sylvia Gray's avowed aim to campaign for women's rights would be tested – in equal opportun-ity for all women everywhere.

Bures WI in West Suffolk had opened up the subject as long ago as 1943. Their proposition 'that men and women should receive equal pay for equal work' had been a notion that gained new credibility thanks to the activities of women during the 2nd War: 'Dangerous jobs, piloting planes and boats, scientific jobs testing delicate apparatus and precision engineering, dull heavy jobs on farms, and in factories, routine jobs in offices and shops, weary jobs on railways and buses, and very many having domestic duties at home as well . . . Is it not manifestly unfair that the reward for all these things should be subject to the prejudice of a bygone age, and that it should continue to be taken for granted that women will work for less? . . . [Consider] the recent case reported in the press of a girl who was apprehended for impersonating a man, her defence being that as Michael she could earn £4 a week, whereas as Muriel she could only earn fifty-five shillings a week. This is the machine age – it is no longer a tussle between nature and muscle. Even on the farm, most of the hard physical work is being done more and more by machine power, and the direction of this power is just as much within a woman's capabilities as it is within a man's.'

Miss Greenwood of Clare in West Suffolk in a beautifully thought-through argument, anticipated that men would actually be worse off in the post-war job market unless they accepted the notion of equal pay because, otherwise, the market would be flooded with cheap female labour. Now that women had demonstra-ted an ability to compete successfully, equality was as much in the interests of their competitors as their own.

As history shows, the achievement of equal pay was a slow process. Eight years after Mrs Green's resolution, equal pay was introduced only among civil servants and teachers. Not until 1975 did the Equal Pay Act come into effect, by which time – not suprisingly – attitudes had considerably hardened. In the media – especially in books, films, television and in the press (all areas where women found early success) – the feminist lobby maintained a high profile during the late '60s and '70s.

This was the era when pressure groups of many creeds first began to form, as Lady Anglesey recalls: 'The idea of pressure groups only goes back as far as the '60s – 'what Bernard Levin calls "single issue fanatics".'

But the WI picture of rural Britain and country-women's rights, on the other hand, was still painted in the colours of the Movement's founders; everything flowed from their spiritual ideals (written into the WI constitution) of fellowship, truth, tolerance and justice. Members felt confident that these ideals offered a position (the best position) in any circumstances how-ever much the world had changed since 1915. Annoying as it may have seemed from the media's point of view, the WI refused to fall in line with the newly voluble feminist lobby. In consequence, in 1975 when the 'equal opportunities' issue finally took discussions a stage further than equal pay, it was not carried on a wave of emotion or cant – the more popular mode amongst pressure groups at that time – but on due consideration of real issues and their possible consequences.

For example, one concern (most unfashionable at the time) was that the role of mothers in the home might – by the acceptance of the resolution – be belittled; young mothers might be encouraged not to fulfil the traditional role of motherhood and go out to work instead, thereby missing a unique experience (bringing up a child) and, possibly, depriving the child as well. Mrs Batty Shaw re-assured the delegates – 'The wording of the resolution does not imply that women may not remain in a home and give full time care to their families if they wish.'

As a further example of the WI approach, some time after the resolution a follow-up discussion was announced by Mrs Laverty of Longhoughton WI. Deliberately playing devil's advocate she organised a discussion at a Northumberland Federation Council meeting and entitled it – provocatively – 'Are Women Taking Men's Jobs?'

The discussion had the desired effect of demonstrating

how multi-faceted was the issue of equal opportunity; it isn't easy for a miner's wife drawing the dole to suddenly embrace the idea of a wider job market just because a new breeze blows in from the affluent, middle-class south: 'Some ladies got up and said, "We don't educate our daughters to a high standard to have them stopping at home with their children all their lives. We don't expect it and they don't expect it." Very valid point. Then there was perhaps a miner's wife, or an unemployed man's wife saying, "It's not right, women shouldn't be allowed to work full time," because they were worried about their husband's future employment.'

In the North East, unemployment was a serious problem, and in many people's minds there remained a real dichotomy between men's work and what women do: 'There are a lot of things which we do think of as men's work. Mining, steel making, this sort of thing . . . I produced statistics showing that there are more women in work in this country than there are in any other country in

A car maintenance class in progress at Denman College. Sign of the times?

Mrs Patricia Batty Shaw, fighting her corner at the AGM.

Europe or America.' The question then arose as to whether it is morally justifiable [i.e. justifiable according to the spiritual ideals of the Movement] for an employer to employ a woman with no financial responsibility to a family in preference to a male family breadwinner: 'People who work in local government or the civil service or a lot of other big organisations, have equal pay, so a single woman is getting the same amount of money as a married man with two children and a mortgage.' Was this morally justifiable, particularly when an employer would very often choose 'two part-time women rather than one school leaver simply because he could save on health stamps'?

The discussion brought out real issues as they appertain in the real world and was a deliberate attempt to prick a bubble of fanaticism. Mrs Laverty laughed when she 'had a phone call from The Womens Equality Commission in Newcastle saying, I couldn't call my talk "Are Women Taking Men's Jobs?" because there was no such thing as men's work, which I thought was quite interesting because this was well before the arrangements for the discussion had been made. Somehow it had leaked out!'

The 1975 'equal opportunities' resolution became one of the Movement's most important successes, its purpose later enshrined in the Sex Discrimination Act, which made it unlawful to treat a man or a woman, on the grounds of his or her sex, less favourably than a person of the opposite sex. And when, later, Jo Richardson MP read out a letter of WI support for the related Sex Equality Bill, a cheer went up in the House for the Movement's work in the whole area of women's rights. In 1977, a main speaker for the resolution, Mrs Patricia Batty Shaw, was elected Chairman of the WI, and as Margaret Thatcher prepared to take office as Prime Minister – Mrs Batty

Shaw was asked by a national newspaper, 'Do you think that women voters regardless of their usual party allegience would be encouraged to vote Conservative because the party is lead by a woman?' She was able to reply: 'Women have thankfully grown out of such simplistic yardsticks, although there may still be a residue of prejudice among men, women will vote for the right person for the job regardless of their sex. If they vote in Mrs Thatcher it will be on the strength of her policies, not because she is a woman.'

The response, expert in its avowal of the wider view, again emphasised that WI interest in the rights of women is an interest in the principle of justice which includes equality and is part of its constitution, while prejudice – the 'positive discrimination' option which was being coaxed by the interviewer – is not. The reasoned voice of the WI has not made it so many friends in the media, where recently it was described as 'a sleeping giant', but it is a voice skilled in creating change through existing channels of power, and in many cases it may succeed precisely because it does not play the media's game.

The progress that the organisation has achieved for women has been especially marked in the area of health, where once again Miss Sylvia Gray's determination proved of enormous value. When one talks to members about the role that the WI has played in improving the nation's health, it is not the well-publicised milk-in-schools campaign of the '30s that one gathers is most significant, nor its research/survey work on the efficiency of the NHS in 1949 and again in 1976, nor even its reputation for being quick off the mark in bringing to public attention important health issues such as venereal disease in 1922, eye transplants in 1952 (long before transplants of any kind became popular), or AIDS early in 1986. Rather, it is the Movement's work in the area of women's health that one finds most pride.

As early as 1921 Lady Denman had supported the Walworth Women's Welfare Centre, and had given money to assist the opening of clinics by Dr Marie Stopes and others. In 1931 Lady Denman was asked by Marie Stopes to become the first Chairman of the Family Planning Association (under its original title, the National Birth Control Council). At that time it wasn't just the Roman Catholic Church that reacted strongly against the concept of family planning (and Dr Stopes' books, *Married Love* and *Wise Parenthood* in particular). Opposition was widespread and owing to the non-party-political and non-denominational constitution of the WI, it was inconceivable that Lady Denman would ever involve the Movement in such a cause, however strongly she might feel about it personally. The issue did, however, strike at the heart of WI social concern. Richer women received planning advice, but for the ordinary countrywomen the situation was often appalling: 'You have to remember,' recalls Nancy Tennant, 'that people in the early days of WI were longing to find out how they could stop having children that they could not afford to have. Otherwise they were having a baby a year, weren't they? which dragged them down.'

Years passed, however, until by 1971, things had so changed, both in the country and in the institutes, that the principles began to seem inordinately restrictive. 'In

Miss Gray, counting the votes at the 1971 AGM when the constitution was altered to permit discussion of party-political issues (which by then most issues were). 'The BBC televised the resolution, but didn't plug in properly – the man said, "Can you put it to the vote again?" I went up and explained to the 6,000 delegates and they agreed, voted again, and passed it with an even bigger majority.'

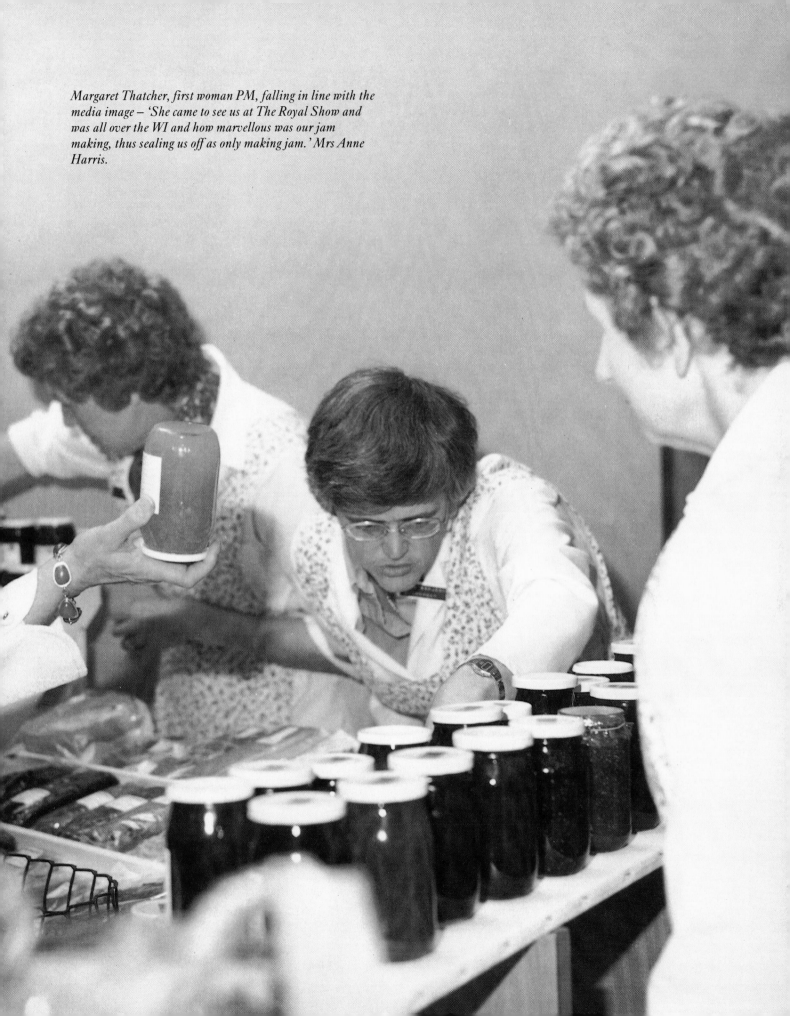

Margaret Thatcher, first woman PM, falling in line with the media image – 'She came to see us at The Royal Show and was all over the WI and how marvellous was our jam making, thus sealing us off as only making jam.' Mrs Anne Harris.

the political context prior to the 1950s,' recalls Lady Anglesey, 'people would say, "I back Labour" or "I back the Conservatives – I accept their policies and that's the sum of my political commitment." In that context the WI could perform a real function.' Now the political game was changing fast; every important issue attracted a party view, and as Mary Castle pointed out at the AGM: 'Many subjects of vital interest and concern to women start by being party-political or sectarian and so we are barred from discussing them.

'There are people who stay out of our Movement because they feel there are many things of interest to them but which they cannot discuss because of our rules. Thus there is a loss to the WI of would-be keen young enthusiastic members; and they lose too, for there is much to be gained from being a WI member, as we who are here today well know.'

Mrs Nancy Crofton Saville also argued strongly to change the rule: 'To be truly non-sectarian and non-party-political is to be back in the "little woman" category, enclosed within the walls of kitchen and nursery . . . If you do not pass the resolution, you are forbidding such matters of particular interest to young members as family planning and abortion (these are sectarian all right), or comprehensive education and the Common Market . . .'

Two years later, Miss Sylvia Gray who, as Chairman of the WI, had presided over the debate, said, 'I have no doubt that this resolution was the biggest and most significant change in our history . . .'

It certainly aroused strong feelings at the time – Mrs Ailsa Struthers took Lady Denman's point of view: 'Madame Chairman, fellow members, up to now I think the great strength of the WI has lain in its detachment from the sphere of political and religious controversy. We have been accused now of being the little woman and confined to the nursery. One has only to read the list of courses at Denman College to know that is not true. There is enough interest there to keep anyone interested for nine lives, let alone one. If anyone wants to discuss party politics or sectarian religions there are plenty of political and religious groups to cater for them.

'We have been accused of not interesting the younger woman. I think our duty as a WI is to interest the younger women on important moral issues like pornography and some of the material on TV and plenty of others. We are certainly not marking time if we concentrate on that.

'This business of Miss Gray not being able to speak on these matters when she represents us on other bodies – well, I do not think anyone has a right to speak on behalf of others on matters of conscience. Matters of opinion, yes. But on matters of conscience, no, not even

if it is a majority vote. We are half a million women. A quarter of us might be divided almost equally and in that case Miss Gray can only give her own opinions and not the opinions of others. She cannot possibly know what a great many of us think on these matters. I am not saying what my own opinion is, because I do not know the opinions of others. I only know the opinion of my own institute. For example, recently the Council of Churches spoke on behalf of other churches all over the world about using force in South Africa against apartheid. Well, this was resented in this country very much indeed and yet they had to agree with it. I do not think the churches or Parliament or anyone else have any right to speak on behalf of matters of conscience.'

The Chairman: 'Thank you. I would only just say in passing that I do not yet know where I have served where I have had to speak for your conscience; it has not really come my way yet.'

Mrs Leslie Hopkins pointed out that if denied freedom of speech in the institutes many women would form other groups – they would not be muzzled: 'Madame Chairman, fellow members, on behalf of the Gloucestershire Executive Committee and in support of several points which have already been made I should like to tell you of an experience which I had a few years ago when, as a VCO, I attended one of our institutes on the edge of Bristol, one of those young institutes where there were upwards of a hundred members, almost all of them under thirty, bursting with enthusiasm, full of life and a real joy to listen to. This was a time when Bristol was in an uproar about comprehensive education: should their schools go comprehensive or should they not? – A matter of vital importance to these young members with their young friends and families coming up to school age. Yet, according to our rules, they could not discuss this in their meeting. So what did they do? They held an extra meeting, a meeting of WI members but not so-called, to talk about this problem, to toss their ideas around and formulate their own opinions and indulge in free discussion.'

Finally, the majority of members attending the 1971 AGM agreed that it should no longer be shackled by the chains of a constitution drawn up to meet the needs of a very different age. Nevertheless the final wording of the new mandate was distinctly mild: While 'the character of the Movement is non-sectarian and non-party-political, this shall not be so interpreted as to prevent women's institutes from concerning themselves with matters of political and religious significance, provided the views and rights of minorities are respected and provided the Movement is never used for party-political or sectarian purposes.'

The new rule immediately released the institutes to

Before the NHS, the health of villagers would often depend on the services of the local nurse.

discuss the family planning issue, and a resolution was prepared by Lady Anglesey and Mrs Gwen Davies for the Anglesey Federation, in 1972, which read, 'This meeting urges the Government to make it mandatory rather than permissive, as at present, for all Local Authorities to provide a full free Family Planning Service.'

When the resolution itself became mandatory, representations were made to the Secretary of State for Social Services, the County Councils' Association, medical associations, and organisations concerned with family planning, and in 1974 family planning services became a normal part of the National Health Service.

The absence of official concern or interest in women's health during the early part of this Century was a legacy of Victorian prudery and male chauvinism, and long before the Anglesey resolution on family planning it was a favourite issue of the WI. From 1925 the WI Movement had fought hard for a better deal for mothers in childbirth, to create pre-natal clinics, make available specialist obstetric advice, improve the midwifery service, and hasten new analgesic services for women in childbirth. Between 1935 and 1943, maternal mortality had been halved, mainly because of improvements in obstetric and midwifery practice, and in 1946 a compre-

hensive maternity service was secured through the National Health Service Act.

The NHS itself was hailed within the WI as the successful culmination of a campaign waged since 1925 for a proper welfare system, free medical treatment for women and, in particular, for the right of married women to health insurance even though they may not be 'gainfully' employed (as the contentious distinction went).

Before the NHS, the health of villagers might have depended upon the services of a local nurse like Nurse Catherine, whose clinic in the Anglesey WI hut was the village health centre of its day. And there was much to be said for such arrangements; people preferred to be looked after by someone they knew, someone of the village rather than a doctor or midwife who might travel in from a nearby town: 'Although the National Health Service meant free medical help for people,' recalls Nancy Tennant, 'ironically it took away from private hands, admittedly unofficial hands, things that had been working perfectly well in many villages. What I am thinking of is our local nursing association which my mother started for three villages. We had our own nurse who came every week, everybody paid sixpence and she went through the cases. Everybody knew everybody, and we would keep in touch with anyone who was ill. Of course all that was wound up and the whole thing was taken away when the NHS was established.'

Nevertheless the cost of good health remained a serious burden for many families before the establishment of a free service, as Miss Comber of Toft WI in Cheshire pointed out in 1943 when recording the Movement's appreciation of Sir William Beveridge's Report (which formed the basis of social security legislation in Britain, including the NHS Act of 1946): 'I think what specially appealed to us was that it treated everyone alike, and that very largely we should ourselves be contributing to our own benefits. Those who till the soil never want something for nothing: they know it would be against nature . . . You and I know that what causes poverty in the home is illness not covered by insurance, and bringing up children on a small wage. We know of families that have spent years struggling to pay off doctors' bills and hating to feel that they owed money. We need insurance for married women. At last, the housewife is coming into her own. The men are recognising that even if she is not what they call "gainfully" occupied, she is of immense value to the community.'

As the Health Authorities worked on plans for the new service, local institutes and federations made their views known on what was required in the villages. Three years after the NHS Act they reported that only 2,294 out of 6,500 villages had NHS surgeries of their own. Where a village had no surgery it was common for sick persons to travel to one several miles away often by means of an inadequate bus service. It was also common, so it appears from a number of institute surveys, for village surgeries to open only two or three times a week and not to have a waiting room, so that patients had to wait outside in the street:

'At Crafthole in Cornwall,' the local institute reported, 'a surgery is open once a week to serve three villages; the doctors live far away and some are not on a bus route.' Binham in Norfolk apparently had no surgery, and if a doctor did visit, 'someone must bicycle to his surgery five miles away to fetch medicine'. In Piddletrenthide in Dorset and Pattingham in Staffordshire, surgery patients 'must wait in the street, and are vocal as to the need for waiting rooms'.

Here in the Movement's early concern for the health of the village were laid the foundations of community health care which has since become a mark of institute involvement throughout the country – fulfilling a need recently exacerbated by policy to discharge patients from mental hospitals into the community. Mrs Rigby of Newton and Field Broughton WI in Cumbria explains how her institute became involved: 'It was over thirty years ago, following the AGM in London in 1957, that our delegate and President, Mrs Mills, reported back to our members a resolution that had been passed,

The NFWI worked hard over many years to secure a milk-in-schools scheme. Their own resolutions in 1934 and 1939 together with Lady Denman's personal efforts in addressing MPs on the subject in the House of Commons eventually bore fruit during the 2nd World War. Thirty years later, as Health Minister, Margaret Thatcher stopped free school milk, and was dubbed 'Thatcher the milk-snatcher'.

Sir William Beveridge and his wife (a WI member) surrounded by well-wishers. The institutes saw his Report as a victory for campaigns they had fought – for health insurance for married women.

expressing the need to remove from patients the stigma of mental illness. One way of attempting to do this was to become associated with a local mental hospital. This was a resolution our members thought they could pursue and the matron of Lancaster Moor Mental Hospital was contacted.

'At this time there were over 500 patients in the hospital who rarely received a visitor or had any contact with people outside. It was suggested that five ladies should be adopted, all of whom had been in the hospital for up to forty years. A decision was taken to invite these and a few more patients to a Christmas party at one of the member's homes, and to remember their birthdays with a card and present. A summer party was also arranged and regular visits organised with the hospital.'

One young patient, Marie, from Hong Kong, was diagnosed as deaf through the care and observation of a visiting member and has since been fitted with an aid that has improved her life immeasurably in her difficult situation. 'Today, many of our hospital friends have been discharged into the community and live in sheltered housing. We do not visit them there but they return to the hospital when we arrange our afternoon tea parties.

The work in the Cumberland Federation spread fast to neighbouring counties. 'It was in 1976 that we were approached by Cumberland Federation regarding hospital visiting,' recalls Mrs Jean Lovell of Wideopen WI in Tyne and Wear. 'Their members attending Newcastle hospitals for treatment are so far from home they suggested that it would be nice if our members could visit them. I volunteered to organise, and now I visit ten to eighteen patients per year. Most of whom stay four to six weeks on Radiotherapy. Occasionally a WI Husband comes to hospital, when I take my husband along – between them they put the world to rights!'

In February 1979, Mrs Rhoda Lee a WI member of Moretonhampstead in Devon, herself felt the warmth of the organisation around her at a moment of terrible loss. 'I have a great many WI memories but perhaps the most important to me, and the most poignant, is very personal. Nearly ten years ago my husband had taken early retirement and handed the farm over to my son and daughter-in-law. For a year we enjoyed our leisure and I was free to do more WI work. Then suddenly our son, an only child, died. We were all devastated, obviously and I wanted most of all to cut myself off completely from the outside world. But my WI friends wrote, telephoned, visited and simply carried me along on a wave of affection and concern in such a way that I was able to get back to normality in a way which would have been impossible without them.

'Since then, I have taken up more and more WI work and responsibility so that it is now a very large part of my life. It has given me an outlet for so many of my interests and even ambitions – but, above all, it has given me loving friends.'

Spiritual support and emotional comfort is only one aspect of WI community health work which covers a wide range of activities including, for example, the recent 'manning' of the 'Heartbeat Wales' campaign set up by the Government 'to tackle the enormous problems of heart disease in Wales,' as Mrs Rhiannon Bevan, WI liaison officer for Wales, explains: 'We were the first voluntary organisation to get involved . . . we helped in major promotions in the main towns of every county in Wales. There was a mobile unit and we did the demonstrations, pulse testing, blood pressure, and so on; we had thousands of people coming.

In the '50s the Movement was invited to become involved in a nationwide education programme about cancer, aimed at calming people's fear of the disease and at encouraging them to recognise symptoms and submit themselves for screening. How apt, therefore, that in addition to a subsequent campaign for a national breast screening service (which, following the Forrest Report, looks set to herald in the first national breast screening service in the early 1990s), the Movement's drive for better women's health should reach a kind of zenith in a campaign for NHS screening for cervical cancer, the most pernicious of diseases that affect women today.

In 1964, Whitchurch on Thames WI in Berkshire raised 'as a matter of urgency' the question of cervical cancer tests, the provision of comprehensive facilities for routine smear tests for cervical cancer. 'It was the WI championing that did it,' recalls Mrs Margaret Pike, Chairman at the time. 'We were the only co-ordinated organisation on that.' Today smear tests are widely available largely due to WI efforts, and the Movement has followed up its campaign at local level, by supporting and organising appeals for Well Woman Clinics.

One example of this is in mid-Essex where Mrs Peggy Wass has organised an Appeal Committee which 'offers to visit and talk to any interested group of Women.' Information is disseminated, monies made available, fund raising events – fashion shows, garden parties (with home-made refreshments, of course) – are prepared. WI members also participate directly by helping with clinic sessions, acting as receptionists, making bookings for appointments, arranging for the professional services of Doctor and Nurse; or as interviewers, using a questionnaire to help a patient relax and decide what she would like to discuss with the professionals.

Chapter Fourteen

THE AGE OF SCIENCE

*'There is no assembly more for
the preservation of the English countryside.'*
PROFESSOR G M TREVELYAN

*The mushroom cloud of the US atomic
bomb which destroyed Nagasaki.*

In 1974 Mrs Pat Jacob, JP, was elected Chairman of the WI. 'Before that time,' she recalls, 'they had never done anything scientific and I wanted to bring science home to ordinary people. Literature and the Arts had all been represented in the institutes, but I felt we were now living in the Atomic Age, and we should help our members to understand about science and not be afraid of it. So I went up and down the country talking to people, and the British Association for the Advancement of Science helped us start a few courses at Denman College. The time was right, you see, people were frightened of the atom bomb and didn't understand that atomic power can be used for good purposes as well as bad. We wanted people to start talking about things of that sort in the institutes. I think it got members to think about these sort of things.'

With the Chernobyl disaster and modern problems of nuclear waste disposal in mind, the resolution from the Glamorganshire Federation in 1977 to postpone building of a fast breeder reactor 'until such time as a more satisfactory means has been discovered of disposing . . . of nuclear wastes' suggests that the education programme went so well that institute members had rumbled the fact that not even the scientists had thought things through – the peaceful use of nuclear power could indeed be as frightening as the bomb, and now they

knew why! In the same year, at the instigation of Harracott WI, the Movement lobbied for priority research into alternative sources of energy. The key element in WI campaigns in the field of nuclear power has been environmental. In 1989, for example, there was an Albert Hall resolution to impress upon the Government the need for controls on the dumping of toxic waste (a term which did seem to include nuclear waste, though as not even the Government inspector present could define 'toxic'; one wasn't sure). Delegates learned that there are some 5,000 dumping sites in the country and only five Government inspectors to police them (and that anyway, safety was the responsibility of local authorities). A member for Bradwell WI told a frightening story of the sudden dumping of asbestos waste in their village and warned that 'tomorrow a toxic waste

'I suppose the thing that I was gladdest about, was to bring science into the Movement.' Mrs Pat Jacob.

The disposal of thousands of gallons of milk following a leak from the nuclear processing plant at Windscale in 1957.

dump could be authorised on your doorstep'. Toxic waste, it seems, is big business; incredibly it is being left to market forces to decide what to do with it.

As always, there are clear precedents for WI policy. At the 1928 AGM, in his 'Preservation of the Countryside' address, Professor G M Trevelyan impressed upon the Movement that 'we are accustomed in this island to think and act in terms of money, we are apt to go on destroying without a thought and to be annoyed or contemptuous if anyone proposes to interfere with public works or private enterprise.'

In recent years, at local level in the villages, the WI has begun to grasp the nettle of destruction in its 'own backyard'. In Newark I was told, 'The environmental farming problems are important to members in the Nottinghamshire Federation, like crop spraying, like stubble burning – that's a big and contentious issue because of the pollution. It's very difficult because we've got a lot of farmers' wives who are members and sometimes the resolutions tend to be a bit divisive because the farmers' wives have to be loyal to their

Are Science and Nature acting in accord? Inset: *Wylfa power station in Cemaes Bay, nestling in the beautiful Anglesey countryside. 'The Island is divided about the proposal for a second station,' says Mrs Stella Taylor who is representing the WI view. At Bryn-y-Maen, farmers have first-hand experience: 'The Chernobyl nuclear accident spread radioactive dust . . . and for a period of time the movement of sheep was prohibited.'*

husbands' business, but they can also see the environmental damage occasionally caused by farmers. Farmers sometimes think that they're being knocked, but they're not – there are farmers and there are farmers (good and bad). Mainly it's a question of both sides understanding, being made aware.'

As in the case of nuclear power, it is tempting to see these environmental problems as due to unbridelled scientific progress and a morality that has not kept pace.

Since the 1920s there has appeared an increasingly wide gulf between the farmer (in his efforts to secure a living) and the ecologist (in his efforts to protect the environment). 'Before the 1st World War,' wrote A G Street from his own experience, 'the farmer's first thought was not whether the crop one was sowing would pay a profit over the cost of production or no. That never entered anyone's head. In good seasons farmers did pretty well, and in bad ones, presumably not quite so well . . . If one attended to one's business decently, one got along all right. Some did better than others, but all got along all right.'

The post-war story of farming is a model of inconsistency and illogic in a scientific age. In 1945, the Government did not repeat the withdrawal of support to farmers which followed the 1st War. Instead – determined never again to lay the country open to siege – it poured money into agriculture to boost production. Subsidies combined with better machinery and other scientific developments (artificial fertilisers and pesticides) and created unprecedented yields. 'The pesticides were brought in when the scientists were the golden boys, when we needed extra production, but nobody realised what it would lead to environmentally,' recalls Lady Fraser. 'I think we are all just suddenly realising what we have done. The rape of the land with pesticides . . .'

Actually, farmers have – for a long time – understood what happened to the soil when fertilisers were used. Again, A G Street, farming and writing in the late 1920s, recorded an older labourer's view: '"That chemical tackle ain't got no proof in it." By "proof" they mean an intangible something, which can best be described as "essential guts" . . . You get good crops for a year or two. Then, for another year or so you get crops which look good, but their yield of grain in comparison with the quantity of straw is disappointing. Finally, you get crops . . . described locally as "kneesick".'

The new scientific additives were to the land like drugs to the human body – momentarily spectacular, addictive, and finally destructive of the soil itself. The problem of chemicals affects all nature: insects and birds, who feed off the pests, even humans who must drink water tainted with run-off from the fields: 'The

'How good is soil that's been sprayed and resprayed with poisons?' Mrs Brady, Cookham WI.

whole subject of pollution,' says Viola Williams, 'is very much an issue. We have had many resolutions at the Albert Hall on nitrates and so on. I think time has caught up with the farmers.'

The policy of subsidies created enormous competition. Farmers borrowed against the rising value of their land to buy more land and gain more subsidies. Before

A 1988 Government survey shows that in 3 out of 10 areas nitrate levels in water will exceed EC limits for 50 years.

Above, *battery farmed chickens –*
'beauty is no longer produced by
ordinary economic processes,' Professor
G M Trevelyan said as early as 1928.

Right: *'I heard about Bovine*
Somatotropin – the injecting of cows to
increase milk yield with no regard to the
effect upon the public – and immediately
informed my WI (Uffculme, Devon).
We have campaigned vigorously on
radio and in the press, and in the EEC.'
Mrs M Hayward.

long they were held captive in a spiral of having to expand and produce more to finance their borrowing.

The result of the expansion, in the east of England, is that intensive, American-style crop farming has had disastrous effects upon the ecology of the environment. Nor is it solely the leeching of the ground with more and more fertilisers (for like a drug, more is needed on every application) and the contaminating of drinking water that are at issue, as Members of Pinbolton WI in Cambridgeshire explain. 'This is one of the many little villages in West Cambridgeshire. There is no big town, there is in fact a rural development area to do with the Cambridge Community Council for development of community life in this very rural part. The area is predominantly agricultural with most of the land devoted to arable farming, cereal crops, especially barley and wheat, with peas, beans and oil seed rape as change crops. Farms are large with highly mechanised farming methods used, which means that comparatively few workers are employed. In recent years many hedges have disappeared, victims of the trend towards intensive cereal farming and increased mechanisation. Farmers view this change as an economic necessity, but ecologists deplore damage to the wildlife.'

A field in East Anglia might today be as big as 500 acres. More than 100,000 miles of hedgerow has disappeared from the countryside since the War, with consequent loss (sometimes extinction) of the flora and fauna whose habitat it was. Another practice arousing strong WI feeling is stubble burning. New residents complain about inconvenience from smoke and smuts. The farmers argue that on the heavy clay soils stubble burning is the only effective method of disposing of waste straw.

The Essex Federation has demanded legislation from the Government to ensure that Essex farmers obey rules for burning stubble. In an impassioned plea, Mrs June Bloom of Langley WI explained that Essex was an intensive corn growing area, and this had caused annoyance, alarm and tragedy after harvest time. She was worried that the number of stubble fires needing attention by the fire brigade had doubled in the last year. Mrs Bloom feared the ruination of the landscape and the destruction of land and wildlife if this situation was allowed to continue. Living in a thatched cottage

A field in the East of England might, today, be as big as 500 acres. More than 100,000 miles of hedgerow have disappeared from the countryside since the last war, with consequent loss of flora and fauna.

Another modern farming practice (right) which has upset village communities is stubble burning. The Essex Federation has demanded action to prevent further pollution and the destruction of wildlife.

surrounded by trees, she had seen 'apples roasting on the trees near the thatched roof.'

In 1960 Cookham WI first raised the effect of using poisonous sprays, insecticides and weed-killers on our food, and in a resolution to speed research into the effects of chemicals in food, in 1962, Mrs Corbett Ashly of Horsted Keynes WI in East Sussex pointed to the sheer stupidity of the course on which farmer and food manufacturer are jointly set: 'We are killing the bees, the birds, the small mammals and we spray our vegetables and fruit leaving minute doses of poison in these and in the soil. And preservatives and colouring matter are added which keep our food from decay, but it is no longer fresh and all the goodness has gone out of it. Of twenty colouring matters which we allow in food only one is legal in other countries as being the only one which has no harmful effects . . . We have a welfare state, with more money in most people's pockets, and we have more cancer, more heart, liver and nervous diseases, and these are the diseases which are affected by the same chemicals with which we are treating our food.'

Mrs Loewenfeld drew our attention to the way 'chemicals deceive us by beautifying and artificially flavouring food . . . hiding age and loss of value . . . The first control on which we should insist is the compulsory statement on labels and packs of all chemicals used.'

As the 1980s turn into the final decade of the 20th Century, there are real signs of improvement in this area. But there seems no fundamental change in a Government that can, in 1989, sanction the sale of irradiated food – another 'hobbyhorse' of the WI. Always it is consumer groups like the WI Movement, which have brought change while the Government stands by. Again, it is successive governments that have artificially bolstered the agricultural industry with subsidies, encouraging expensive, unhealthy, chemical production methods, high yields, wheat mountains, butter mountains and milk lakes. 'If someone offers you a really good subsidy to increase your wheat yield, are you going to say no?' asks Viola Williams.

At least one 5,000-acre farmer agrees that the Government is to blame – 'It's crazy subsidising me to produce at high cost wheat which nobody wants. The solution should surely be to produce less wheat using less fertiliser and fewer chemicals.'

'Conservation is the keyword,' said one WI member, 'and organic farming a good second.' People say a return to organic farming would be too expensive. Currently, between £3,000 and £5,000 million of our money is spent on the industry each year. In 1988, Southwell WI campaigned for the Government to use some of the budget to fund farmers during transition to organic food production. And in 1989, the principle of the strategy

has been applied in a trial scheme to pay farmers in East Anglia to restore habitats of flora and fauna – hedgerows, flower-rich grassland – which have been destroyed by intensive farming practices.

The scientific revolution that has occurred in farming since the war has affected things other than the physical health of the land and its people, however; it has changed the nature of villages too. Sylvia Gray tells of the change that modern farming has brought to her village of Burford in Oxfordshire: 'Years ago Burford was a much more self-contained, much more active place than it is now. Some WI members were farmers and if they weren't, they had great agricultural leaning round here. They were working on farms. That's what altered the character of the place – when agriculture became so much more mechanised. Today all the farms round here are very big but there are fewer of them. Very little farm land has actually been sold for development as it's all a conservation area around here. What has changed is that all the people who used to live in the houses worked on the farms and that is no longer the case. Now we have got much more of a retired population who bought up these Cotswold cottages, and many more weekenders. But of course that hasn't happened overnight and people have had time to take it in their stride. It has just been a continuing process, and now nobody thinks about it.'

The same might be said of villages throughout the English countryside: 'All the people that lived here, worked here,' says Mrs Evans of Follifoot in Yorkshire. Besides farmers of course there were others who enabled the village to be self-sufficient – Follifoot 'boasted among its 500 inhabitants a tailor, a cobbler who made as well as mended villagers' boots and shoes. The village could dress its own stone, build its own houses, plaster its own walls, paint its own woodwork, shoe its own horses, bury its own dead.' But the main employment came of course from the farms: 'One farm employed fifty people.'

The mechanisation of farming – scientific progress – cut employment drastically. In 1946 there were 739,000 full-time agricultural workers; today there are just over 100,000. 'Change is inevitable,' write members of Redberth and District WI near Tenby in Wales, 'but it has come rapidly to what is by nature a conservative community. The mechanical age has taken away something which can never be replaced. What it gives in speed and efficiency it takes away in friendliness and neighbourliness. Haymaking and Harvest were great social events. Neighbours came together and helped one another without stint. They were very aware of their dependence upon one another. The Haymaking and Harvest suppers which followed the work of the day

Farming – then and now – from the Bryn-y-Maen WI scrapbook: 'The corn harvest has come through all the changes, from being cut by scythe and made into sheaves by hand, to being cut by binder. Sheaves were made into stooks and left out to ripen . . . Finally they were carried to the stack yard and made into ricks or stacks.'

Today any crop is harvested by combine harvester. The first time one of these machines worked in Bryn-y-Maen was in Ffirth Ysgol on 4th September 1952. It is registered in the school log as the boys were taken to see it working and it belonged to Gloddarth Farm. 'People wondered how it could cut, thrash, grade and sort out the weak seeds in one operation. It was the beginning of the end of the thrashing machine and all the labour it involved.' Mrs Angela Jones.

were enjoyable events.'

Quotas, Government offers of 'set-aside', and diversification grants designed to encourage farmers not to farm – to plant forests that are changing the face of the countryside or to turn to tourism – seem to underline the unnaturalness of what has come to pass. Mrs Joy Foot: 'I am a farmer with a quota, and we are limited in the nature of our diversification, that's why we take in Bed and Breakfast. It's something I thought I would never do, but I am doing it of neccessity.'

In Hawes in the Yorkshire Dales – Herriot Country – tourism is big business: 'In 1923 farming was the staple industry in Hawes – they were hill farmers (sheep). Looking back I can see that the changes began to occur about twenty years ago,' says Mrs Norah Worth, 'changes which have combined to make Hawes not just a market town but a tourist attraction now. There are holiday cottages or people doing "B and B" all over. And this has meant that the people who run it as a tourist attraction are crying out for the young people to do the jobs – in shops, in hotels, in guest houses, cleaning holiday cottages; there's no shortage of work for young women in Hawes.'

'What is interesting in Norfolk,' says Mrs Batty Shaw, a rural Development Commissioner, 'is that in the 1930s the Scottish farmers were coming down here because land was cheap, but the reverse is now happening and Norfolk farmers, because of the agricultural situation, are tending to sell up and go to Scotland and their farms are being bought by, not necessarily Londoners, but those that are wealthy enough in the metropolis. However, farmers are perhaps not so badly affected by restrictive regulations as in, say, Cumbria and Northumberland where diversification has

had a direct effect upon the life of villages. They are given something like £80 per acre not to use their land, which in turn affects how much employment can be offered by farmers. They are simply not needing the same people to work the land, which affects what is happening in the villages because if your farm workers are not able to spend money on services and new shops and things, then the whole community is affected.'

The WI foresaw some of the effects that an increasingly technological industry, economic in manpower, would bring to the life of villages. As early as 1941, Lady Denman left no doubt as to its position: 'We are pledged to study the changes taking place in agriculture, some of which have come to stay. We share the responsibility for seeing that in future agriculture is given as important a place in national life as industry.'

Mrs Lystra M Berrett observes what those changes have meant to the village of Steeple Ashton in Wiltshire: 'Farming has changed radically here. There are now only two dairy herds in the whole parish. In 1949 there were at least sixteen; many of them small-holders milking a dozen or so cows by hand. One farm yard now has fourteen houses on it, another Council bungalows for the elderly. The arable acreage has become the greater part of all the farms; numbers of hedges have been destroyed to enlarge fields. Nearly all the ponds have gone, and what we still notice is the loss of all our elm trees. Mechanisation of farming has also meant the loss of hayricks and strawricks with their thatch; the small bales are now giving way to big bales and fork lifts on tractors. Silage has mainly taken over from hay. Beef cattle with continental breeds and crosses have displaced the Dairy Shorthorn and the British Fresian. Sheep have come back but there are no pigs. The pigs that

were kept by one farmer in large numbers have gone, fifteen years ago. Milk churns are not used; all milk being collected by tanker from bulk tanks on the two dairy farms. The footpaths across the fields are difficult to follow and often ploughed up or blocked; in spite of the County Councils way-marking signs. They have deteriorated greatly since 1949.'

In the 1950s, Lady Denman's successor, Lady Albemarle, recognised a need to re-vitalise industry in the villages, even if not agriculturally based, and as Chairman of the Development Commission co-opted the WI to help sustain a parallel social development: 'When I took over (at the Development Commission, now The Rural Development Commission), we were just beginning to get advance factories into villages, alternative employment. I really started that when I was Chairman. I remember going up to Lincolnshire and meeting the farmers there who were frightfully suspicious of us building factories, they thought we would take all their employment. But in my day, because we didn't have an enormous grant, it was quite a modest thing. Now they get a lot of money from the Government and there is a new Act of Parliament superseding the one that we worked from, which rather limited us to industries more related to the countryside. The Development Commission also financed The Rural Industries Bureau which made grants and loans to craftsmen. I brought them together and made them into one thing, The Council for Small Industries in Rural Areas – COSIRA – which now has its headquarters at Salisbury. We gave grants to the WI, administrative grants because we always said that you cannot have economic development in the countryside without parallel social development and we use the WI a one of our instruments of social development in the villages.'

Today, in Wales, the process is continuing with the WI taking an ever more direct role. Mrs Rhiannon Bevan: 'Craft industries are coming back to rural areas. In mid-Wales especially there has been a lot of encouragement to set up small enterprises. Recently we had our first and only community WI Manpower Services Education programme. It was to encourage men and women to be trained in skills so that they could set up small businesses. You see heavy industry has disappeared from Wales. The Manpower Services were providing us with the money. The Local Education Authority were mounting it and we were providing classes according to the needs of the people. Sometimes the people didn't know what kind of skills to be trained in, so we made a variety available from cobbler to computer operator.

'We had a manager, who was a WI member, and we interviewed and employed about ten part-time workers who recruited people in the field, finding the tutors.'

In Eastgate, County Durham, besides sheep farming and beef farming which still obtain, local industries include the mining of minerals or, perceptibly on the increase, tourism. One notices even as far north as the Weardale valley that tourism is the villager's great hope for the future. On a farm in Westgate I shared my breakfast table with a man informed that a multi-million pound ski resort was about to be built near there (an extraordinary idea for these parts, but quite true I discovered later), and he was on the look-out for a business property to service the thousands of tourists that would soon flock to this strip of beauty barely known.

One can see the logic of the enterprise. Perhaps, just as the farmers of Hawes have turned to James Herriot for

Far left: Mrs E Everitt's cottage at Hunstanworth in Durham – 'We didn't pay £300 for it – now they're going for up to £50,000 or £60,000.'

Left, in Weardale, beef and sheep farming and mining (minerals mostly) still exist happily side by side, but tourism is catching up, observes Mrs Kathleen Ward of Eastgate – 'We were the original tourist industry here, with our caravan site. The "in" thing these days is to buy a converted barn and commute into the town. It would have been frowned upon years ago when men used to walk from Teesdale over to Weardale and bring their "wallet" of food for a week. The cottage (right) a builder uses as a holiday home.'

their salvation, so other landscape painters and novelists will be used to draw crowds to the areas that have inspired their work. Again, we may not have Benidorme's sun or America's Disneyland, but we do have some of the most beautiful and varied countryside in Europe and a cultural heritage readily accessible in our monastries, castles, ancient 'digs' and stately homes . . . The logic is plain, but the feeling one has is that if we have come to a point where our heritage is for sale, what next? As we look at what past generations have handed on to us, it cannot fail to occur to us to ask what we are conspiring to leave our grandsons and daughters? There's economic sense but a strange sort of finality about the exploitation of a culture.

In areas where subsistence industries have not been replaced, villagers have had to leave to find work elsewhere, and a new population has come in. Depending on the location of the village, the new people may be commuters, they may be elderly people coming to the country to retire, they may be town people buying holiday homes or even permanent homes, but rarely do they supply work opportunities for the natives or, so it would seem,

lend very much to the life of the village.

To all outward appearances Embleton on the North East coast of Northumberland doesn't seem to have changed a great deal in the seventy years that its WI has thrived, though the quarry is no longer the employment focus of the village. 'Our biggest problem now is the development of the village into holiday homes,' said Miss Bolton who had been part of a group of people that had done a survey and discovered that 25% of their houses are now second homes. 'A few incomers support the village and feel some sort of responsibility to the community, but there are quite a lot of people that have been coming here for a number of years that we still don't know.'

I put it to the Embleton institute that patterns of life are changing, that people born in the country want to go to work in the towns to make money and maybe return to the country later on. There is a big change, a big social change in progress and the natural reaction is to try and put the brakes on it. They listened politely and asked whether I was looking to buy in the area . . .

At the other end of the country a member of the

Embleton, a haven for holiday homes.

Cornwall Federation Executive told me, 'The sort of people who have come in are not the sort of people who have done or would do anything for the whole area. All of this detracts from the highly focused life of a village, just as the closure of village schools has.'

In Oxfordshire Lady Brunner points to escalating house prices as the root of the problem for villagers: 'Today the countryside is full of people from towns and they don't join in anything. This is Yuppyland here, and it's tragic really because when we came here fifty years ago the Chilterns were the "back-of-beyond". There was a little railway to Henley, but there was no electricity in the village until the summer we came [1937]. Everybody was friends and everybody joined everything in the village. But now the houses change hands at a tremendous rate. You don't pay Capital Gains tax on selling your home so everyone in the past ten years has been engaged in buying a house, adding on a wing, living in it for about three years, and then selling it for an extra £100,000. And of course they don't join in.'

Mrs Hubbard of Follifoot WI: 'House prices in Follifoot in Yorkshire have doubled, nearly tripled in the last year. It affects the young people who cannot afford to stay where they belong and they'd very much like to. We have been astonished at the prices this year (1988). A lot of dwellings have been let as holiday dwellings whereas they would have been jolly nice as homes for the young ones. The escalating house prices haven't benefited anyone. You can't "cash in your chips" and make a profit unless you move to a poorer quality place in a different area. Mr Burge has just moved, he sold up and has gone up to Bishop Auckland area, but that's because he's retiring and his wife is a diabetic so she wanted to live up near her sister.

'The point ·about the holiday cottages is that it encourages a transient population – they don't belong to the village or get involved. We must preserve the community spirit or you become a dormitory and there would be no one left to keep it nice.'

Mrs Evans explains that the institute believes it is its purpose to ease the integration of in-comers: 'We're small enough still to be a caring community and still have a great deal of community spirit. I'm a member of

Follifoot WI looks out on village school and bungalows for the elderly, for which the institute fought.

Radwinter, Essex, 1966
'There is a strong sense of community and a great pride in belonging. It has been little touched by development . . . It is, as Miss Mitford wrote of her village,

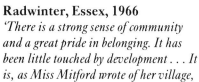

"a little world of our own . . . where we know everyone, and are authorised to hope that everyone feels an interest in us." The village is kept neat and tidy by our seven Road Men (top right, George Halls), who see to the roads, hedges and grass verges. Our Post Office is unique in having an all-female staff (left, Violet Turpin), our milkman, besides delivering milk, also kindly takes messages (above left, Bob Baynes).'

Radwinter, 1985.
The M11 has welcomed the village into commuter country; it's only a 90 minute drive into London. From the outside, it's not too dissimilar, but half Radwinter's population has moved there in the last 10 years. 'You no sooner get to know them than they are off,' says WI member Cicely Fordham. 'No youngster getting married could afford to buy a house here,' says Bob Baynes, 'And they're not building Council houses.' Difference in incomes between residents and in-coming commuters is causing some tensions. Harmony is assisted by a thriving WI and the village school.

the Parish Council and like to keep my finger on the pulse and particularly to welcome new people. We send a letter early on to new people, tell them they're welcome, tell them their talents are very welcome, and any ideas will be taken on – please join in and help us – and that I'm sure that's why they've come to live in the village. It works with 80%, there's very few who use Follifoot just as a dormitory; most people join in.'

Besides acting as a catalyst in the community, the WI flexes its muscle on housing committees too – Mrs Batty Shaw: 'Housing is the greatest worry rural areas have at the moment. One would think that if there was a farmhouse or a farm building being converted that it would be a property that could be bought by the young, but usually it is so expensive that it goes to the richer second-home buyer.

'It is a most serious problem. Every county has a Rural Community Council (or its equivalent) which falls under the umbrella of ACRE. They work with voluntary and statutory bodies – District Councils, County Councils,

'The presence of a constable is a good thing for a community.'
Mrs Patricia Batty Shaw, JP.

Parish Councils, WI, Age Concern and so on – to look at what the problems are for people living in rural areas. Housing Associations have now been set up to use money being put through the Housing Corporation by the Government to build new reasonably priced houses which they will rent to the young. There is then no question of that house being sold out of our hands, somewhere can be provided for young people to live in their village. You usually find a WI member sitting on the Rural Community Council.'

The Warwickshire Federation is unique in having its own Housing Association, the brain-child of ex-Chairman Mrs Mollie Lodder. Following a resolution at the annual Warwickshire Council Meeting, financial aid was forthcoming in the form of a grant from the Exchequer paid through the Local Authority. Full mortgage facilities were made available and, says Mrs Goodey, County Secretary, 'Now we are financed entirely by rents paid by our tenants. "Friends of the Housing Association" was formed – they hold social functions to raise money for extras. The finances are completely separate from Federation funds and there are now two converted houses, one with thirteen flats and the other with fourteen.'

Along with the erosion of the traditional land-based rural economy, many villages have suffered a parallel dismantling of the social infrastructure; the hubs on which community life once turned – the school, the village shop, the post office, sometimes – as in the village of Hett in Durham – even the church itself. Four hundred sub-post offices had closed in the two years prior to 1971 when Mrs Anne Walker spelt out the implications of the closure of the Chignalls and Mashbury office in Essex – 'It means that mothers with young families and senior citizens have to go into Chelmsford, five miles away, with only two buses a day, rising bus fares and a four-hour wait in town for the return bus.' Elsewhere, the village bobby has gone, the vicar is shared by three or four other villages; even the village shop, a traditional meeting place and information centre, has very often succumbed to economic pressures. The church, the village and WI hall, the pub, the shop, the post office, the school, these are places of exchange, social, spiritual, even cultural exchange which make the difference between a collection of inhabitants and a happy community. Often it is the going of the village school which illustrates most poignantly the nature of loss to the village community.

St Wenn in Cornwall fought hard to keep theirs, teachers and parents getting together to ensure that it was kept open. Why? 'When the small children go there, their mums take them to school and they go and they

The church, the school, the farm, original hubs of village life.

fetch them and they meet together. It is a social thing as well. The fact that they are being brought up in their own village has a good effect on them in later life. Also it means that the parents get very involved in the schooling, because if your child has to be bussed to school four miles away you can't get so involved with his education. The village teacher knows more about the whole life of the child and can provide more individual treatment as a result.'

As a JP, Mrs Batty Shaw, sees the run-down of village schools as but one aspect of a deprivation which has had a disastrous effect upon the security as well as the happiness of village communities: 'Well, you see, villages have changed haven't they? If you look back over the last thirty years there have been tremendous changes. You have lost the squire, you have lost the rector, you have lost the village bobby. The squire and the rector were looked at as leaders and nowhere has a natural leader come forth. Active community citizenship is the latest thing for villages. I think that is inevitable now. My bench is at our market town where we have a dear old bobby, a constable who walks up and down the street each day and knows everybody. He knows all the gangs and all the rest of it, and our crime rate is quite low compared to a lot of other market towns who don't have the same set up. You see the presence of a constable is a good thing for the community. If we haven't got the money to have it then we have all got to be more helpful ourselves to each other. The whole philosophy at the moment is self-reliance and competition. Some can cope, and some simply cannot. A good, strong WI in a village is a great asset in that climate.

Chapter Fifteen
MIRROR TO THE FUTURE

*'What is wanted is to grow
a contemporary culture from the old roots.'*
T S ELIOT

*Lucy Freeman – an Old member of 16. 'I joined Old WI
when I was 14 . . . I have learned how to glass engrave, play
skittles, and joined a yoga class, but above all I have become
accustomed to public speaking which has been invaluable –
being a member of the WI is fun.'*

In 1965 Isabelle Gardner of the Northumberland Federation said: 'A new type of countrywoman is emerging in the area adjacent to our own great city, Newcastle-upon-Tyne. Young and vital housewives whose husbands do not wish to live in the city itself are members of large housing estates on the outskirts. They may have cause to wonder to which community they belong although they live almost in the country, their houses are not in the village, and if the spirit of a village life is lacking, so are the shops, cinemas and restaurants of the city. We in Northumberland are therefore going ahead by forming institutes in these new estates.'

'The point about the WI,' says General Secretary Mrs Anne Ballard, 'is that its membership reflects the developing social patterns of the country as a whole.' 'When the institutes began,' agrees Pat Jacob, 'they were all in villages, but by the '60s many towns had expanded and absorbed villages. Where that happened, or villages were joined together into towns through development, institutes survived, they weren't closed just because they had changed from being rural to being urban.'

It seems that Lady Denman's warning, implicit in her

Traditional country ideals come to the towns: Bilton is a suburb of Harrogate. The WI, just 3 years old, chose the Nidd Valley viaduct as their institute symbol – 'Several of us belong to a conservation group and the money that's been raised has been used to reclaim areas – you can now enjoy the walk right along the Nidd.' But what unites the membership in Bilton are the activities – 'we had 66 different events last year' – and the feeling of belonging. 'Bilton's quite a community of its own, we're very proud of our community spirit. What we enjoy about the WI is the fellowship.'

AGM speech at the end of the War, had come to pass: 'Some planners believe that the ordinary small village has no future and that people can only be happy in a community with a population of two or three thousand.'

She was right too about the effect the new communities could sometimes have upon peace of mind, as Mrs Aileen Spencer recalls: 'Having been uprooted and brought to live on a new housing estate in Whitley Bay when my two children were babies, life became a very lonely and friendless existence. Then after seven years, and still without real friends I was asked to join a new WI that was being formed and from then on life has been completely different, and I have found a host of good friends and also learned quite a lot about other people and their way of life.'

Up until 1965 the WI was pledged in its Constitution not to institute membership in any place with a population larger than 4,000. The Movement had been committed to the so-called '4,000 rule' since its inception. Early in its history certain towns had expressed eagerness to form institutes, but although some WI centres were formed in towns (for example in Cornwall as meeting places for members of very isolated institutes on market day), the idea of urban WIs was frowned upon and actively discouraged. Indeed, in 1929, in order to block any moves to form urban WIs, the NFWI took part in deliberations which resulted in the formation of the National Union of Townswomen's Guilds.

But in 1965, faced with a *fait accompli* – there were

Liz Roberts from Wendover put the WI fellowship ideal to the test: 'As a WI member, wherever you go you can find a friend. I proved this walking 259 miles from the edge of Berkshire to Liskeard in Cornwall with my 6-year-old Labrador bitch Vicky, staying with a fellow WI member every night. 1978 was NFWI's "Good Health is Good Fun" year, and although I was not expecting to be sponsored, friends and colleagues were so insistent, I was able to send the National Federation £150 and the Cheshire Home in Liss £200. I wanted to use only footpaths and bridleways and avoid the towns. I bought fourteen maps with which to plan my route and as usual the WI turned up trumps . . . After 16 days I reached my destination. Vicky and I had had a marvellously warm welcome wherever we stopped. We were the most pampered tramps in all England.'

already institutes existing in areas with populations in excess of 4,000 due to post-war expansion – Chairman Mrs Gabrielle Pike steeled herself to presiding over a constitutional change which would have far-reaching effects upon the organisation. 'I shall be in the middle of this controversy,' she said at the time, 'and I dare not say which way I think it will go. It will be a tremendous decision to take which could affect us for years to come.'

When the decision had been taken, Mrs Frances Charlton, like many other County Chairmen, interpreted the resolution to the letter: 'We went into the housing estates looking for membership. We weren't very popular in some places. It was supposed to be a countrywomen's organisation, but I think you have got to remember that a lot of people living on these housing estates were country girls, that had lived in the country, gone to work in the town, had married and had come to live on the estates around about Newcastle and didn't know their next-door-neighbours.

'I can remember forming a WI in the west end of Newcastle on a new estate and we got them all to wear a label with their name and address and you saw them looking at the labels and saying, "You live in our street and you only live three doors away from me," and I think opening a WI did a tremendous amount for the people living on these estates. Yes, we got some great WIs out of those estates, and the lovely thing about it was that the really rural WIs were getting smaller through death and people leaving the countryside, and our membership would have gone down drastically had we not formed institutes in the estates and it helped our income too.'

Did Mrs Charlton notice any difference about these urban institutes? 'They were much more social gatherings. But I think they still slotted in very well. When we wanted help for council meetings, for stewarding and all that sort of thing there was a great willingness. They wanted to help and they wanted to be part of something. You got the odd one where the membership dropped because we didn't do the things that they thought that perhaps we ought to do – the more social side of things.'

Today many of the old guard remain unconvinced of the wisdom of spreading into the towns. Miss Viola Williams: 'I can remember as far back as I have been with the WI, we have always been fighting for the rural side of the Movement against the semi-urban and urban side. I think there is a danger of losing our identity. Let me give you a parallel example. The International Council of Women, which started in the 1890s purported to get together the womens organisations from all round the world. By the mid-twenties it was terribly obvious when they got together that the problems they were discussing were urban problems, not rural problems, so a group of them got together and said, "We want to discuss rural problems." That is why the Associated Countrywomen of the World started in 1930, for the rural organisations as against the urban organisations. And I have been very worried in the last few years that the WI, which was one of the very important founder members of ACWW, is now becoming more and more urban.

'I hope it survives as at least a spokes-organisation for rural women. An awful lot will depend on who we have as our leaders, as it has in the past. At the moment (1988) we have an absolutely first class National Chairman, Agnes Salter, who has got her feet in

Is traditional craftsmanship an anachronism today? 'Where are the heirlooms of tomorrow or the consumer goods of the future, if no true craftwork is done today?' asked Mrs Batty Shaw at the 1970 AGM. A WI member added, 'Only a handful of people know all the secrets of these things . . .' For others, the sense of loss is characterised by a fear that the modern world will extinguish the ideals of craftsmanship in a flood of nostalgia. 'The National Trust has a blacksmith and welder here,' says Lady Brunner. 'He's not at all quaint; he does welding for bigger firms. It would be a great pity for our rural base to become a picturesque centre for tourism.'

manure. She is a countrywoman through and through, she came into the WI through the markets.' Sadly, Mrs Salter died during the preparation of *Village Voices* – but, as Miss Williams suggests, her special empathy with the rural membership is treasured by many.

Is the movement of institutes into towns a reflection of change in the community or is it really the membership game that all big organisations must play? After all, does not the demise of farming and the parallel depression in parts of the rural community offer the organisation the very best reason to concentrate its efforts there, than it has had since the Movement's inception in 1915?

Lady Albemarle: 'These days I think that the WI (like all other organisations) has become obsessed with membership numbers. Possibly they will go down but as long as they are meeting a need of the rural woman and supporting rural life and building up rural life and

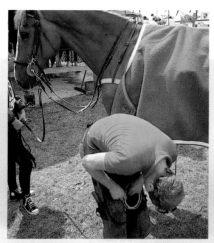

Horse-shoeing at the Royal Welsh Show.

Sheering at Staverton Fayre.

Shires on show, and Dufton stone-walling.

making it fun and interesting for people to live in the countryside and helping people to know each other in the countryside, then they are doing a much more important job than simply increasing their numbers.

'When I went to Australia when they had the big anniversary of the WI out there, I saw that they always had had WIs in the towns as well as way out in the countryside. But members tended to be countrywomen who had gone to live in the towns, because there, in Australia, they had this particular problem that they had to send their children into the towns to be educated. The town WIs would look after the country children while they were in the town. So there was an excuse for it. That makes sense to me.'

What would Lady Denman, her immediate predecessor as Chairman of the WI, have done? 'It's awfully hard to say what Lady Denman would have thought about the development of the WI into towns because she was gifted of a very enquiring mind and things have changed enormously in the countryside since her day. Perhaps she would have felt that it was a good thing, I don't know.'

Mrs Anne Harris, Chairman from 1981 to 1985, believes that 'a lot of members of the Clapham WI, of which my daughter is President, are estranged rural people. They do very much the same sort of things but they are not rural of course, so it is much more difficult for them in London. Even though London is a collection of villages, each WI doesn't quite grow out of the neighbourhood as it would do in a rural village, but a lot of the conservation ideas come from the towns, for example, and the more they can understand the country, the better.'

In 1965 Mrs Pike emphasised the movement into the towns as providing an extension to the organisation's community work – 'More and more institutes are springing up on council estates and in the last year or so sixteen branches have been set up to help give an interest to patients in mental institutions. WI gets people out of often isolated homes, provides meals for spastic children, takes old people on outings and looks after any one who is ill and alone and on their own in the village. They are fighting for changes on the law about abortion. One big question at their AGM at the Albert Hall tomorrow is whether all this sort of work should be done on a rather more official basis than it is at present. They are thinking of liaising more closely with the Citizens Advice Bureau.'

A decade and a half later, when Anne Harris was elected Chairman she was asked what plans she had, 'and I did say that one of the things that I would like to do is to do something about membership, to get an improvement, and so we asked Strathclyde University to do a survey. I realised we needed to see not only what WIs thought, but what people outside felt about the WIs. Strathclyde went

Anne Harris. 'Lady Denman would have defended our rural roots but used the development into towns to all our benefit.'

both to the institutes and the woman in the street to ask her how she perceived the WI and what she would feel she would get out of it. "Friendship" was a big thing everywhere and for the woman in the street, "being able to do something for the community", "being a voice in the community".'

The survey led to a fully orchestrated WI promotion – ably masterminded by the present Chairman, Mrs Jean Varnam, JP – with the stated aim of attracting new members, perhaps a new type of countrywoman, perhaps not a countrywoman at all, for out of the promotion came the new London Federation of WIs. 'The promotion was a three-year affair and moved on three themes: women and education, women and health, women in public life. It was a success measured in terms of new members,' recalls Anne Harris. The promotion culminated in a huge exhibition at Olympia – "The Life and Leisure

Exhibition". The WI Annual Report describes it as follows: 'the emphasis of many exhibits was on action and participitation. Visitors were encouraged to have a go – on a ski slope, under a car bonnet, on a computer, or making theatrical costumes.' It seemed to mark a departure, a change towards sport, leisure, club activities . . . the kind of activities which Mrs Charlton had noted were popular among the new urban institutes. 'It did definitely start a new direction, or at least, a difference in emphasis,' agrees Anne Harris. 'You see both the Strathclyde survey and the younger people joining the WIs – this is what they wanted, sports of all sorts . . . This was the way we were advised to go about it. Remember, the promotion was about membership and we felt that we could encourage people in this way and then they would come and see what else was in the WI. We did of course have other things at the exhibition, we had quite an important area where people in public life came just to chat, answer any sort of questions that might be asked.'

The Exhibition, though very much a success in refuting the 'jam and Jerusalem' image to which – through ignorance –the media had clung since the 2nd World War, did not sustain its promise in terms of increased membership. Anne Harris is the first to admit that 'there was a jump in the membership graph after the promotion when the membership actually rose for the first time in a long time. But I fear we didn't follow it up, doing all the things that we set out in the promotion. People would join for a certain reason that we had been promoting, but when they found that perhaps the particular institute they had joined simply wasn't that sort of institute – you see they are very different one from the other, with different emphases – they'd be disappointed.'

The extraordinary thing about the history of the WI is the nature of its growth. It grew fast because it responded to a need in the rural community, not because a group of people drew up a plan to increase membership. The statistics of membership show that the institutes which emerge naturally, organically as it were, from a community are the ones which last and prosper. This is true everywhere, even in Malaya, as Viola Williams recalls:

'When you went into a village to start a WI you started by aproaching the Chief – that was absolutely vital. The Chief would consult his men and if the men thought it was a good idea, then you could get to the women . . . But one of the most interesting things was that after a couple of years (and especially after Independence) the WIs that lasted were the WIs that were not started by the District Officers' wives and often not the ones started by us. They were the ones that were started by the communities themselves. Those had started very often because the men in one village had discovered that the people, the children in the next village were better fed and better clothed because they had a WI who were showing them how. Then the Chief would get in touch with us and say "Could you come and start a WI?" The WI is today one of the biggest organisations in South East Asia and is multi-racial.'

There are no more Chiefs in the villages of England and Wales, but there seems every reason to expect that institutes will evolve organically from urban communities as successfully as in the countryside, partly because of the number of rurally minded townswomen, partly because the concerns of town and country dwellers are becoming increasingly similar, but most especially because the values on which the Movement are based

'"The Life and Leisure Exhibition" did definitely start a new direction, a different emphasis . . . The younger people joining the WIs – this is what they wanted, sports of all sorts.' Mrs Anne Harris. Right: *The Essex Bowls Championship, 1988.* Far right: *Katrina Savage of Bellingham WI on a sponsored parachute jump: 'I suppose the younger members are getting a bit more adventurous.' The Exhibition, held at Olympia, gave rise to institutes in London: 'The new institutes were both surprising in resembling so clearly their more rural counterparts, and a challenge in the way some rightly questioned established procedures.' General Secretary, Mrs Anne Ballard.*

A Countrywoman's Garden, Chelsea, 1988

The garden was designed by Jaquie Moon, member of Burton and Puddington WI, Cheshire, and constructed by John Ravenscroft's team at Bridgemere Garden World, where it can now be seen. The exhibit won the Gold Medal and the coveted Wilkinson's Sword at the Chelsea Flower Show in 1988. It was a prime example of excellence in the institutes and a wonderful expression of the Movement's rural roots bearing fruit in the nation's capital. But, as Chelsea neared, the project seemed to court disaster. John Daly, who was to build the cottage, broke his wrist three weeks prior to the event, and then the lorry transporting the building material was over-loaded and sank to its front axle in the mud, needing two tractors to free it. On arrival, 'I just dug and dug and dug, some nights until midnight preparing the soil,' recalls Mr Daly. 'We dug down to about 15 inches which was a great advantage, most exhibitors don't do that. But it's the difference between building a garden and building a display.' As a result, the plants, which had been transported in refrigerated containers, looked their best, especially the wild flowers, a breathtaking feature of the garden. More recently Jaquie's garden has won The Lawrence Medal for the best exhibit at any RHS show in 1988.

fill a vacuum in so many lives, as never before.

Of course the issues which concern the WI and bind institutes together to a national purpose have never been exclusively rural; some – like the countrywoman's education, or the village post offices – have been, but others – such as equality of opportunity – clearly affect all women everywhere. Again, with farming no longer the primary rural occupation and with the increasing transportability (via fax and computer) of occupations from town to country, we are as a nation far less readily divisible into town and country folk. Finally, as evidenced in the results of the 1989 EEC parliamentary elections, town and country folk share a concern about our natural environment, as at no other time in our history.

The WI were quick to appreciate this social development, peculiar to our time. For several years from 1970, a WI Town and Country project, aimed at increasing understanding between urban and rural areas, was run with the help of a grant from the Carnegie United Kingdom Trust. It was a conservation project in Conservation Year, and it illustrated perfectly how matters of crucial importance to rural dwellers could be shared and developed in co-operation with the towns. Mount Rayleigh WI in Essex had injected new impetus to the work on conservation in 1969 with a resolution which resulted in the County Federations coming together in a huge national event called 'This Green and Pleasant Land?'. The event, mounted in 1972, pulled together all strands of WI conservation policy in a hugely successful publicity exercise which attracted entries from both urban and rural institutes. It showed how the cross-fertilisation of ideas could benefit both communities.

The life of the institutes has always been a learning process. But nowadays with external adult education courses widely available, and with the success of the organisation's own college, less educational work than before is undertaken in the institute meetings. Many of the older members regret this, and recall how effective the instructor demonstrators were, and how much they would look forward to them, not just to learn but to participate . . . I have tried to show that the original education policy of the Movement was only partly practical, that its other crucial function was cultural – the lectures, the crafts, the exhibitions, the demonstrations, the village scrapbook competitions, even the country dancing and singing, and village pageants, they all kept people in touch with their rural roots.

In many parts of the WI this policy continues today – the word 'Wales' in the following quote could be substituted for a number of counties in Britain – Mrs Rhiannon Bevan: 'Our policy at the WI is to help people to understand what Wales is all about. We have Welsh culture courses, and courses in the history of Wales. We

WI scrapbooks (like the one below) are unique archives of local history, detailing the roots of a culture which is as often expressed today in projects concerned with our future. In 1972, Eton Wick and Boveney (right) won the film section of the conservation exhibition, 'This Green and Pleasant Land?', with their 8mm film, 'Sweet Thames Run Softly'.

have a "Welsh Week" every so often, and every year we have a week-end conference gathering when we tend to put on courses about folk lore, folk dancing, traditional Welsh cooking, the history of the vernacular etc. We want people to really understand what Wales is all about.'

Today the WI's vision remains that of a country composed of small, caring communities, each aware and protective of its own identity, but conscious that it is part of a greater whole – the values of the WI radiate from rural, urban and city institutes to the world. And as political power recedes from the localities to Westminster, as the modern drive towards an efficient, but soul-less monoculture gathers pace, it is never more important that the Movement does not 'cease from mental fight', in defence of values which it holds dear.

In the final analysis, the voice of the WI is not a voice of nostalgia for the traditional English village but a voice for the values which it embodied. As society has become increasingly technological, urbanised, alienated, 'un-natural' – the values of English rural life (a primitive prompting, perhaps, from 'England's mountains green') have acquired an elemental, even spiritual dimension. This fusion of Land and God is expressed in the WI's choice of William Blake's *Jerusalem* as anthem sung at the start of every institute meeting. The new urban WI that told me, 'We only sing *Jerusalem* once a year, we haven't time for it,' was showing how busy it is, but I felt sad that no one there could say what the anthem was about.

Town and city WIs are, like all institutes, branches on the WI tree, albeit farthest from the root source of the Movement, which lies deep in the rural culture of 'ancient time'. 'Whatever else changes,' said Chairman Mrs Jean Varnam in her 1989 AGM address at the Albert Hall, 'our aims and ideals, our basic beliefs and philosophy remain as they were – and always will.'

'You see,' concludes Mrs Bevan, 'There's a greater need now more than ever for an organisation that provides stability. At the WI we have a strong foundation from which we can derive a direction, a point of view, whatever be the needs of different people.'

From the voices I have listened to, I would say that that direction has never changed: whether in singing, acting, dancing or fighting for the rights of women everywhere, their purpose is to maintain a sense of collective cultural inheritance, born of the soil, of natural rhythms, which is indissoluble from the spirit of a people.

'The countryside is part of our lives whether we live in town or countryside.' Mrs Helen Stroh, North Yorks West Federation.

And did those feet in ancient time
Walk upon England's mountains green?
And was the Holy Lamb of God
On England's pleasant pastures seen?
And did the Countenance Divine
Shine forth upon our clouded hills?
And was Jerusalem builded here
Among these dark Satanic Mills?

Bring me my bow of burning gold!
Bring me my arrows of desire!
Bring me my spear!
O clouds unfold;
Bring me my Chariot of Fire!
I will not cease from mental fight,
Nor shall my sword sleep in my hand,
Till we have built Jerusalem
In England's green and pleasant land.

William Blake

EPILOGUE

In the Autumn of 1989 the WI issued a statement of policy – headed 'What Future Our Countryside?' – which summarises many of the environmental and village issues on which members have voiced their concern throughout this book, and particularly in Chapter 14. Comment and recommendations for action on matters relating to the rural economy, modern farming methods, conservation, rural housing, health, transport and village schools, underline the Movement's continued and ever more necessary commitment to its rural base. This, in spite of the fact that the last twenty years have seen a marked spread of its membership away from the countryside into urban areas.

However, the Movement's changing profile and in particular the modern context in which today's members live, have over the past decade or so exercised the minds of the WI leaders considerably, and found expression in two new policy developments – one in the field of education, and the other, more recently, in changes to the Movement's constitution.

'The changes that are occurring in the WI reflect a major change in the expectations of its membership right across the board,' says Chairman Jean Varnam. 'Forty years ago there was only the WI in a village. Now, there could be ten organisations for women – specialist groups such as local studies and local history groups, flower arranging clubs and so on. As a result we have given great thought to developing a quality programme across a wide range of subjects. For some time now we have been sending out training officers from the centre, from London to the institutes. These officers have been through Certificate courses and been assessed by the National Federation so that when they go out into the field they really are very competent indeed. We can now call upon the services of a tutor for almost any subject that a group might wish to study, be it craft, home economics, public speaking, committee work, "how to run a business", computer studies, and so on. In the WI you can have as much or as little as you want of what we have to offer. Our responsibility is to provide the opportunity.'

General Secretary Anne Ballard takes up the point: 'Today, many members want more than a certificate, they want training that will lead to some form of income earning. In the 1950s, fewer women worked, they were happy to perfect their skills, excellence *per se* was enough. Now, many are part of two-income families. Anything that the WI teaches should offer those members the opportunity of employment later on. We are building a bridge to take them from work in the institutes to starting a small business or working with whatever skill we can provide. Again, we are working with the National Council for Vocational Qualifications and so structuring some courses that the WI Certificates exempt successful members from part of the City and Guilds Certificate examinations.'

At Denman College – 'that unique blend of learning, friendship and fun,' as Mrs Varnam describes it – developments are also reflecting the shift (evident both in and outside the WI) towards education-with-a-purpose. The Principal, Miss Pauline Brown, MA, heads a team dedicated to the idea of the College becoming a real force in women's education. While, over the past few years, improvements to college facilities and interior décor reflect the demands of contemporary members for a pleasing environment where learning is fun, the College team also recognises an increasing demand for 'straight education,' says Mrs Ballard. 'What is beginning to ferment is the idea of Denman developing its potential as an educational resource centre,' so that members when they have completed a course can be advised how best to pursue their interest in the localities. 'Education is a root thing in the Movement,' concludes Mrs Ballard. 'In 1986, advancing the education of countrywomen became part of the WI's main purpose along with improving and developing the conditions of rural life. And "country-women" was re-defined to include all women wherever they may live, who are interested in the promotion of the arts, crafts and science associated with rural life.'

The needs of the contemporary member are also behind some of the changes in 1990 to the WI's constitution. Members will be encouraged to be flexible in calling their meetings at times that suit working women. And the old idea of the single monthly meeting will be enhanced to include additional meetings at which particular interests and involvements may be developed in more concentrated fashion. Again, it will no longer be necessary to have a minimum number of eight members serving on an institute committee, a rule which has led to the closure of institutes in areas where already busy members simply do not have the time to meet committee responsibilities. These and many other legal, financial and practical changes reflect the needs of 'a society which is very different from that of 1915,' as Mrs Varnam put it.

But Mrs Varnam was at pains to point out that the ideals and values of the Movement remain the same. The changes simply release constraints on the membership in order that they may more easily exercise their responsibility to society. 'If we look over almost three-quarters of a century we can see "responsibility" running as a strong and powerful element through our entire history. And the need for a WI is greater today than it's ever been.'

We spoke about a few of the areas in which the WI is meeting its responsibilities in what Rhiannon Bevan had described (in Chapter 15) as 'no longer a stable community'. Having attended the AGMs in both 1988 and 1989, I was aware that the rising tide of violence to women was of special importance. In 1958, a resolution by Summerbridge WI in Yorkshire deplored the increasing number of crimes of violence and sexual assault. It resulted in the then Home Secretary appealing to the WI to play an active part in 'curing this social evil'. But, increasingly, the Movement has come to recognise that effective change must come from Government itself. A resolution by Lowdham WI in Nottinghamshire in 1979 called for stronger deterrents, another in 1988 by Sefton WI in Lancashire, urged more adequate sentencing, and in 1989 Old Heathfield in East Sussex called upon the Government to introduce legislation for compulsory DNA testing in areas where violent crime is committed. In thirty years, the Movement's thinking had moved from alerting the Government and the Judiciary to the problem, to making positive suggestions about how to go about solving it. At last, it seems that some progress is being made. Following meetings with 'the Minister at the Home Office, with the Lord Chancellor and the Board of Judicial Studies, we have every reason to believe that reforms will be forthcoming,' said Mrs Varnam.

'We are also actively engaged in the plight of the socially deprived and unemployed. After extensive training in London we sent out officers – people with a very great knowledge of tutor leadership – to run courses for community action leaders who had taken voluntary roles with little or no knowledge about how to lead their particular group, how to serve it best. We helped by showing them how to organise, how to set up conferences, how to go about campaigning, or how to gather useful information to pass on to their people.

Recently, too, there has been an ever increasing energy evident in the Institute's international work. 'We've been doing a great deal of work with both ACWW and UNICEF. UNICEF very often have people "on the ground" who implement the funds we have raised. Our recent project in the Maldives is a case of such co-operation. Because there are so many islands, by the time a doctor can reach an emergency case it's often too late, so together we implemented an educational programme for one bright woman in each area to

be qualified to assist in such cases until help can arrive. Earlier there was a project in Lesotho, sinking water wells, and an educational project in Botswana. And in 1989 we launched a three-year project in the North East of Brazil.'

Marcia Beer, Head of International Affairs at the WI, describes this as 'the focus of WI international activities over the next three years. It is a three-point project which will be undertaken through UNICEF in the very poorest area of Brazil. It is mainly for women, and concerns health education, income generation, and literacy classes, all of which are designed to raise the self-esteem of women in a largely "macho-male" context. So, there are very real parallels with what the Movement did for women in Britain all those years ago.'

In Europe, the WI has had a presence since Britain joined the EEC, as Mrs Varnam describes: 'Through COFACE – the confederation of family organisations within the European Community – we have members sitting on almost all the committees. For example, we have just finished a project with the EEC Consumer Committee, standardising the safety of children's toys and children's equipment. As a result of the knowledge we have gained in Europe we recently ran a series of conferences all over Britain – not only with the WI but with many other organisations – about the effect of the free market in 1992. Our speakers were our own EEC representatives, and sometimes local Euro-MPs – the conferences were well supported, very well organised and extremely effective in disseminating information.

'I just want to mention, too, that over the last ten years a number of Federations have been actively engaged in dialogue with ethnic groups in this country. They have been invited to our meetings and we have been along to theirs. As yet we have made little impact. The problem has been that many of these communities are very self-sufficient and some have very well run groups of their own. Husbands – especially in the Asian communities – while they may be happy to allow their wives to attend an ethnic group, can be wary of looking "outside". But the interesting thing is that we are finding that if you arrange a meeting for the husbands, explaining what the WI is, then there is a much better chance of their allowing the womenfolk to come in.

'This is something we want to work hard for in the future. You see since 1915 our strength as a Movement has resided in the diversity of our membership – different backgrounds, different age groups. When we speak, we have an unprejudiced view. We also have a whole view of society – we are not and never will be "single issue". That is why our voice is welcomed and listened to by Government and by all the organisations with whom we work to seek change.'